Exploring Apple Mac

Sonoma Edition

Kevin Wilson

www.elluminetpress.com

Exploring Apple Mac: Sonoma Edition

Image courtesy of Dr. A. Kent Christensen CC license: BY-SA, iStock.com/golibo, PeopleImages, ymgerman. Photo 130859010 © Kaspars Grinvalds - Dreamstime.com. Photo 103557713 © Konstantin Kolosov - Dreamstime.com. Yuri Arcurs via Getty Images

Publisher: Elluminet Press
Director: Kevin Wilson
Lead Editor: Steven Ashmore
Technical Reviewer: Mike Taylor, Robert Ashcroft
Copy Editors: Joanne Taylor, James Marsh
Proof Reader: Steven Ashmore
Indexer: James Marsh
Cover Designer: Kevin Wilson

eBook versions and licenses are also available for most titles. Any source code or other supplementary materials referenced by the author in this text is available to readers at www.elluminetpress.com/resources

For detailed information about how to locate your book's resources, go to www.elluminetpress.com/resources

Table of Contents

About the Author

With over 20 years' experience in the computer industry, Kevin Wilson has made a career out of technology and showing others how to use it. After earning a master's degree in computer science, software engineering, and multimedia systems, Kevin has held various positions in the IT industry including graphic & web design, programming, building & managing corporate networks, and IT support.

He serves as senior writer and director at Elluminet Press Ltd, he periodically teaches computer science at college, and works as an IT trainer in England while researching for his PhD. His books have become a valuable resource among the students in England, South Africa, Canada, and in the United States.

Kevin's motto is clear: "If you can't explain something simply, then you haven't understood it well enough." To that end, he has created the Exploring Tech Computing series, in which he breaks down complex technological subjects into smaller, easy-to-follow steps that students and ordinary computer users can put into practice.

Acknowledgements

Thanks to all the staff at Luminescent Media & Elluminet Press for their passion, dedication and hard work in the preparation and production of this book.

To all my friends and family for their continued support and encouragement in all my writing projects.

To all my colleagues, students and testers who took the time to test procedures and offer feedback on the book

Finally thanks to you the reader for choosing this book. I hope it helps you to use your mac with greater understanding.

Have fun!

Introducing MacOS Sonoma

MacOS Sonoma, named after California's wine-rich Sonoma County, was unveiled on September 26th as version 14.0 of Apple's desktop operating system for Mac computers.

The operating system is equipped with tools and functionalities that resonate with a broad spectrum of users, from everyday tasks to specialized professional work, especially in the creative domain.

At the heart of macOS lies Darwin, an open-source Unix-like operating system. It's powered by the XNU kernel, which oversees memory allocation, process management, disk activities and CPU resource distribution.

Above this layer is the Quartz windowing system which manages graphical rendering.

The graphical user interface known as Aqua, utilizes the Quartz graphics layer to deliver its distinct visual style and allows users to interact with menus, icons, and windows.

Let's take a look at some of the new features.

What's New?

Sonoma looks similar to its predecessor and introduces some new features, enhancements, and refinements to the Mac. Let's take a look at some of these new features.

New slow-motion screen savers of breathtaking locations from around the world. When you log in, they seamlessly become your desktop wallpaper.

Add widgets to your desktop from the new widget gallery. Access iPhone widgets on Mac with Continuity. Widgets fade for better focus and adapt to your wallpaper colors.

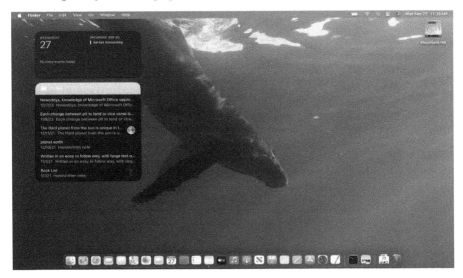

Chapter 1: Introducing MacOS Sonoma

Video Conferencing Enhancements such as Presenter Overlay Keeps you part of the conversation when sharing your screen.

A new stay in frame feature controls the composition of your video when using Studio Display or iPhone as your camera.

New Screen Sharing picker allows you to easily share an app or even multiple apps when on a video call.

Safari now allows you to create a profile allowing you to keep your browsing separate for things like Work and Personal.

You can add web apps to your dock. Add any website to the dock as a web app.

Messages allows you to find messages faster by combining search filters. Share your location or request a friend's location directly within your conversation.

View a full-width PDF right in Notes as well as quickly add links from one note to another.

Game Mode automatically gives games top priority on the CPU and GPU of your Mac.

Communication Safety includes protections for sensitive videos and photos with Sensitive Content Warning option to blur sensitive photos and videos.

There are also visual improvements, and various other minor changes. You'll find a full list on Apple's website.

```
www.apple.com/macos/sonoma/
```

Apple Silicon

In recent years, Apple have developed their own processor chips for the Mac such as the M1, M1 Pro/Max/Ultra, and M2, M2 Pro/Max/Ultra.

Apple Silicon chips combine the CPU, Graphics Processor (or GPU), memory (or RAM), SSD drive controller, and a neural engine which is a component designed to use machine learning and artificial intelligence for tasks such identifying objects in photos, or applying an automatic filter to a picture, analysing videos, voice recognition, and so on.

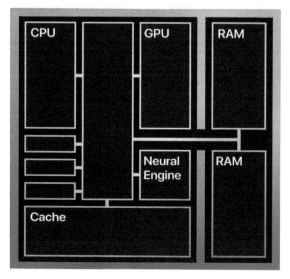

All these components are integrated onto a single chip, known as a system on a chip (SOC), and is why Apple Silicon is much faster and more efficient than using the Intel chips in previous macs.

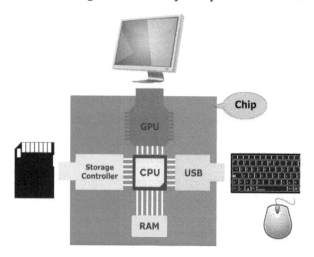

M1 (2020)
- **Mac Models:** MacBook Air, MacBook Pro (13-inch), Mac mini
- **CPU Cores:** 8 (4 Performance Cores + 4 Efficiency Cores)
- **GPU Cores:** 7 or 8
- **Neural Engine Cores:** 16
- **Transistors:** 16 Billion
- **Unified Memory Capacities:** 8GB or 16GB
- **Memory Bandwidth:** 68.25GB/s

M1 Pro (2021)
- **Mac Models:** MacBook Pro (14-inch and 16-inch)
- **CPU Cores:** 8 or 10 (6 or 8 Performance Cores + 2 Efficiency Cores)
- **GPU Cores:** 14 or 16
- **Neural Engine Cores:** 16
- **Transistors:** 33.7 Billion
- **Unified Memory Capacities:** 16GB or 32GB
- **Memory Bandwidth:** 200GB/s

M1 Max (2021)
- **Mac Models:** MacBook Pro (14-inch and 16-inch)
- **CPU Cores:** 10 (8 Performance Cores + 2 Efficiency Cores)
- **GPU Cores:** 24 or 32
- **Neural Engine Cores:** 16
- **Transistors:** 57 Billion
- **Unified Memory Capacities:** 32GB or 64GB
- **Memory Bandwidth:** 400GB/s

M1 Ultra (2022)
- **Mac Models:** Mac Studio
- **CPU Cores:** 20 (16 Performance Cores + 4 Efficiency Cores)
- **GPU Cores:** 48 or 64
- **Neural Engine Cores:** 32
- **Transistors:** 114 Billion
- **Unified Memory Capacities:** 64GB or 128GB
- **Memory Bandwidth:** 800GB/s

M2 (2022)
- **Mac Models:** Mac Mini, MacBook Air (2022), MacBook Air (15-inch, 2023), MacBook Pro (13-inch, 2022)
- **CPU Cores:** 8 (4 Performance Cores + 4 Efficiency Cores)
- **GPU Cores:** 8 or 10
- **Neural Engine Cores:** 16
- **Transistors:** 20 Billion

- **Unified Memory Capacities:** 8GB, 16GB, or 24GB
- **Memory Bandwidth:** 100GB/s

M2 Pro:

- **Mac Models:** Mac Mini, 14-inch MacBook Pro, 16-inch MacBook Pro
- **CPU Cores:** Up to 12 cores (includes up to eight high-performance cores and four high-efficiency cores)
- **GPU Cores:** Up to 19 cores
- **Neural Engine Cores:** 16-core (based on the enhanced custom technologies mentioned)
- **Transistors:** 40 billion
- **Unified Memory Capacities:** Up to 32GB of fast unified memory
- **Memory Bandwidth:** 200GB/s

M2 Max:

- **Mac Models:** 14 and 16-inch MacBook Pro models
- **CPU Cores:** 12 cores (same next-generation 12-core CPU as M2 Pro)
- **GPU Cores:** Up to 38 cores
- **Neural Engine Cores:** 16-core (based on the enhanced custom technologies mentioned)
- **Transistors:** 67 billion
- **Unified Memory Capacities:** Up to 96GB of fast unified memory
- **Memory Bandwidth:** 400GB/s

M2 Ultra:

- **Mac Models:** Mac Studio, Mac Pro
- **CPU Cores:** 24 cores (consists of 16 next-generation high-performance cores and eight next-generation high-efficiency cores)
- **GPU Cores:** Configurable with 60 or 76 next-generation cores
- **Neural Engine Cores:** 32-core Neural Engine, delivering 31.6 trillion operations per second
- **Transistors:** 134 billion
- **Unified Memory Capacities:** Up to 192GB of unified memory
- **Memory Bandwidth:** 800GB/s

You can stay up to date with the latest Macs and their specifications on Apple's website.

`www.apple.com/mac/compare`

How do apps function with different hardware architectures? Applications are typically developed with specific hardware architectures in mind. For instance, Macs with Intel chips (such as the intel core i7) utilize the x64 instruction set, whereas Macs with Apple Silicon (such as M1 or M2) use the ARM instruction set. Essentially, these two instruction sets are like two different languages.

To address this problem and ease the transition over to Apple Silicon, Apple introduced Rosetta 2. This acts as a translator, allowing apps that were developed for Intel-based Macs to run on Apple Silicon Macs. Given that Intel chips use the x64 instruction set and Apple Silicon chips use the ARM instruction set, these apps wouldn't natively run. To do this, Rosetta 2 uses dynamic binary translation. This means it translates the Intel app's x64 instructions into ARM instructions. This translation is done the first time you install an Intel based app, and it converts the entire app to a new version optimized for Apple Silicon.

You might encounter terms such as "native apps" and "universal apps". A native app is an application that has been developed to run on Apple Silicon (M1, M2) without needing any translation. It can fully harness the power and efficiency of the new chips. Universal apps are applications designed to run on both Intel and Apple Silicon without modification. These apps often contains binaries for both Intel-based Macs and Apple Silicon Macs.

While Rosetta 2 does an impressive job translating Intel-based apps for Apple Silicon, native apps will generally offer better performance. This is because they're optimized for the new architecture, taking full advantage of its capabilities.

Apple has provided developers with tools and resources to help them transition their apps over to Apple Silicon. As a result, many popular apps have already been updated or are in the process of being updated to support the new chips natively.

While Apple has committed to supporting Intel-based Macs for several years, they will eventually phase out updates and support for these older machines. This is a natural progression in technology, similar to how Apple transitioned from PowerPC to Intel in the past.

With the transition to Apple Silicon and the push for universal apps, Apple has also emphasized the idea of unified app purchases across the App Store. This means that developers can offer a single purchase that provides the app across multiple Apple platforms, including macOS, iOS, and iPadOS. This is especially relevant as the line between Mac apps and iPad apps blurs, with Macs running Apple Silicon being able to natively run iPadOS/iOS apps.

2

Setting up Your Mac

In this chapter we'll take a look at updating to MacOS Sonoma, as well as:

- Powering up and starting your Mac for the First Time
- Internet, WiFi & VPNs
- Connecting Peripherals
- Other Email Accounts
- Additional Users & Login Options
- Passwords
- Setup Apple Pay
- Touch ID
- Dark Mode & Light Mode
- Setup your Mouse & Trackpad
- Dynamic Desktop, Wallpapers & Screensavers
- Managing Displays
- Setup Universal Control
- System Audio
- Pairing Bluetooth Devices
- Fonts
- Time Machine Backup
- Transfer Files from PC or Mac

To help you better understand this section, take a look at the video resources. Open your web browser and navigate to the following website:

elluminetpress.com/using-mac

Updating to MacOS Sonoma

MacOS Sonoma is a free update to all compatible Macs. If you are updating your Mac, you'll need to check whether your Mac is compatible, as older Macs won't receive the update.

According to Apple, the following Macs will be able to run MacOS Sonoma:

- MacBook Pro introduced in 2018 and later
- MacBook Air introduced in 2018 and later
- Mac mini introduced in 2018 and later
- iMac introduced in 2019 and later
- iMac Pro (from 2017)
- Mac Studio introduced in 2022 and later
- Mac Pro introduced in 2019 and later

If your mac supports Sonoma, you'll likely receive an update notification automatically once Sonoma is released.

Go to the Apple menu, select 'System Settings'.

Select 'general' from the list on the left, then click Software Update.

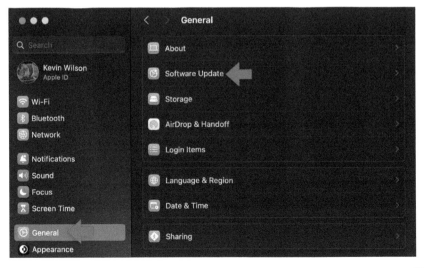

Chapter 2: Setting up Your Mac

When MacOS Sonoma is available it will appear in the updates list.

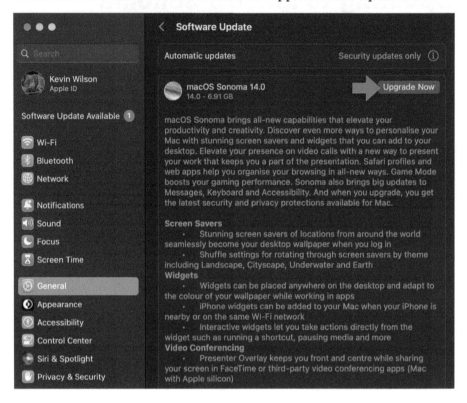

The update process will take some time, and your mac will reboot.

After downloading, the installer will automatically open. Follow the on-screen instructions to complete the installation.

If the Sonoma doesn't show up in the system updates, you can also download it from the App Store. To do this, click on the Apple menu on the top left, then select 'app store'.

In the search field on the top left of the screen type in

MacOS Sonoma

From the search results, click 'view' next to 'macos sonoma'.

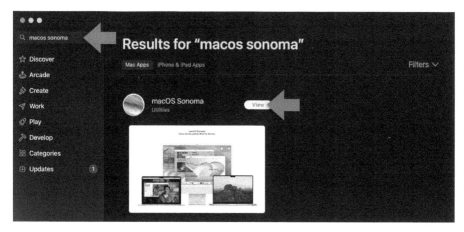

Then click 'get'.

Follow the on screen instructions.

Power Up

The power button on the mac is on the top right of the keyboard on a Macbook Air and Macbook Pro.

 or

On the Mac Pro, you'll find the power button on the top panel.

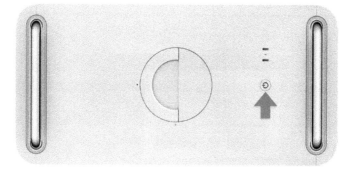

On the iMac and Mac Mini, the power button is situated on the back panel.

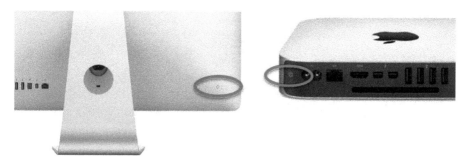

Press the button once to start up your mac.

You can also use the power button to force your mac to shut down in the event of a crash or lock up. Hold the button until the screen goes blank. Only use this option if you're having problems.

Login

If there are multiple accounts you'll see these at the bottom of the screen. Select your user account. The user to sign in will be visible. Press the esc key to see the whole list.

Use Touch ID or use Apple Watch to unlock and log in. If you don't have these setup, type in your mac password.

Power Down

To power down your mac or send it into sleep/standby mode, go to the Apple menu on the top left of the screen.

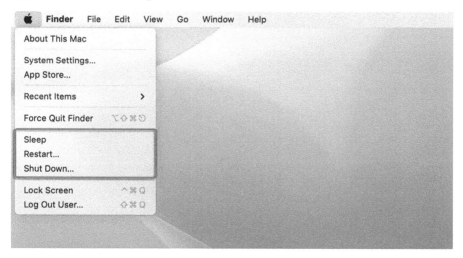

From the menu, click 'shut down' to shut down and power off your mac. Click 'restart' to reboot your mac.

You can also click 'sleep', this will put your mac into standby mode and is convenient if you use your mac on the go a lot and don't have time to wait for your machine to start up.

If you are using a Macbook laptop, you can just close the lid and your Macbook will go into sleep mode.

Starting your Mac for the First Time

When you turn on a new mac for the first time, you'll need to go through some initial steps to set up WiFi, select language, regional preferences and sign in with your Apple ID.

To begin, select your country of residence. Click 'continue'.

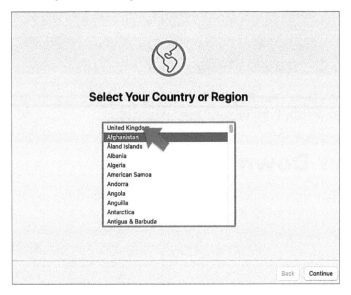

Tap 'continue' on the 'written and spoken languages' page.

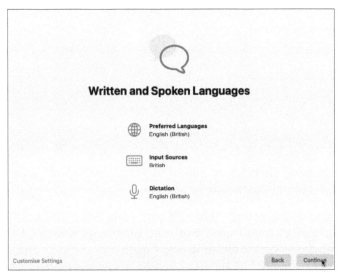

If the language settings aren't correct, tap 'customise settings'.

Click 'not now' on the accessibility screen. You can configure these later in the settings app if you need to make any changes according to your needs.

Select your WiFi network and enter your password when prompted. Your Wi-Fi password is usually printed on the back of your WiFi router.

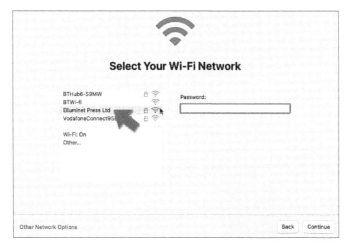

Click 'continue' on the 'data & privacy' screen.

Chapter 2: Setting up Your Mac

Click 'not now' on the 'migration assistant' screen. You can transfer data from an old machine later.

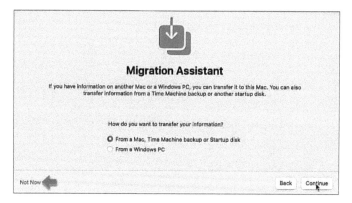

Sign in with your Apple ID email address and password. Click 'continue'.

You may be prompted to enter a verification code. This code will be sent to another Apple device such as your iPhone or iPad. On your iPad or iPhone tap 'allow', then copy the code into the boxes on your Mac.

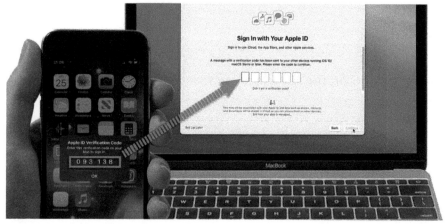

Accept the 'terms and conditions', click 'continue'.

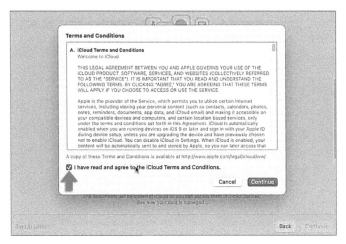

Create your computer account. This is the account you'll use to log into your Mac and it is different from your Apple ID account. Enter a password, then click 'continue'.

Click 'customise settings' on the 'express setup' screen.

Chapter 2: Setting up Your Mac

Enable location services. It is safe to enable this and it will allow you to make use of location based services such as maps, local news, and weather. Click 'enable location services on this mac', then click 'continue'.

Click 'continue' on the 'analytics' screen

Click 'continue' on the 'screen time' page.

Enable Siri, click 'continue'.

Then on the next screen, click 'not now', click 'continue'.

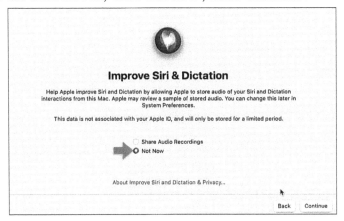

If you're using a Macbook with a finger print scanner, you will be asked to set up your finger prints so you can log into your Mac. Click 'continue' and follow the instructions to register your finger print.

Chapter 2: Setting up Your Mac

Select your look. You can choose from light mode or dark mode. Dark mode is good for low light conditions and night time viewing. It removes most of the bright white color from the screen. Click 'light' or 'dark', or select 'auto' to use light mode during the day, and dark mode during the evening.

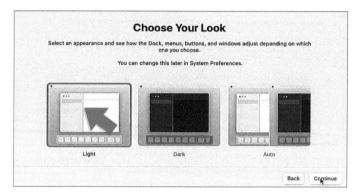

Give your Mac a few minutes to complete the setup.

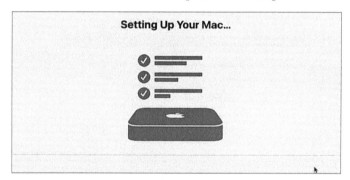

You'll land on the desktop when the setup finishes.

Now you can start to use your Mac.

Apple ID

An Apple ID is an account used to access various Apple services, including the App Store, Apple Music, iCloud, iMessage, and FaceTime. It incorporates the email address and password used for signing in, along with contact, payment, and additional information required for these services. Note that the Apple ID is different from the account used to sign into your Mac.

Create a New ID

To create an Apple ID open safari and go to the following website:

`appleid.apple.com/account`

Fill in the form with your name, country and date of birth.

Create Your Apple ID

One Apple ID is all you need to access all Apple services.
Already have an Apple ID? Find it here ›

First name   Last name

COUNTRY / REGION

United States   ⌄

Birthday

Enter an email address you want to use as your Apple ID. *Keep a note of this email address and password, you will need it if you want to purchase Apps from the App Store, use iCloud, Apple Email, iMessage, Apple Music and the iTunes Store.*

name@example.com

This will be your new Apple ID

Password

Confirm password

Apple will send a verification email to the address you used as your Apple ID. Find the code in the email and enter it in the verification window on your screen. Do the same with the phone verification text message.

Once your email is verified, your Apple ID is created and ready to be used with Apple services.

iCloud

iCloud is a cloud storage service developed by Apple. iCloud enables you to store your email, messages, documents, photos, and music on Apple's remote servers. This enables you to share data between your devices and with other users.

If you haven't signed in, go to system settings, click 'Apple id' and enter your Apple ID username and password if prompted.

From here you can change your iCloud settings. Use the panel on the left hand side to navigate between the sections.

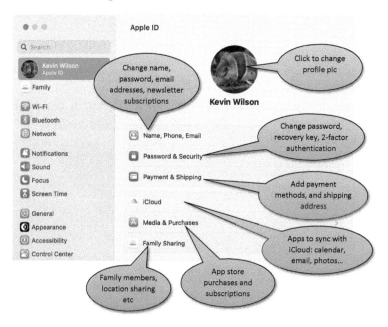

Select 'name, phone, email' to change iCloud password, or your name. To change your password, click 'password & security'. To add payment methods, select 'payment & shipping.

Underneath you'll see a list of all your Apple devices, such as iPhone, iPad or another Mac. Here, you can click on a device and see info such as serial number, and show the location on the web.

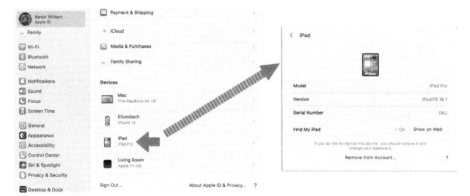

If you need to sign out, click 'sign out' on the bottom left.

iCloud Drive Setup

Go to system settings, click 'Apple id' and enter your Apple ID username and password if prompted. Select 'icloud' from the panel on the right.

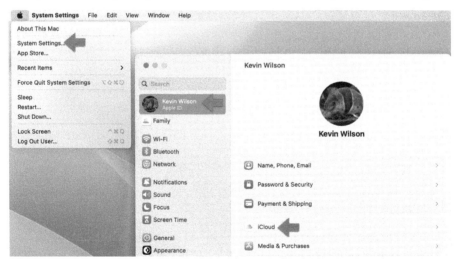

To change which apps store documents on data on iCloud, click 'iCloud Drive'.

Chapter 2: Setting up Your Mac

Click on 'options'

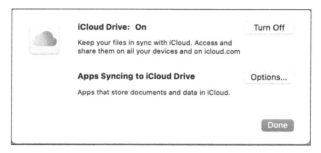

Select your apps you want to use iCloud Drive.

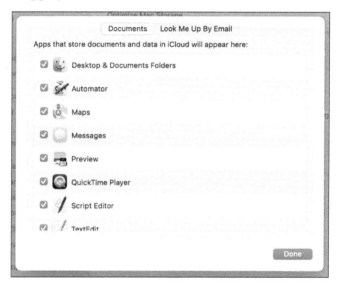

These apps will save data to iCloud Drive rather than to your Mac.

Click 'done'.

Storage Management

iCloud Storage Management allows you to manage what data is saved on your iCloud Storage. To manage your iCloud storage, go to system settings, then select your 'Apple id'.

Click on 'icloud'.

At the top of the window, select 'manage'.

At the bottom of the window, you'll see a chart showing a breakdown of the space used on your iCloud Storage. Click 'manage'.

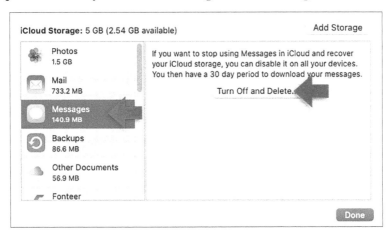

Here, you'll see a more detailed breakdown of the apps using storage on iCloud and the amount of space they've taken up. Now the data stored on iCloud isn't the app itself, it's the data such as your messages, photos you've taken, device backups etc.

Click on the app to view details and delete any data. This is useful if your iCloud storage is running low.

Click 'add storage' if you need more than 5GB of iCloud storage. There is a charge for larger storage plans.

Setup Internet

There are various ways to connect to the internet, the most common being WiFi. You can also connect using an ethernet cable.

WiFi

To set up your WiFi, select the WiFi symbol on the status menu on the right hand side of the screen. From the drop down, click 'other networks'. Select the network you want to connect to (SSID).

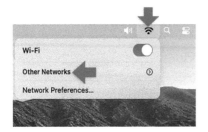 

In the dialog box that appears on your screen, enter the WiFi password (sometimes called a network key).

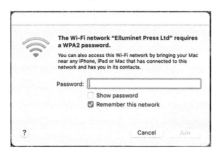

On a home network, your WiFi password is usually printed on the back of your modem, access point, or router.

If you don't see the WiFi icon on the top right, go to system settings and select 'network'. Click 'WiFi' on the right hand side of the window, then click 'network name'. From the list select the network you want to connect to.

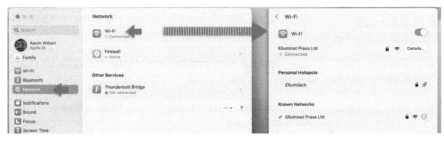

Using an Ethernet Cable

If WiFi isn't available, and you use a cable modem to get online in your home, you can use a cable.

Here is a typical setup.

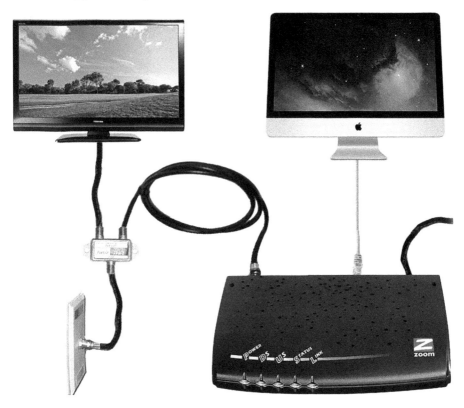

Your coax cable coming into your home is usually split using a splitter. One cable will go to your TV and the other will go to your modem.

Your computer will connect to your modem using an Ethernet cable.

Chapter 2: Setting up Your Mac

Plug one end of the Ethernet cable into your modem, then power up your modem and allow it to connect to your ISP.

Plug the other end into the Ethernet port on your computer, as shown below.

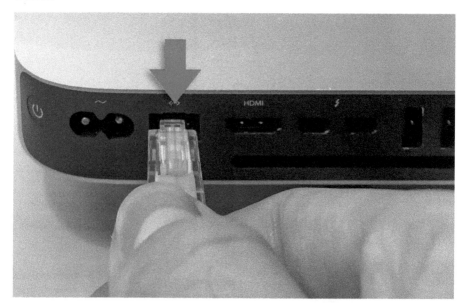

Your mac should connect automatically. To check, go to system settings.

Select 'network' from the list on the left. Click the 'i' next to Ethernet on the right.

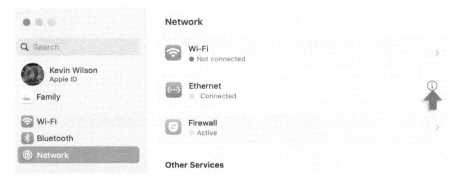

Select 'TCP/IP'. Make sure IPv4 is set to DHCP and your computer has picked up an IP address. Or if you need to enter settings manually change 'configure IP' to manual.

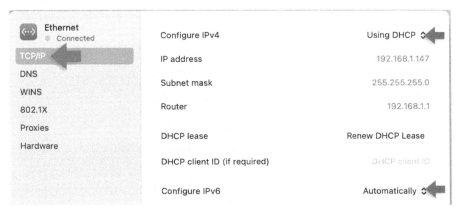

If you need to change the DNS settings, select DNS from the list on the left, then enter the IP addresses for the DNS servers.

Similarly if you need to add a proxy server, click on proxies, then enter the proxy server details

Phone Tethering

Tethering allows you to share your iPhone's data connection with your Mac. To set this up, on your iPhone go to the settings app and tap 'personal hotspot'. Toggle 'personal hotspot' to on, then enable your bluetooth.

On your Mac, your iPhone appears in the WiFi menu as another network.

In this example the iPhone is called 'iPhoneAPC3', so I'd select that one from the WiFi networks.

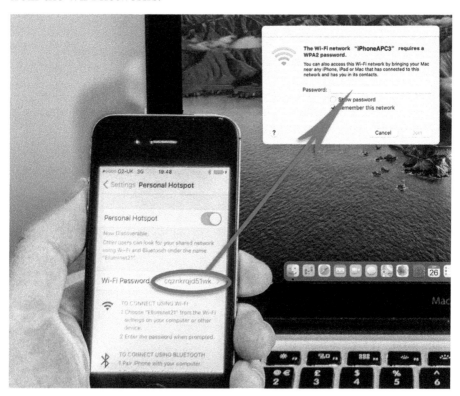

When prompted on your Mac, enter the WiFi password shown in the personal hotspot settings on your iPhone, as show above.

Mobile USB Modems

If you use your Mac on the go a lot or travel frequently, you should also consider using 3G/4G/5G LTE mobile data modem. You can get these from a phone provider such as AT&T, Verizon, o2, T-Mobile, etc.

When you buy these from your phone provider, you can take out a contract or pay as you go in the same way you'd buy a cell/mobile phone.

You'll need to follow the instructions from your phone supplier for specifics. However the procedure is very similar.

You'll usually need to install a piece of software to manage your device.

Plug your dongle into a USB port on your Mac.

Double click the icon that appears on your desktop.

Open the folder called 'Mac' if there is one, then double-click the setup package. Follow the instructions on screen.

Once installed you can use the connection manager to connect to your service.

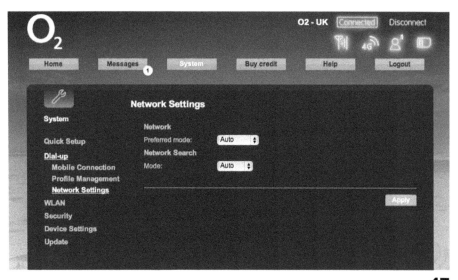

Virtual Private Networks

A Virtual Private Network (or VPN) is a secure connection where data is send and received over the internet through an encrypted tunnel. This means you can browse the internet anonymously and your data is safe on unsecured networks such as public WiFi.

Your Mac   ISP   VPN Server

Using a VPN Service

There are various different VPN services available. Eg Windscribe. Windscribe is a good starter service as you get 10GB of free data a month. To use the service, you'll need to download the app. Go to:

```
windscribe.com/download
```

Scroll down, click the 'mac' icon under 'windscribe for your computer'.

Click the downloads icon on the top right of Safari, from the drop down double click the download to begin.

Follow the on screen instructions to sign up and activate the service. You'll find the VPN app on launch pad - click to start the app if it isn't already running. Click the icon on the top right of the screen. In the drop down window, click the switch on the top left to turn on the VPN.

Manual Setup

Open the system settings then select 'network'. Click the '+' icon on the bottom left

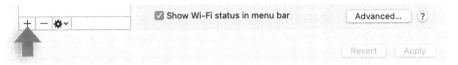

In the 'interface' drop down, select 'VPN'. Then in 'VPN type' select the kind of VPN connection you want to set up. Get this info from your VPN service or Administrator. Give the connection a name, click 'create'.

Select the interface and enter a name for the new service.

Interface: VPN

VPN Type: IKEv2

Service Name: VPN (IKEv2)

Cancel   Create

Enter the server address and the remote ID for the VPN connection. Get this info from your VPN service or administrator.

Server Address: vpn.elluminetpress.com

Remote ID: vpn.elluminetpress.com

Local ID:

Authentication Settings...

Click 'authentication settings'. In the drop down box, select method of authentication: username or certificate. Get this info from your VPN service or administrator.

Authentication Settings:

Username

Username: username

Password: ••••••••

Cancel   OK

Click 'ok'. Click 'advanced', under the DNS tab, click the '+' on the bottom left and enter a DNS server address.

49

Connecting Peripherals

You can connect peripherals such as external drives, scanners, and printers. You connect peripherals using a USB cable. On the side panel of the Macbook, you'll find your USB ports. These will be USB-C ports. On the side panel of your Macbook, you'll see these ports.

If you need standard USB ports, or HDMI, then you can get a hub that plugs into the side of your Macbook.

These USB-C hubs are available at most computer stores and online.

The USB-C hub will allow you to use the USB-A type used on the most common peripherals.

On the back panel of the iMac. Here you'll see your USB ports, ethernet, headphones, and an SD card reader so you can read memory cards from digital cameras.

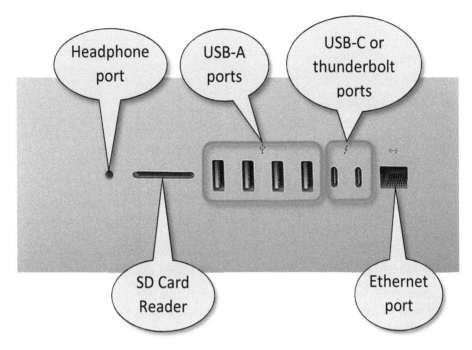

The back panel of your mac mini 2018. Here you'll find your USB ports, and HDMI port for plugging in a monitor, ethernet, and a headphone jack.

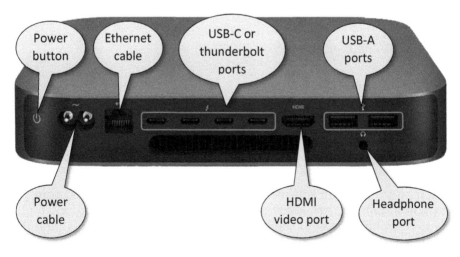

You'll also find the power buttons and power cable ports.

System Settings

System settings is the control panel for your mac. Here you can personalise your system and change settings.

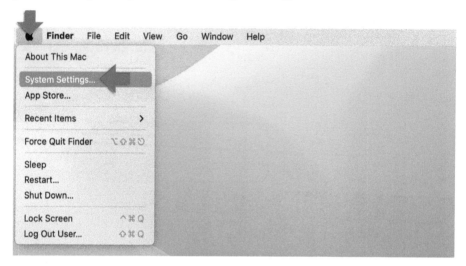

To open your system settings, click the Apple menu on the top left hand side of your screen, and select 'system settings'.

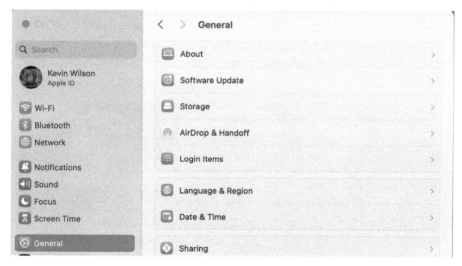

You'll notice that the settings are grouped into categories according to their function and are listed down the left hand side. So for example, if you're looking for WiFi settings, select WiFi, if you want to adjust the sound settings, select 'sound' and so on. Here is a brief explanation of what each of the sections in the system settings panel does and where to go when you are looking for a setting.

Apple ID. You can manage various aspects related to your Apple ID account and iCloud settings such as synchronizing photos, documents, and app data across devices, controlling iTunes Store, App Store, and Apple Books. You can also update personal information, security settings, and payment methods. You can manage iCloud storage usage and backups, as well as Family Sharing, shared purchases, subscriptions, and location sharing with family members.

Wi-Fi. Allows you to manage your wireless connectivity. Turn WiFi on or off, connect to available networks and manage known networks. You can also configure advanced network options such as TCP/IP settings, DNS, and proxies.

Bluetooth. Allows you to enable/disable bluetooth and change settings, or pair a bluetooth device.

Network. Manage both WiFi and Ethernet connections, adjust advanced network settings such as IP addresses, TCP/IP settings, DNS, proxy servers, and VPN configurations.

Notifications Notification center settings, alerts, banners and which apps are allowed send notifications.

Sound. Adjust settings for speakers and microphones, choose system alert sounds and other sound effect settings. Adjust the overall system volume as well as individual app volumes.

Focus. Allows you to create sessions without interruptions from other apps, notifications or messages.

Screen Time. Provides a detailed reports of device and app usage, the ability to set limits for app usage and schedule downtime, and implement content restrictions and privacy settings.

General. Allows you find information about your mac, system software updates, storage, airdrop/handoff, login items, language/region, sharing, time machine, restore mac defaults and select a startup disk.

Appearance. Change desktop wallpaper, dark/light mode, accent colors and sidebar icon colors

Accessibility. Manage screen readability, voice over, speech, etc.

Control Center. Add/remove control center modules such as WiFi, bluetooth, sound and display controls.

Siri and Spotlight. Configure, Enable/disable Siri. Preferences for system wide search settings.

Security & Privacy. Allows you to control which apps have access to location, contacts, photos, and other data, manage FileVault, Firewall, and Gatekeeper, and set a password for sleep or screen saver.

Desktop & Dock. Allows you to adjust the size and position the Dock. You can customize settings for the menu bar, Hot Corners, Mission Control, desktop, stage manager, windows and widgets.

Displays. Allows you to adjust the display resolution and scale to optimize the clarity and size of your on-screen content. You can manage color profiles and calibrations. If you're using multiple displays, you can configure settings to ensure a seamless transition between each screen.

Wallpaper. Allows you to change the desktop background to an image of your choice.

Screen Saver. Change screen saver settings.

Battery. Shows battery health, as well as on screen usage, enable/disable low power mode

Lock Screen. Allows you to enable/disable screen saver lock time, when to turn of displays and user switching options

Touch ID. If you're using a Macbook with Touch ID, you can setup or add finger prints to unlock your Mac

Users & Groups. Allows you to add, delete, and manage your user accounts on your Mac, configure automatic login, display login window options. These accounts are used to log into your Mac.

Passwords. Manage all saved passwords from Safari and other apps you have signed into.

Internet Accounts. Allows you to add and manage internet accounts such as email, calendar, and contacts.

Game Center. Allows you to add your gaming accounts, see your friends activity, profile privacy, nickname, etc

Wallet & Apple Pay. If you're using a Mac with Touch ID, you can add credit cards to use in the App Store or on the Web

Keyboard. Set keyboard shortcuts, keyboard country layout settings & dictation.

Trackpad. Set pointer track speed and sensitivity, as well as multi touch gestures.

Printers & Scanners. Add printers or scanner devices, as well as device settings.

Search System settings

On the top left of the settings window, you'll see a search field.

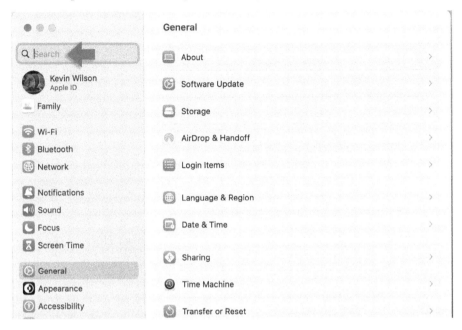

Type in the name of the setting or device you want to change. In the drop down menu, you'll see suggested settings. Select the closest match.

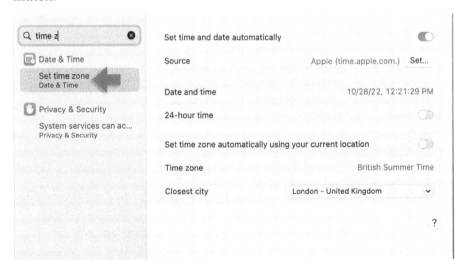

This will take you to the section in the system settings where you can adjust the setting you searched for.

Add a Printer

Click on the Apple menu on the top left of your screen. From this menu, select 'System settings'.

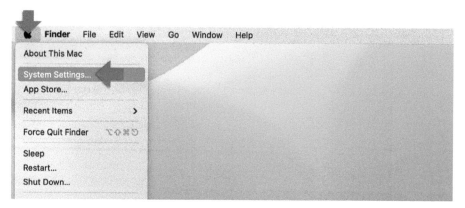

From the list on the left select 'Printers & Scanners'. Here, you'll see information about current printers and devices.

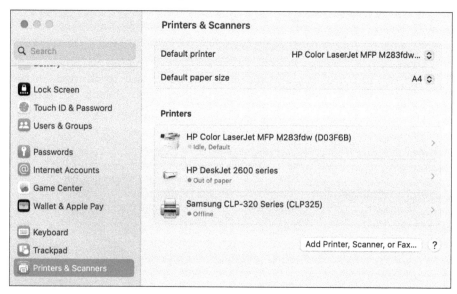

To add a new device, click 'add printer, scanner, or fax' on the bottom right.

In the box that appears, MacOS will scan for connected printers; whether they are connected via USB or WiFi.

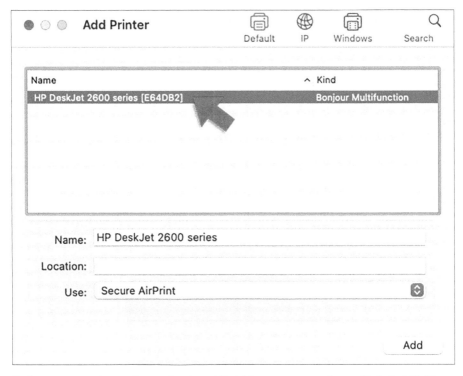

Select your printer from the 'use' list if necessary, then click 'add'. Your mac will download the driver from its own driver library.

You'll see your printer appear in the 'printers' list.

You'll also find a new print center to manage your printer and print jobs. To access it, open finder, select 'applications', then click 'utilities'. Double click on 'print center'. Have a look at the 'print center' bonus

elluminetpress.com/mac-os

Also, have a look at the printer demos at:

elluminetpress.com/using-mac

57

Connect Printer to WiFi

Nowadays you'd connect your printer to your Mac using WiFi. It is difficult to give specific instructions on printer setup as each model of printer and each manufacturer has its own method. However, I will provide some general guidelines you can use to get started.

If your printer is brand new, you'll need to connect it to your WiFi. Printers with LCD panels display step-by-step instructions for setting up the wireless connection when you first turn on the printer. So read the instructions for specifics on how to do this.

If your printer doesn't have an LCD panel, use the WPS method. You can use this method if you have a WPS button on your router - as shown in the photo below. Refer to the printer's quick start guide to find the exact procedure for your printer model. Usually you have to press and hold the WiFi button on your printer for a few seconds, then go to your router and press the WPS button.

If your router doesn't have a WPS button, you'll have to select your WiFi network (SSID) and enter your WiFi password on your printer. You'll need to refer to the printer's instructions on exactly how to do that on your particular printer.

Other Email Accounts

You can add all your email accounts such as Gmail, Yahoo, Microsoft and any email accounts you may have. To to this, open system settings.

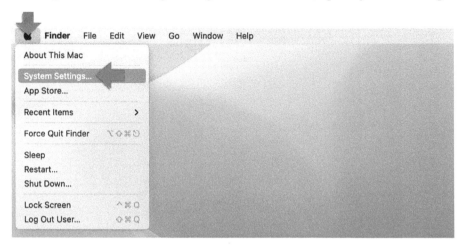

From the list on the left hand side, select 'internet accounts'.

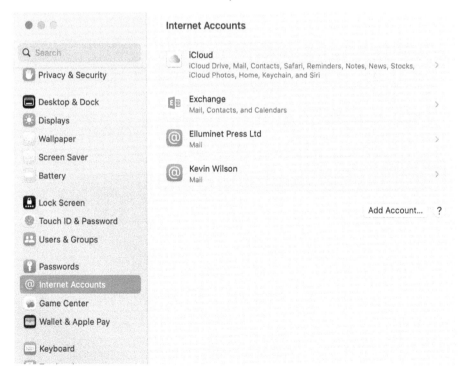

To add a new account, click 'add account' on the bottom right.

If you have a Gmail account, click 'google'. If you have a Microsoft Account use 'exchange'. For yahoo mail select 'yahoo'. For any other email account click 'add other account' at the bottom of the list. In this example, I'm adding my Gmail account. So I'd click 'google'.

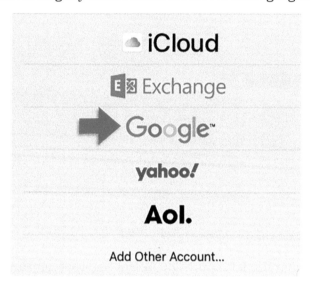

Click 'open browser' on the popup prompt.

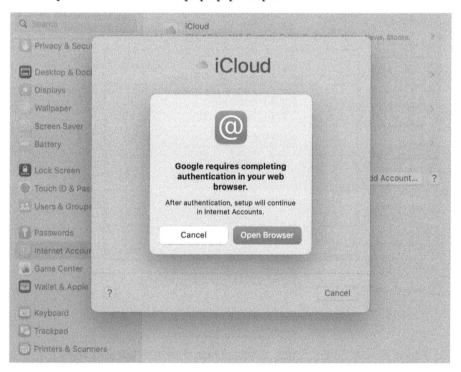

Sign in with your Gmail email address and password. Click 'next'. On the next screen click 'allow' to give macOS permission to access your Gmail account.

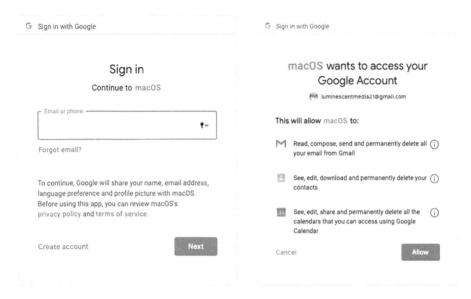

Click the tick boxes to select what you want to sync between your mac and your Gmail account. You can bring over your email, contacts, calendars and notes. All these will be added to your mail, contacts, calendar, and notes apps on your mac.

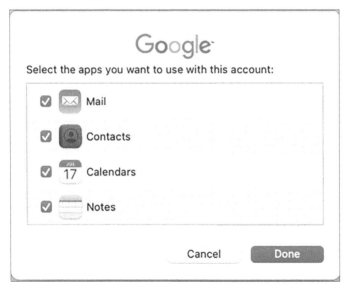

Click 'done' when you're finished.

Additional Users

You can create multiple user accounts for all those who use your Mac. So you could create one for each family member.

To do this, open the system settings. Click the Apple menu on the top left, then select 'system settings'

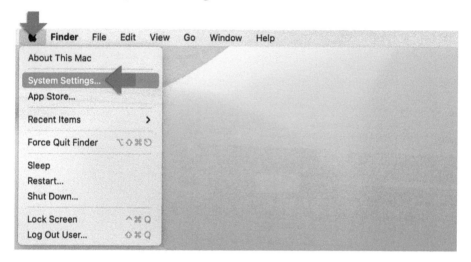

Click 'users & groups' from the list on the left. Then click 'add account' on the right.

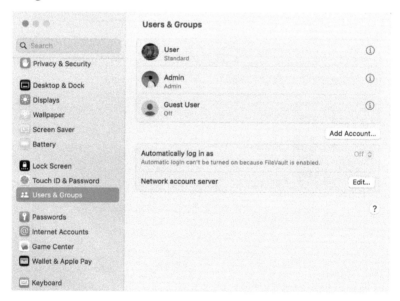

Enter your mac username and password if prompted

Fill in the details in the 'new user' form.

New Account: Standard

Full Name: |

Account Name:

This will be used as the name for your home folder.

Password: Required

Verify: Verify

Password Hint: Hint (Recommended)
(Recommended)

? Cancel Create User

For 'new account', set it to 'standard'. Only use 'administrator' if you want to allow this user to change system settings or install apps.

Enter the user's first and second names into the 'full name' field. Your mac will automatically create an account name.

Enter a password for this account in the 'password' and then again in the 'verify' fields.

Click 'create user' when you're done.

Login Options

To do this, open the system settings. Click the Apple menu on the top left, then select 'system settings'

Chapter 2: Setting up Your Mac

Select 'general' from the list on the left. To open an app at login, select the '+' icon underneath the 'open at login' section. Select an app to run. If you want to remove an app, select the app from the list, then click on the '-' icon.

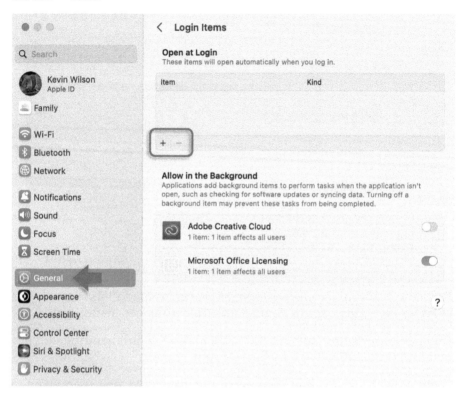

Underneath, you can enable/disable apps that run in the background. Just toggle the switch next to the app name.

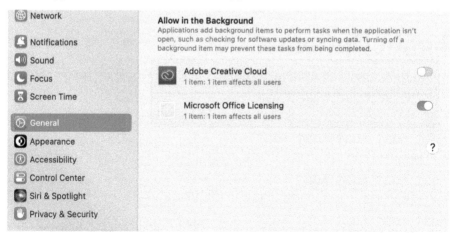

Change Passwords

You can change your mac password and your Apple ID password from the system settings.

Mac Password

To change your mac password - the password you use to unlock your mac, click the Apple menu on the top left, then select 'system settings' from the menu.

Select 'users & groups' from the list on the left. Click the 'i' icon next to the user account you want to change.

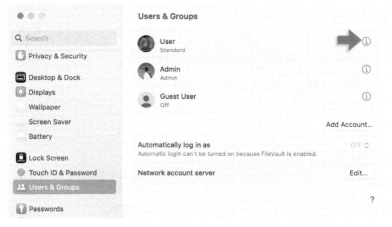

Click 'change password'.

In the dialog box that appears, enter your current password in the 'old password' field, then enter your new password into the 'new password' and 'verify' fields.

Click 'change password' to confirm.

Apple ID Password

To change your mac password - the password you use to sign into your Apple ID, App Store, etc, click the Apple menu on the top left, then select 'system settings' from the menu.

Click your Apple ID account at the top left.

Click 'password & security' on the right hand side.

Click 'change password'.

In the popup dialog box, enter your new password, then click 'change'.

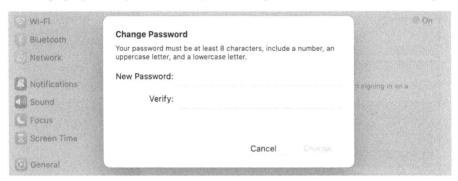

Password Manager

A passwords section is available in the system settings. This section groups all your saved logins and passwords from various websites and services into one place, so they're easier to manage.

To view your passwords, click the Apple menu on the top left, then select 'system settings'.

Select 'passwords' from the list on the left. Enter the password you use to sign into your Mac. Or use touch ID if enabled.

Here, you can manage your passwords. Here at the top you'll see 'password options'. Using this setting, you can enable or disable autofill, which allows apps to automatically enter passwords for signing in.

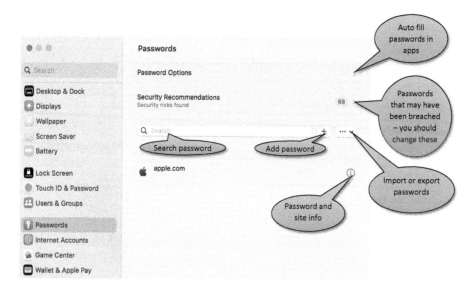

Underneath you'll see a 'security recommendations' section. This is a list of passwords that have appeared in data breaches, or passwords Apple consider to be weak or easily guessed. You should go through this list and change the passwords on the various sites.

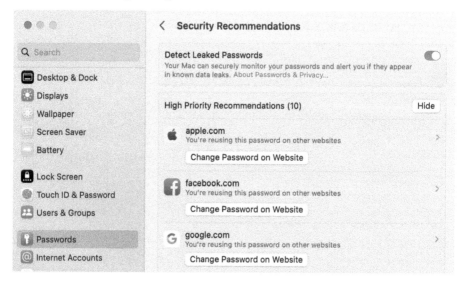

Back on the passwords screen, select 'i' icon next to the site on the right hand side.

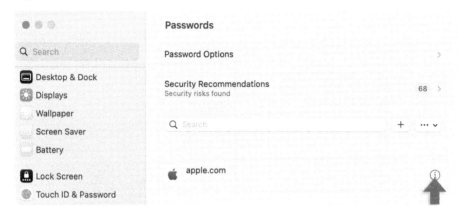

If you click 'edit' on the right, you can change the username & password that has been saved. Click 'change password on website' to change the password on the actual site. Click 'create strong password' if you want your Mac to generate a random password for you.

You'll see an alert under the 'security recommendations' section any of your passwords appear in a data breach, or are considered weak or easily guessed. If you want to share the password with someone else, click the 'share icon on the bottom left of the window.

Click 'done' when you're finished.

Setup Apple Pay

To set up Apple Pay, go to the settings app on your iPhone, scroll down and tap 'wallet & Apple pay'. Then tap 'add card'.

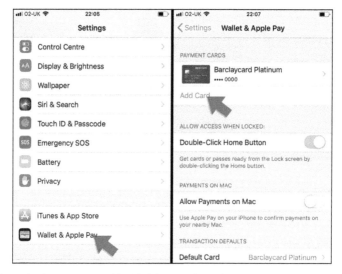

If you already have a credit/debit card registered with your Apple ID, then Apple pay will ask you to add this one.

If this is the card you want to use, then enter the 3 digit security code and tap 'next' on the top right. Hit 'agree' on the terms and conditions. Your card will be added.

If you want to add a different card, tap 'add a different card' underneath.

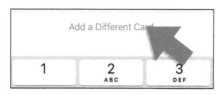

Position the card so it fills the white rectangle on your screen. Apple Pay will scan your card and automatically enter your details

If you can't get the camera to scan the card, tap 'enter card details manually' then key in your card number, exp dates, and so on.

Tap next. Check and confirm your card details. Make any changes if necessary, so the details match those on your card. Tap next, then tap 'agree' to the terms and conditions.

Now you'll need to verify your card. Some banks use different methods, so read the instructions on the screen. In this example, the bank will send a code via SMS to the phone number registered when the bank account was opened. Tap 'next'.

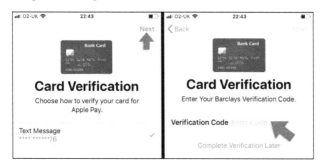

Check your SMS messages and enter the verification code in the field. Tap 'next'.

Setup Apple Pay on a Macbook

If your Macbook has a touch sensor on the top right of the keyboard, then you can use this method to set up Apple pay. Open system settings and select 'wallet & Apple pay'.

Under 'transaction defaults', you can add your shipping address, email, phone number and so on. This will be passed to the retailer when you make a purchase.

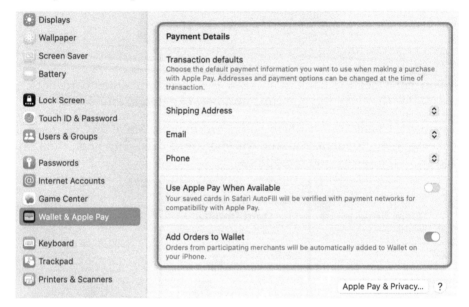

Enable 'use apple pay when available' if you want to use Apple Pay to pay for things in Safari. Enable 'add orders to wallet' to automatically add orders made on other Apple devices.

To add a payment method, click 'add card' on the top right.

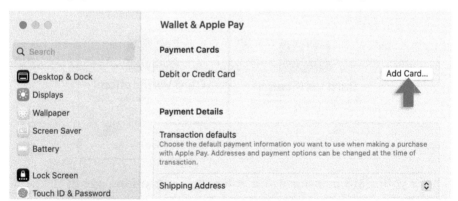

Point the front of your card at your camera. Position your card in the white rectangle. Allow your Mac to identify the card. Click 'next'.

Check and amend any details if necessary. Click 'next'.

Verify the expiration date, then enter your 3 digit security code.

Click 'next'. Your bank will verify your information (follow any instructions or prompts that may appear).

After your bank has verified your card you can use Apple pay.

Touch ID

You can use Touch ID on a mac that has a touch sensor such as a Macbook air or Macbook pro.

Click the Apple menu on the top left, then select 'system settings'

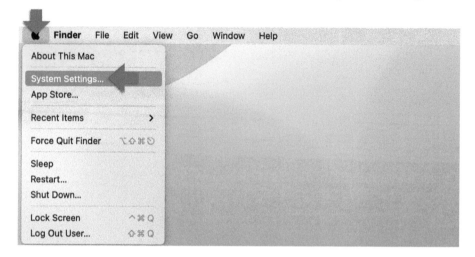

Click 'Touch ID & Password' from the list on the left.

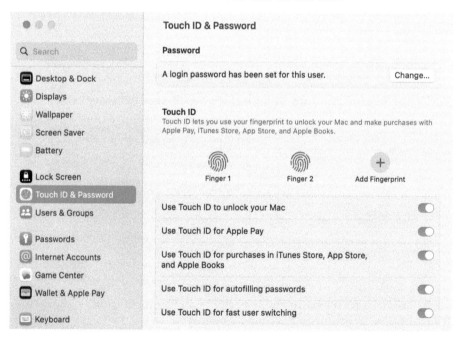

Select all items under 'use touch id for'. Click 'add fingerprint'.

Now scan the finger you most likely use to turn on your mac - eg index finger.

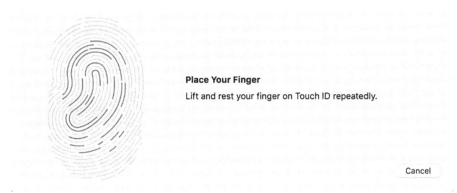

Place Your Finger

Lift and rest your finger on Touch ID repeatedly.

Cancel

Rest your finger on the touch sensor, remove your finger, then rest your finger on the sensor again. You'll need to do this multiple times until your Mac tells you the procedure is complete.

Once complete, click 'done'.

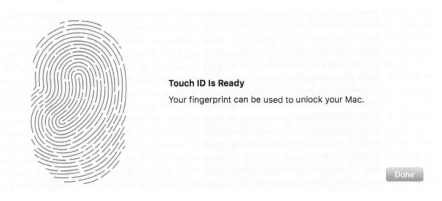

Touch ID Is Ready

Your fingerprint can be used to unlock your Mac.

Done

You'll now be able to unlock your mac with Touch ID, use Apple pay to pay for things on the web, or Apple Store.

Changing the Appearance

To change the appearance such as dark/light mode, accent colors, scroll bars, icon sizes and so on, open your system settings then select 'appearance' from the list on the left.

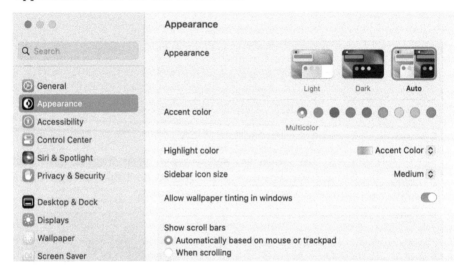

Dark Mode & Light Mode

Dark Mode is designed to put less strain on the eyes and is intended to make reading a computer screen easier. Here in the screen shot below you can dark mode on the left and light mode on the right. Dark mode has a high contrast visual look with dark backgrounds and white text.

To enable dark mode, change the 'appearance' option to 'dark'. You can also set the appearance mode to 'auto'. This means you'll get light mode during daylight hours and dark mode at night.

Accent Colors

You can change the highlight colors and accents. These are the colors of active tab, focused input texts, checked boxes, and so on. If you need to change these, select a color in 'accent color' and 'highlight color'

App Sidebar Icon Size and Wallpaper Tint

This changes the size of the text in the sidebars in various apps such as mail, photos, music, settings and so on

Scrollbar Behaviours

You can adjust when scroll bars appear such as automatically when you move your mouse, when you scroll the window, or set them to always visible. You can also select what happens when you click inside a scroll bar

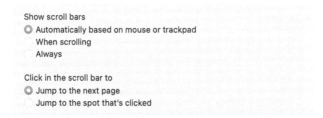

Setup your Trackpad

Personally I find the default settings on the trackpad to be very unresponsive and hard to use. So I tweak the settings in the system settings.

Open your system settings. Click the Apple menu on the top left, then select 'system settings' from the menu.

Select 'trackpad' from list on the left hand side.

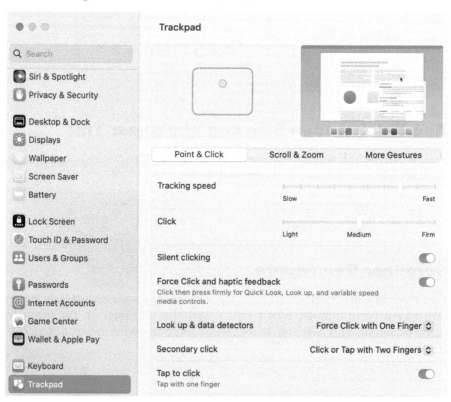

On the point and click tab, move the slider at the top to adjust the pointer tracking speed. Move the click slider to set how much pressure you need to put on the trackpad to click. Turning off silent clicking turns off the artificial click sound when you click on something.

Enable 'force click and haptic feedback to show previews or quick look when you press the trackpad harder that for a click. Enable 'tap to click'. This allows you to use the tap feature to select something, rather than trying to click the left button on the trackpad.

On the 'scroll & zoom' tab, disable 'natural scrolling'. So when you run your fingers down the trackpad your page scrolls down with you instead of up. This makes it a lot easier to navigate through pages on websites and other applications. You can also enable/disable zoom and rotate.

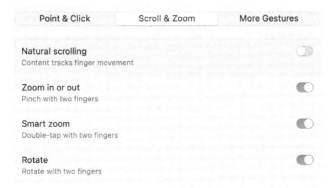

On the 'more gestures' tab, you can configure two and three fingure gestures for turning pages, swiping between apps and so on.

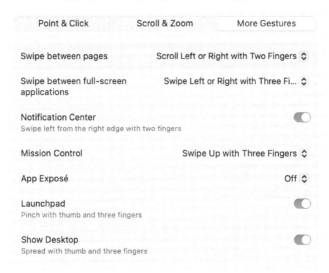

You can enable the two finger swipe from the left edge of the trackpad to show notification center, or configure a gesture to open mission control, launch pad and mission control.

Setup your Mouse

Personally I find the default settings on the mouse to be very unresponsive and hard to use. So I tweak the settings in the system settings.

Open your system settings. Click the Apple menu on the top left, then select 'system settings' from the menu.

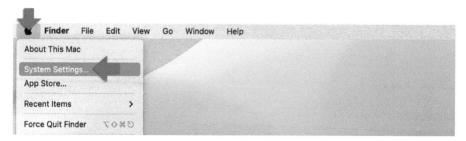

Select 'mouse' from the list on the left hand side.

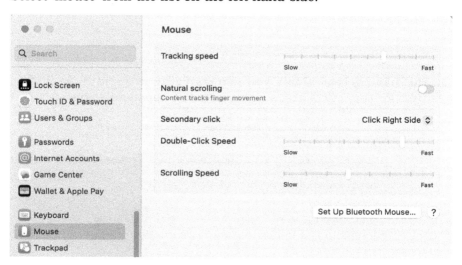

Disable 'natural scrolling', so your pages move in the right direction when you scroll up and down.

Increase the 'tracking speed' until you have the desired mouse pointer speed when you move the mouse. This will make it less strenuous on your wrist. You can also adjust the double click speed - this is how quickly you have to click the button, and the scroll speed, this is how many lines of a page scroll at a time

If you have a bluetooth mouse, Click 'set up bluetooth mouse'. See "Pairing Bluetooth Devices" on page 96.

Screensavers

Sonoma introduces new screensavers that are designed to enhance the visual experience for users.

Click the Apple menu on the top left, then select 'system settings' from the menu. Then select 'screensaver' from the list on the left. The Show as Wallpaper option means the screensaver will be displayed as your desktop wallpaper when it activates. The 'Show on All Spaces' means that the screensaver will be visible on all virtual desktops (Spaces) that you have created.

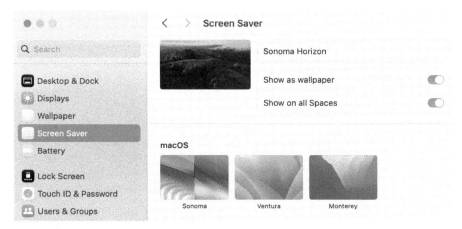

In the screensaver settings, you'll see a list of available screensavers. Click on a screensaver to select it.

The new screen savers feature breathtaking locations from around the world and been captured in high resolution to provide a mesmerizing visual experience. Scroll down and select one of the themes from below

These screen savers seamlessly become your desktop wallpaper when you log in. This means that the beautiful scene you were watching as a screen saver can continue to grace your desktop, providing a cohesive visual experience.

To change the time delay before the screensaver shows, select 'lock screen settings' from the list on the left. See page 82.

Lock Screen

The lock screen is the screen that shows when your machine goes to sleep, when the screensaver shows or locks due to inactivity. You can customise this screen.

To do this, open the system settings, select 'lock screen' from the list on the left hand side.

Here you can change the amount of time before the screensaver starts, and how long before your display goes off when running on battery or power supply.

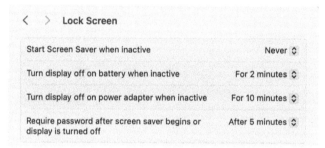

Further down, you can select the size of the clock, and whether to show password hints when you mistype a password, or whether to show any messages or notifications on the lock screen.

Underneath, you can change how to display the log in screen. Whether it is a list of registered users or just a username and password field.

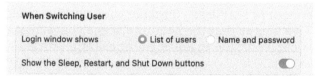

You can also set whether you want to show the sleep, start and shutdown buttons on the lock screen. Just toggle the switch.

Wallpaper

A wallpaper is a digital image or set of images that is used as a desktop background on your screen. Wallpapers are also used as a background on the lock or login screen. To change the wallpaper, open system settings, then select 'wallpaper' from the list on the left.

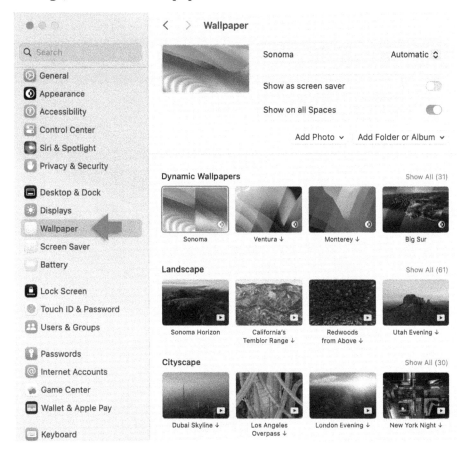

You'll see various different wallpapers to choose from. Dynamic wallpapers change automatically based on certain conditions such as time of day, weather, system events or user activity.

Sonoma introduces some visually stunning wallpapers. You'll see these listed in various categories such as landscapes, underwater, earth and so on. These are not just static images but dynamic, moving visuals that play in slow motion, providing a serene and visually appealing backdrop when your Mac is inactive. The wallpapers are linked with the new screensavers, see page 81.

Just click on the thumbnail preview to select the wallpaper.

Using your Own Photos

You can change the background image/wallpaper on your desktop to anything you like. Perhaps a loved one? Child? Or a picture from your last vacation, or outing with a friend? You can use a photograph taken from your iPhone or iPad. To do this, open the photos app on your mac.

Double click the photo you want to use.

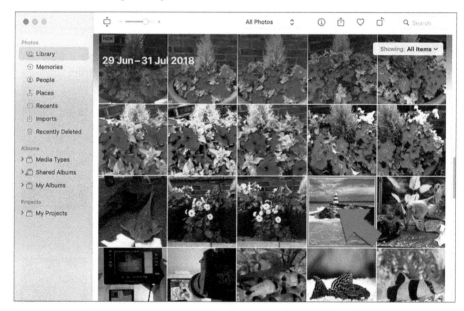

Click the share icon on the top right, then select 'set desktop picture'.

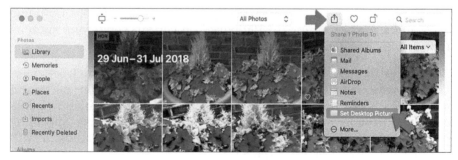

Your picture will appear on your desktop.

Managing Displays

You can manage the displays you connect to your mac. You can also connect multiple displays to your mac. This could be another monitor, projector or TV.

Open your system settings. Click the Apple menu on the top left, then select 'system settings' from the menu.

Select 'displays' from the list on the left. If you have one display, you'll see it appear at the top. If you have multiple displays, you'll see them listed at the top next to the 'arrange button'. Click on the display you want to configure.

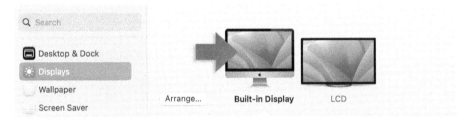

Mirror or Extend

Here you can adjust the settings for that display. If you have multiple displays, click on 'use as'.

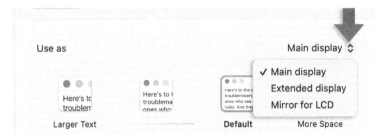

This will allow you to use the currently selected display as your main display, or mirror the display to the second screen, or extend your main screen onto the second screen. Useful if you want to present something on a projector, an external display or TV.

Resolution

For some external displays, you can set the resolution. Note, macOS usually sets most of these things automatically, but you can change them from here if you need to. For example, if I want to change the resolution of my LCD display. Select the display from the top

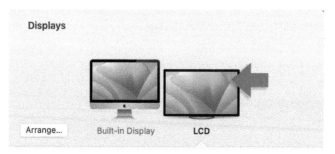

Select 'default for this display' to set the best settings. If you need to change the resolution, select 'scaled' and select the desired resolution from the popup list. If you don't see the resolutions, click 'advanced', then select 'show resolutions as list'.

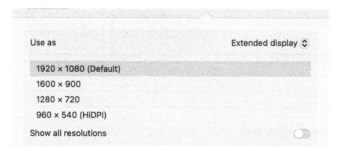

Arrange Multiple Displays

If you have multiple displays you can arrange them. To do this, click 'arrange'. Note the 'arrange' button only appears if you have multiple displays connected.

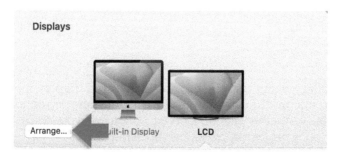

Each display connected to your mac is represented with a rectangle. Your main display is marked with a translucent line along the top as we can see below.

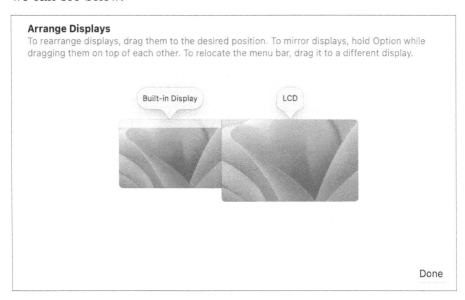

Arrange the rectangles to match the physical arrangement of your displays.

So for example, my second LCD display is on the left hand side of my main build in display - as shown below.

The rectangles in the 'arrangement' window should match the physical arrangement. This makes it easier to drag apps, files or folders to your second display while you're working.

The LCD in the arrangement window is on the wrong side, so I'll need to drag it over to the left.

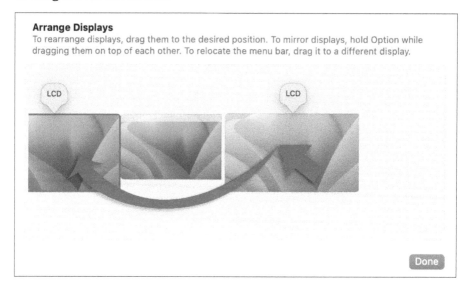

Arrange Displays
To rearrange displays, drag them to the desired position. To mirror displays, hold Option while dragging them on top of each other. To relocate the menu bar, drag it to a different display.

LCD   LCD

Done

Color Profiles

Select the display from the thumbnail list along the top. From the color drop down, you can set the color profile for your particular display. MacOS will normally select the best color profile for your display, however you can select another one here.

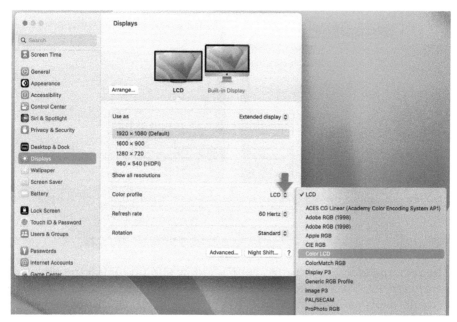

Screen Calibration

You can also calibrate your display. This is useful if you do a lot of graphic design or photography. To do this, scroll down to the bottom of the color profile drop down menu, then select 'customise'.

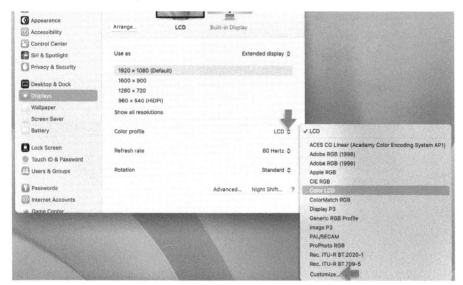

Click the '+' icon on the bottom left of the window.

Follow the on screen prompts from the calibrator to calibrate your screen.

Night shift, removes the blue light to make it easier on your eyes. To turn it on, click on 'night shirt', select 'sunset to sunrise' to enable night shift mode in the evenings.

Setup Universal Control

This feature usually works automatically when compatible devices are nearby. Here below is our little setup. Below, we have an iMac on the left with a Macbook Pro next to it. You can also use an iPad.

To set up Universal Control, on one of your Macs - I'm going to start on the iMac - click on the Apple icon on the top left, then select 'system settings'.

Select 'displays' from the list on the left.

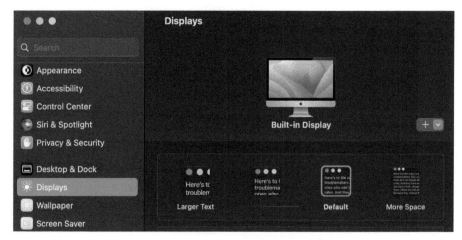

Click on the '+' on the right hand side. From the dropdown menu, select the machine you want to link to, in this demo my Macbook. *We want to link the keyboard and mouse so we can use the same keyboard and mouse across both machines. We also want to extend the screen onto the MacBook.*

Click 'arrange' on the left hand side.

Chapter 2: Setting up Your Mac

Arrange the displays on the screen to match your physical setup. My Macbook is on the right, so I moved the 'Macbook' icon to the right of the iMac icon.

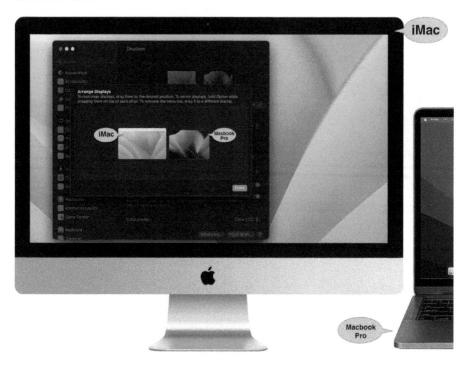

On the bottom of the 'displays' main screen, click on the advanced button.

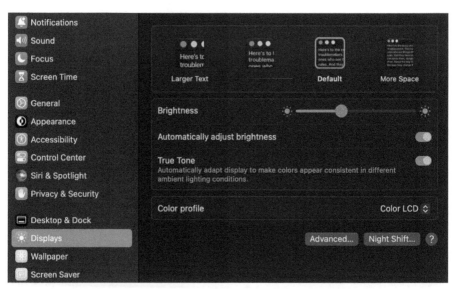

Here, you can allow your mouse pointer to switch between nearby Macs and iPads.

Here, if you turn this option off, you allow your mouse pointer to move freely between your Macs and iPads.

If you turn this feature on, you'll see a purple marker when you move your mouse pointer to the edge of the screen. You'll need to push through to get to the other Mac or iPad.

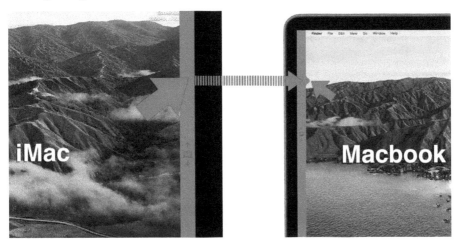

Select automatically reconnect to allow your Mac to connect to the iPad or Mac when you move them next to each other.

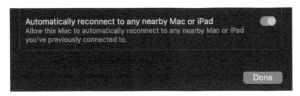

Click 'done', when you're finished.

See page 176 for info on using Universal Control.

System Audio

You can manage your audio devices such as external speaker systems, microphones, and system sound effects.

To do this open your system settings. Click the Apple menu on the top left, then select 'system settings' from the menu.

Select 'sound' from the list on the left.

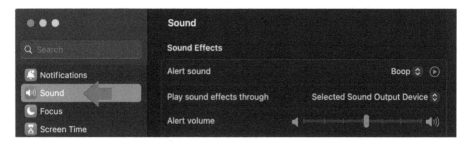

Here you can select a sound to play for system alerts, select the audio device to play the sounds through, alter alert volume, play a sound when you start your mac, enable/disable system interface sound effects, play a sound when you change the volume and adjust the main system volume.

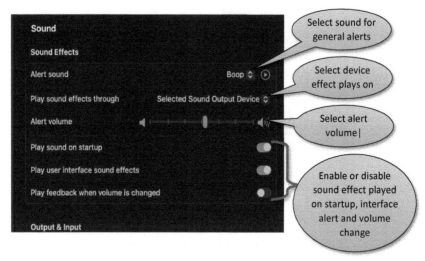

Further down the window, you can manage the audio output devices, such as headphones and speaker systems, as well as the internal speakers on your mac.

To do this click the 'output' tab. Select the one you want to send audio to.

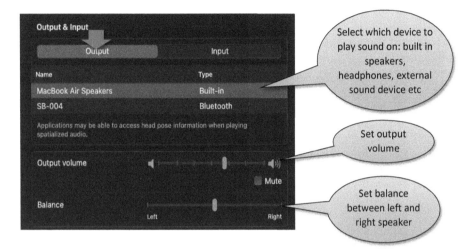

The 'input' tab lists all your audio input devices such as a microphones and any 'line in' device that is connected to your mac. Select your mic.

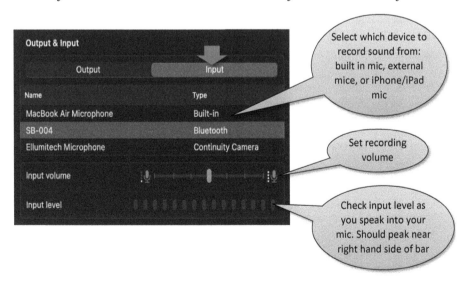

Talk into the mic, if it is working correctly you'll see the 'input level' spike as you speak.

Pairing Bluetooth Devices

You can pair bluetooth keyboards, headphones, and most bluetooth capable devices.

To pair a device, first put the device into pairing mode. You'll need to refer to the device's instructions to find specific details on how to do this. On most devices, press and hold the pairing button until the status light starts flashing. This means the device is ready to be paired with your Mac.

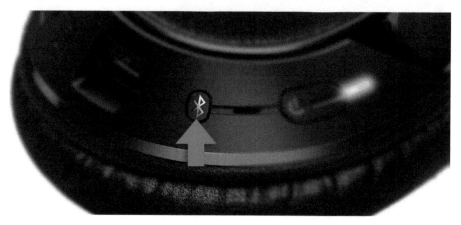

On your Mac, open the system settings. Select 'bluetooth' from the list on the left. Use the switch at the top to turn on bluetooth if it isn't already. Any new devices will be listed under 'nearby devices'

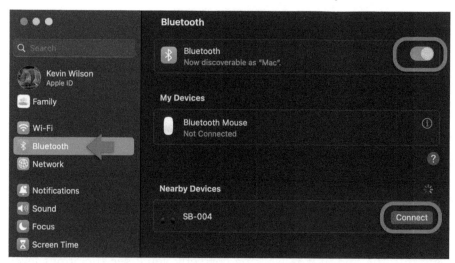

Hover your mouse over the device, you'll see a 'connect' button appear. Click on this to connect your device.

Once connected, your device will appear under the 'my devices' section.

If you want to remove a device, click on the 'i' icon next to the device.

Then from the popup window, click 'forget this device'.

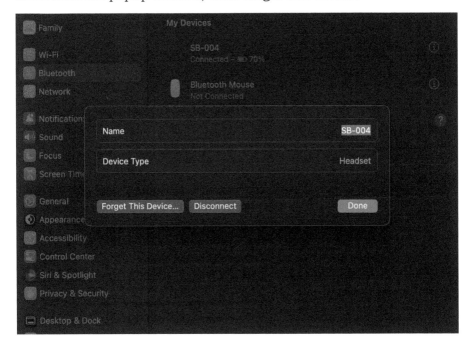

If you just want to disconnect the device but not remove it click 'disconnect'. This will allow you to reconnect your device if you need to later. If you click 'forget this device' you will need to pair the device again if you want to connect it later.

Fonts

You can manage fonts installed on your mac, and install new ones. To see all your fonts, open launchpad and click on the 'other' folder.

Then select font book.

From here you can install new fonts and see samples of fonts already installed on your mac.

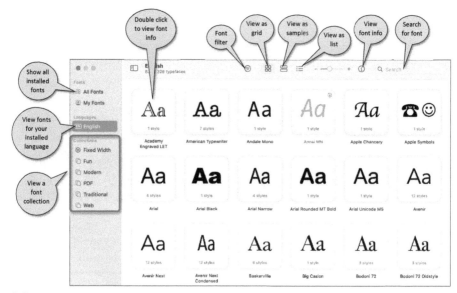

You can download countless fonts from the internet such as `dafont.com`, `1001fonts.com`, `myfonts.com`, and so on.

To install fonts you've downloaded, drag and drop the font files (.TTF, .OTF and .FON) from finder to 'all fonts' in fontbook. *Many font files are compressed as a zip file, make sure you double click on the zip file to extract the fonts.*

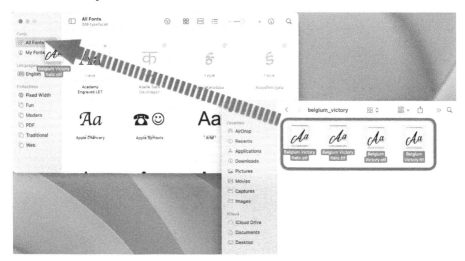

The font will be available in your apps. Within fontbook, you'll find the installed font under 'my fonts' on the left hand panel.

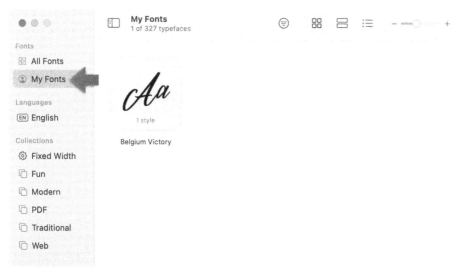

Double click on the font to see more info. From here, you can test your font, type in a sample and see what it looks like.

Find My

This feature allows you to pinpoint your Mac's location and is quite useful if you have misplaced your Mac or had it stolen.

Setup

First you need to activate it on your Mac. Click the Apple menu on the top left, then select 'system settings' from the menu.

From the list on the left, select your 'Apple id'. Click on 'iCloud'.

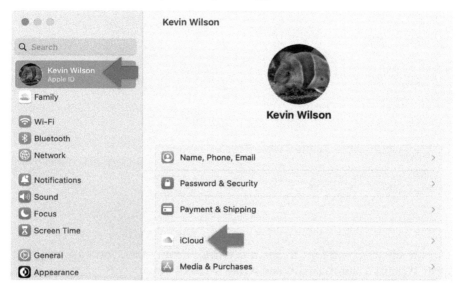

Click 'turn on' if 'find my mac' is off.

Make sure both options are turned on. Click 'done'.

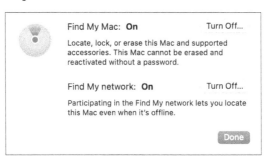

Make sure location services is turned on. To do this go back to system settings main screen and select 'security & privacy'.

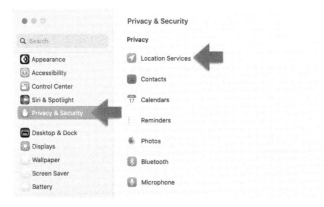

Then click 'enable location services'.

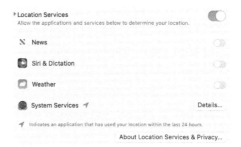

Chapter 2: Setting up Your Mac

Locating & Taking Action

On any device - iPad, Mac or PC, open your web browser and navigate to:

www.icloud.com

Click 'sign in', then sign in with your Apple ID. Scroll down, select 'find my' from the iCloud control panel.

You can locate all your Apple devices. Select the name of your device from the drop down menu in the top middle of the screen.

You'll see a green dot appear on the map. This is the current location of your device.

On the left hand side of the screen, you can take action. Here you can click 'play sound' to play an annoying sound on your device wherever it might be. This helps you to locate it if you've lost it in your house somewhere, or annoy a thief if they have possession of it.

You can also remotely lock your device or put it into lost mode. This locks your device and tracks its location.

Finally you can erase your device completely. This will remove any personal data that is stored on your device.

102

Sharing Locations

You can share your location with friends and family. To share your location, open launchpad, then click the 'find my' app

Select 'share my location' on the bottom left of the 'people' tab.

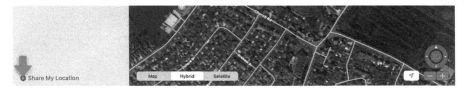

Enter the Apple ID or phone number of the person you want to share your location with. Tap 'send'.

Choose to share your location for One Hour, Until End of Day, or Share Indefinitely.

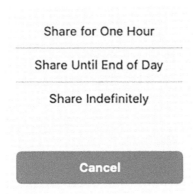

The other person will get a prompt on their device. This will allow them to share their location with you.

Check Someone's Location

Open launchpad, then select the 'find my' app. Select the 'people tab' then click on the person's name.

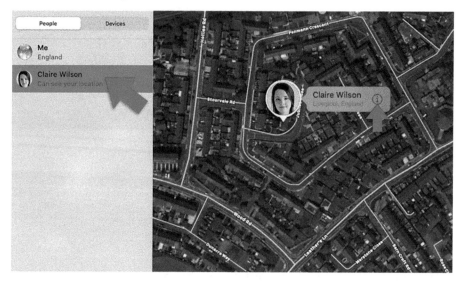

You should see the person's location appear on the map on your mac. Click the 'i' icon on the name tag to show the person's location information.

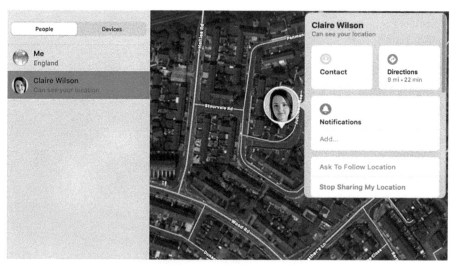

Click 'contact' to send the person a message, click 'directions' to see directions to the person's current location, click 'notifications' to add a notification when the person arrives at your location, leaves their location or any other specified location.

Time Machine Backup

The Time Machine allows you to create backups of your files to an external hard drive.

Have a look at the backup demo at:
`www.elluminetpress.com/mac-sys`

Setting Up Backups

To use Time Machine, get yourself an external hard drive. You'll need at least 500GB - 1TB in size. Connect your external hard drive to a USB port as shown below.

Click the Apple menu on the top left, then select 'system settings' from the menu.

Select 'general' from the list on the left. Then click 'time machine'

From the time machine window, select your external drive. My drive is called 'Data', so I'll select that one. The drive is usually labelled with the manufacturer's name or model. Click 'set up disk'.

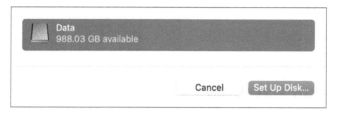

Here, you can encrypt the backup data if you need to. This allows you to enter a password. If you don't want to set a password, turn off the encrypt backup option. Underneath you can specify the amount of space on the disk you want to allocate to the backup - usually the whole disk. If you want to change this, click 'custom', then use the slider to allocate space for backup. Click 'done', when you're finished.

Make sure you use a blank external hard drive and not one that contains any important files. Time Machine will ask you if you want to erase the disk, click 'erase'.

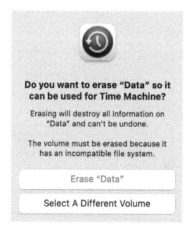

You'll see the backup drive appear in the time machine settings. The backup automatically backs up your files every hour. If you want to change this, click 'options'.

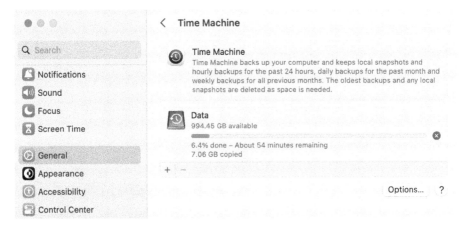

Here, you can set the 'backup frequency' to weekly or monthly, or manually. If you want the backup to run when plugged in only, turn off 'backup on battery power'. Click 'done' when you're finished.

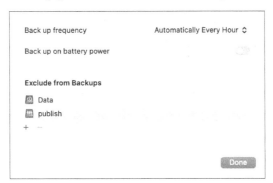

Whenever you want to back up, just connect your external hard drive and the backup will start automatically.

Note, the backup will not work unless the external drive is connected to your Mac. Make sure you connect your hard drive at least weekly, or daily depending on how much work you do.

If not, click the Time Machine icon on the menu bar on the top right and select 'backup now'.

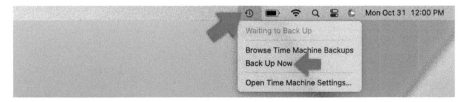

Select 'open time machine settings' to change backup settings or add/remove drives.

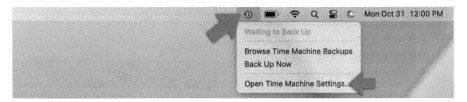

You'll see the backup status in the time machine window. Here you can change drives, or remove drives. Just click on the '+' on the bottom left to add a drive, or to remove a drive click on it in the list, then select the '-' icon on the bottom left.

To change backup options, click 'options'. If you want to exclude a particular folder, click on the '+' on the bottom left. Select the folder or drive to exclude.

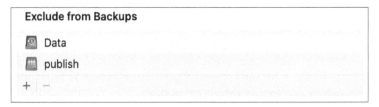

Restoring Items

First, plug in your external hard drive you used to back up. To restore something click the icon on your menu bar as shown below, select 'browse time machine backups'.

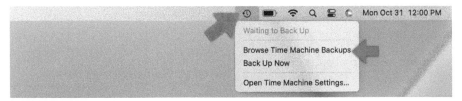

Look for the file in the finder window shown below.

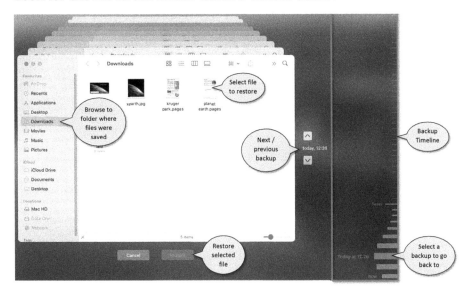

Using the timeline on the right, select what date or time to go back to.

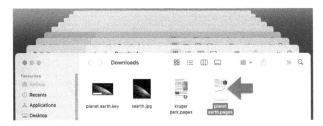

When you have found the file, click restore on the bottom right of the screen. The file will be restored to its original location.

109

Transfer Files from a Windows PC

If you have used a Windows machine in the past and have moved to a Mac, you can transfer your files using the Windows Migration Assistant.

Before you start, make sure your Mac and PC are connected to the same network (or the same WiFi).

First you need to prepare your PC. You'll need to download the migration assistant. Go to the following website and download the program.

`support.apple.com/kb/DL1978`

On your PC, run the migration assistant installer in your 'downloads' folder and run through the installation. Once installed, run the migration assistant - you'll find the icon on your desktop. Click 'continue'.

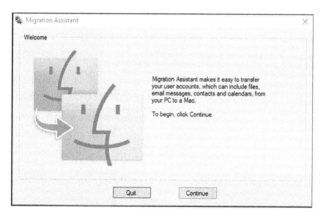

Now when you reach this screen. Go start the migration assistant on your Mac.

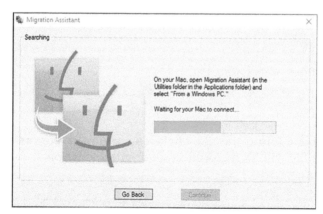

On your Mac start the Migration Assistant. You'll find it in finder -> applications -> utilities. Enter your mac username and password when prompted. Follow the prompts until you get to the migration page. Select 'From a Windows PC', then click Continue.

Click 'continue' to close any other open apps.

On your Mac, select your PC from the list of available computers. Click 'continue'.

When both computers display the same passcode, click 'continue' on your PC and Mac.

Chapter 2: Setting up Your Mac

Your Mac will the drives on your PC and build a list of files to transfer. When the scan is complete, select the files that you want to transfer to your Mac then click 'continue'.

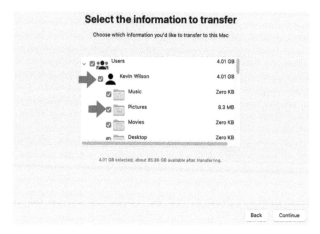

You can watch the progress and estimated time remaining on both the PC and your Mac. This might take a while.

When transfer completes, you'll find a new user account. Set a password, and sign in with your Apple id. Run through the setup prompts. You'll find all the files you transferred in finder under your home directory. Go to: Mac HD -> users -> username.

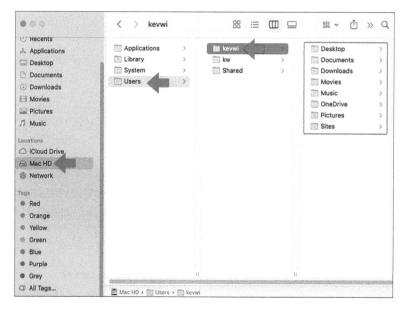

You can move these files to the directories you want them in, eg pictures in the pictures folder, or music in the music folder and so on.

112

Transfer Files from an old Mac

First, you'll need to make sure both your Macs are on the same network, or the same WiFi.

On your old Mac, open the Migration Assistant. You'll find it in the utilities folder in your finder applications. Click 'continue' and follow the prompts.

When you get to the transfer screen, select 'to another Mac'. Click 'continue'.

On your new Mac, open the Migration Assistant. Click 'continue' and follow the prompts.

When you get to the transfer screen, select 'from a Mac', click 'continue'. Select your old mac from the options. Click 'continue'.

Select the files you want to transfer then click 'continue'.

When transfer finishes on our new Mac, the login window will reappear. Log into the account and follow the prompts.

3

Getting Around your Mac

In this chapter, we'll take a look around MacOS Sonoma. We'll explore

- The Desktop, Menu Bar, Dock, Stacks & Launchpad
- Spaces & Mission Control
- Finder & Basic File Management
- External Drives
- Networking & iCloud Drive
- Managing App Windows
- Spotlight Search
- Notification Center, Control Center & Stage Manager
- Handoff & Universal Control
- Shortcuts
- Focus Mode
- Using Siri, Voice Control & Dictation
- Using Apple Pay on your Mac
- The Mac Keyboard & Keyboard Shortcuts
- Making Trackpad Gestures & Magic Mouse
- The Touch Bar
- Screenshots & Screen Recording
- Split Screen Mode
- Keychain

To help you better understand this section, take a look at the video resources. Open your web browser and navigate to the following sites:

elluminetpress.com/using-mac

The Desktop

The desktop is the main work area on your mac. It's the equivalent of your workbench or office desk, hence why it is called a desktop.

Let's take a look at the different parts of the desktop.

On the top left of your desktop, you'll find the Apple menu. From here, you can shut down or restart your mac, open settings, the app store, lock your screen, and log out.

Along the top of your desktop you'll find the menu bar. On the left hand side you'll find your application menu, and on the right you'll find your status bar.

On your desktop you may find icons for a disk drive or any file you have saved to the desktop. This will depend on how you use your mac.

Along the bottom of your desktop you'll find the dock. Here you'll find your apps, you can also pin apps to the dock. You can resize the dock to suite your needs - make it smaller to give you more space, or make it bigger if you can't see the icons clearly.

Desktop Widgets

Sonoma introduces the ability to place widgets directly on your desktop. This provides quick access to information and functions without needing to open the respective apps.

To add widgets, right-click on an empty space on your desktop. From the context menu, select 'edit widgets'.

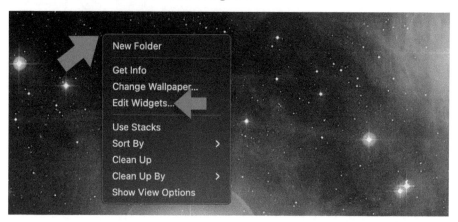

In the widget gallery, you'll see a variety of widgets available for you to add to your desktop. Browse through the widgets and find the one you want to add. Click and drag the widget you want to your desktop.

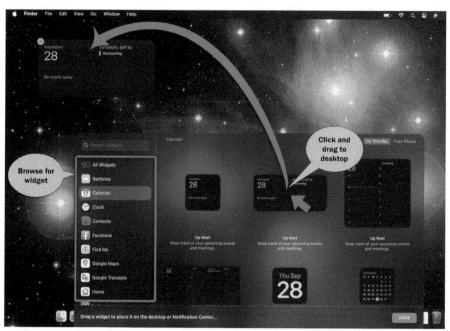

If you want to add widgets from your iPhone to your Mac desktop, ensure that both devices are signed in with the same Apple ID and have Bluetooth and WiFi turned on. In the widget gallery, there should be an option on the top right to access and add iPhone widgets. Select the desired iPhone widget and add it to your desktop.

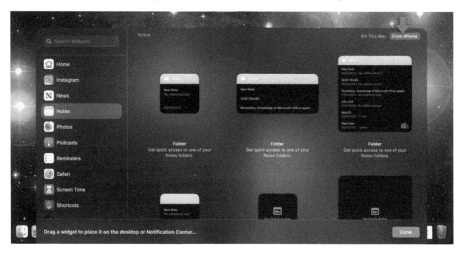

Once you've added the desired widgets, you can close the widget gallery. To do this, click 'done' on the bottom right of the widget gallery.

Once the widget is added to your desktop, you can edit it. To do this, right click on the widget. You can make the widget small, medium or large. To remove a widget, select 'remove widget'.

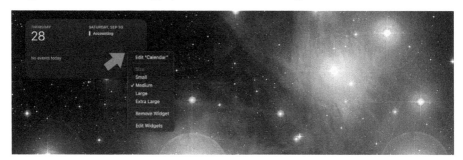

You can also move your widget around. Click and drag it to your desired location on the desktop.

Widgets on your desktop are designed to fade into the background when you're working on other tasks, so they won't be obtrusive. They'll come back into focus when you're on the desktop.

The Menu Bar

You'll find the menu bar along the top of your screen, and it looks like this:

One thing to notice about the menu bar is it changes according to which application you have showing on your screen. For example, the finder app will have its own menu, iMovie will have a different menu. Keep your eye on the top left hand side of the menu bar as it will have the name of the application currently running in bold type.

Application Menu

The left hand side of the menu bar contains the menu for the app you're currently using. In this example I'm running Safari.

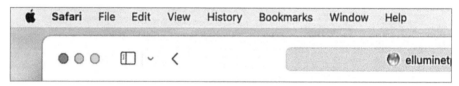

The name of the app appears in bold next to the Apple menu. There are several other app menus, often with standard names such as File, Edit, Format, Window, and Help. Many of the commands in these menus are standard in all apps. For example, the 'open' command is usually in the 'file menu' and the 'copy' command is usually in the 'edit menu'.

Some apps have extra menus with more specific commands native to that app.

Status Menu

The right hand side of the menu bar contains the status menu.

This menu gives feedback on the status of your computer and gives you quick access to certain features - for example; you can quickly turn on WiFi, do a spotlight search, change the audio volume, see date & time, access control center and you can also check messages in notification centre.

If your menu bar is starting to get a bit crowded, you can remove items. To do this, hold down the command key and drag the icon off the menu.

The Dock

The dock has short cuts to applications, such as Music or Photos App. If the app you are looking for isn't here, it will be in the applications folder in finder or on Launchpad.

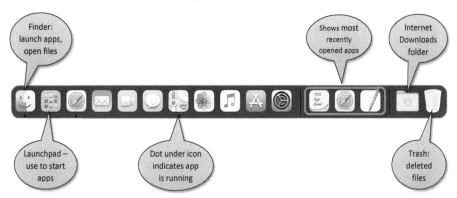

The apps along the left hand side of the dock represent apps installed on your system. You'll see the finder, siri, and launchpad, along with a few others. On the right hand side you'll see a divider and three apps - these are your most recently used apps and they change according to the apps you use on your Mac.

The next icon on the right is your downloads stack - this is where you'll find the files you've downloaded off the internet.

This folder is called a document stack as it opens out allowing you to see the names of the files without opening the folder, as shown above.

119

You can also add other folders as stacks to the right hand side of the dock. I'm going to drag my 'documents' folder from the finder window, and drop it next to the 'downloads' icon on the far right of the dock. This creates a stack.

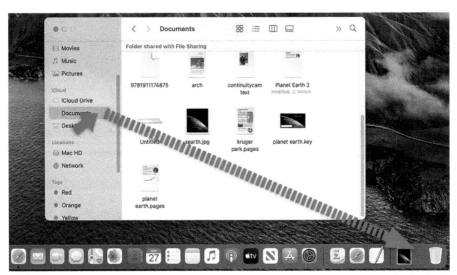

You can also add an app you use a lot to the dock. For example let's add the Chess App to the dock. Open finder, select 'applications' from the panel on the left, then drag the app's icon to the dock.

I'm going to place it between the Maps App and the Contacts App. The icons on the dock will part to allow you do drop the app.

You can also re-order apps on the dock. To do this, click and drag the app to a new position on the dock.

Stacks

You can organise cluttered files on your desktop by automatically stacking them into groups based on the file type - so images are stacked in one pile, documents in another, and so on. To activate desktop stacks, right click on the desktop and select 'use stacks' from the popup menu.

The documents will be stacked neatly on the right hand side of the screen. To open any of the stacks, just click on the icon.

You can also group your stacks by file type (kind), date, or tags. To do this, right click on the desktop and go to 'group stacks by'. From the slide out menu, select an option and see what happens

Launchpad

Launchpad lets you see, organize, and easily open apps installed on your machine. The icons are organized into pages. To access Launchpad, click the icon on your dock, shown below. You can also press F4.

To launch any application, just click on the corresponding icon.

You can organize your applications into folders in Launchpad. Just drag and drop one icon on top of another. For example, you can drag all your reference apps together such as dictionary and calculator into a folder.

Give the folder a name if required. Click the name and type a new one.

When you need to find them you just click on the folder when you open launchpad.

You can also search for apps using the search field at the top of the screen.

Select the app from the results.

If you have a lot of apps installed, you will have multiple pages of apps. Click the page indicators at the bottom of the screen to move between pages.

You can also swipe two fingers across your macbook trackpad.

123

Spaces & Mission Control

If you use a lot of apps at the same time, your desktop can get a little cluttered. Mac OS has a feature called spaces, that allows you to organize apps onto different virtual desktops called spaces. It's like having more than one desk in your office - different projects will be laid out on different desks. Back on your mac, you can have a desktop that has your email and web browser open, another desktop you could be working on a presentation in Keynote and an accompanying report in Pages App. Another desktop could have photos open and so on.

To open mission control, press F3 on your keyboard. To create new virtual desktop, click the '+' icon on the top right of the screen.

Open the apps you are going to work on. Eg safari web browsing and email.

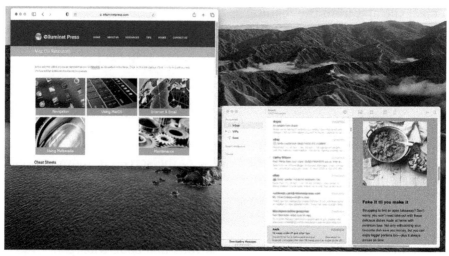

Press F3 again. Click the '+' sign at the top right of the mission control screen to create another virtual desktop. Click the desktop thumbnail that appears on the top bar to switch to that desktop.

On this desktop I'm going to work on my 'international modern architecture' project. For this project, I need Pages and Keynote. So I'd open these apps.

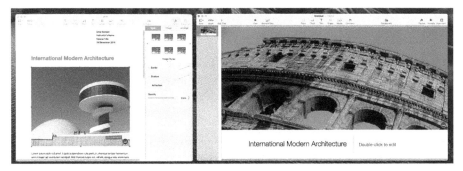

To shift between spaces swipe using 3 fingers on the trackpad on your MacBook. Or press F3 on your keyboard and click the desktop icon at the top of the screen to switch to it.

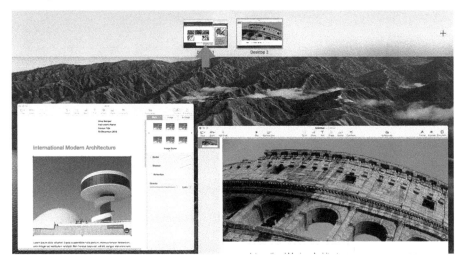

Now when you want to do some web browsing or check your email, you can go to desktop 1, to carry on with your project go to desktop 2.

Finder

This is where all your documents, letters, photographs and favourite music are stored. The finder is like your filing cabinet.

You'll find the finder icon on the far left hand side of your dock.

The finder window is divided into three main parts.

The toolbar across the top of the window contains icons you can customise the way files are displayed. The sidebar which you can use to choose locations and devices on your computer. The main contents, the large pane where all the files and folders are displayed.

Lets take a closer look at the different parts of the finder window.

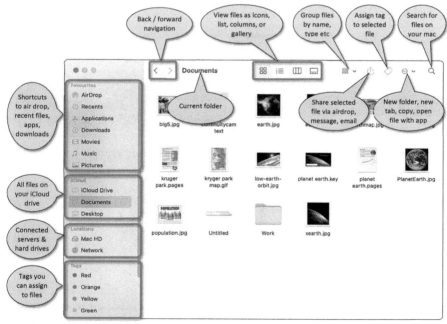

File View Style

The four icons at the top of the finder window allow you to display your file icons in different formats. You can display them as icon view, list view, column view, and gallery view.

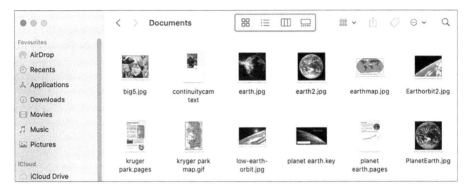

Lets take a look at each view...

Icon View. To enter icon view, click the first icon on the top of the window as shown below. This view is useful for scanning through photographs or videos.

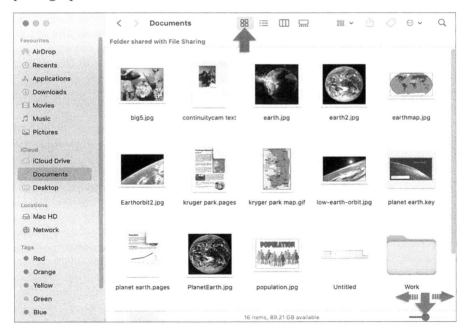

The slider on the status bar along the bottom of the window will resize the icons and previews. If you don't see the status bar, go to the view menu and select 'show status bar'.

127

List View. To enter list view, select the second icon on the top of the screen, as shown below.

This is useful for looking through documents and file names. You can sort the list according to name, size date, or type - just click on the column headers.

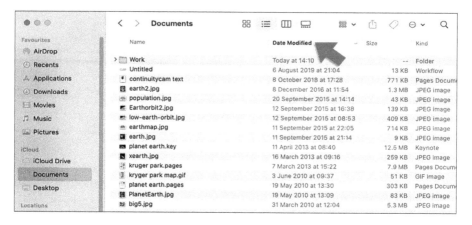

Column View. To enter column view, select the third icon on the top of the screen, as shown below.

This is useful if you are looking through files that are stored in lots of folders, as you can open up the folders in each column and view the contents side by side.

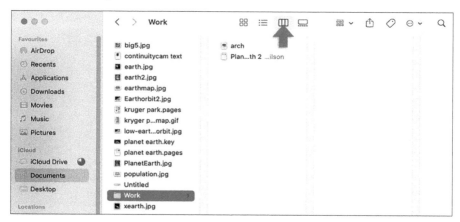

Gallery View. To enter gallery view, select the fourth icon on the top of the screen, as shown below.

This is useful for scanning through photographs, videos, documents, or music. Thumbnail previews of the files appear in the bottom third of the window with a larger preview of the selected file in the top half of the window.

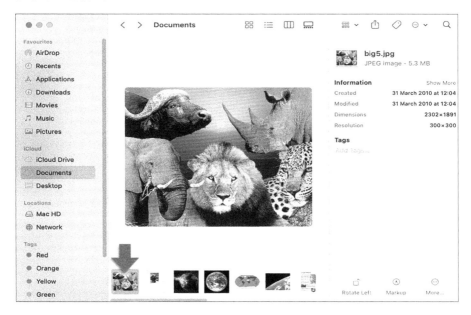

On the right hand side you'll see some details about the file such as date created, date modified, resolution and tags. This is the preview pane.

To hide or show preview pane, go to the view menu, then select 'show preview' or 'hide preview'.

Finder Settings

You can customise finder to your own needs. To do this, in finder, click the 'finder' menu and select 'settings'

Along the top of the window you'll see four tabs. From the 'general' tab you can select which icons to show on the desktop - your external hard disks, flash drives, and your internal hard disk, as well as any CD/DVDs and server shared folders you're connected to. You can also select which folder appears automatically when you open finder.

Under the 'tags' tab, you can customise your tags. See "Tags" on page 132 for more information.

Under the 'sidebar' tab, you can customise the shortcuts you see listed down the left hand side of your finger window. Click the check boxes next to the shortcuts you want to add, remove the tickbox next to the shortcuts you want to remove.

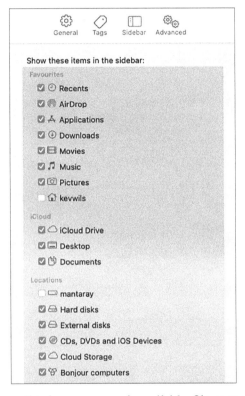

From the 'advanced' tab, you can show/hide filename extensions, set finder warnings, keep folders on top of other windows, and the default search location when using finder search.

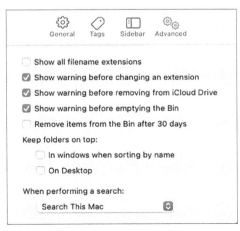

Tags

Tags allow you to place markers onto your documents so you can find them more easily. First, rename the tags to something more meaningful. To do this, open finder, click on the finder menu on the top left, then select 'settings'

Click on the 'tags' tab at the top of the settings window.

You will see a list of the color tags, and a few more at the bottom such as, 'Work', 'Home', and 'Important'.

To change the color of a tag, click on the little bubble and choose a color.

To change the name of the tag, click on the tag title, and type your new tag name.

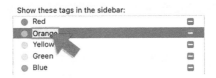

To create a new tag, click the '+' icon on the bottom left and enter a name.

Enter a name for your tag, eg 'work'.

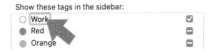

Assign a color.

Add the tag to the shortcut menu. To do this drag the tag over the tag you want to replace in the favourites section at the bottom of the window.

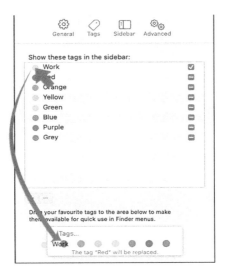

The favourites section shows up on the left had pane in finger under 'tags', and in the shortcut menu.

Tagging Files

To tag a file, click the document you want to tag then select the tags icon. From the list, select the tag that describes the category of your document, eg work.

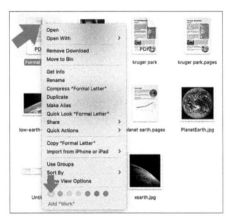

You can also use a keyboard shortcut to tag files quickly. Select the file, then press Control 1 - 7 to add the tag. Control - 0 clears tags.

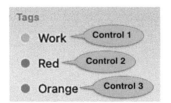

The control keys relate to the order in the 'tags' list on the left hand side.

Quick Preview Files

When browsing through your files in finder, you can preview the file without opening it. This works well with photos, documents and videos.

To preview a file, click the file to select it, then press the space bar on your keyboard. A window will popup displaying a preview version of the file.

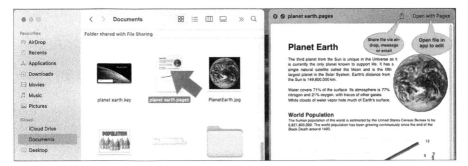

On the toolbar along the top, you can open the file in the appropriate app to edit it, or you can share the file via email or social media.

Markup in Finder

Markup allows you to annotate documents and photographs just by opening up a preview, rather than opening the file in an app.

In finder, select the folder the image or document is saved in. Right click on the icon. From the popup menu go down to 'quick actions', select 'markup' from the slideout.

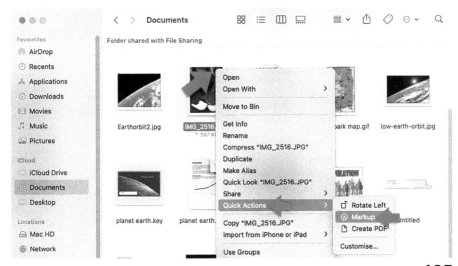

Once the markup screen appears, you can add text, shapes and color.

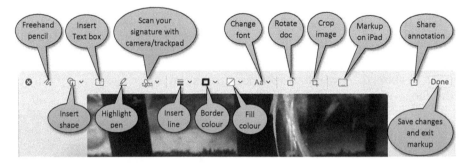

I'm going to add a shape. Click the small down arrow next to the shape icon and select a shape.

Draw the shape on the image, and double click inside it to add some text.

To change the size, color and font, click the small down arrow next to the font icon on the toolbar. From the drop down menu, you can select a font, change the color and size, change the typeface to bold italic or underlined, and also change the text alignment.

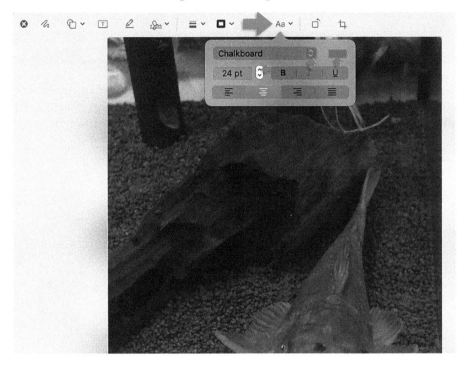

Click 'done' on the top right of the toolbar when you're finished, or click the 'share' icon to send your file with the annotations to someone else.

Markup using your iPad

You can also send documents and images to your iPad for annotation. To do this, select the finder app on your dock.

Select the folder where the document is saved. Right click on the document, go down to 'quick actions', then select 'markup' from the slideout.

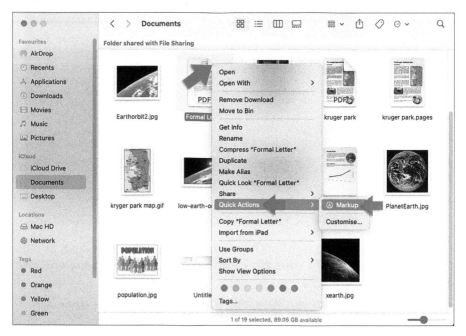

You can use the markup feature on images such as jpeg, or png, and PDF documents.

You'll also find the markup tools in the preview screen. Select document, then press space bar.

Now on your iPad, you'll see the markup screen appear. *If it doesn't appear automatically, click the 'markup on iPad' icon on the top of the toolbar on the markup window on your Mac.*

On your iPad, use your finger or the pencil to annotate your document. You'll see a live update on your Mac as you do so.

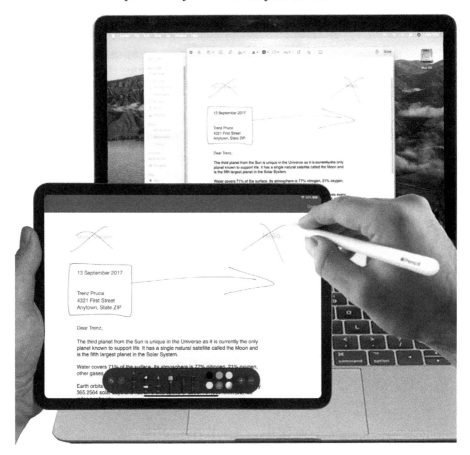

On your iPad you can select different pens, highlighters from the toolbar along the bottom of the screen, as well as change the size and opacity.

Tap 'done' on the top right of your iPad screen when you're finished.

Click 'done' on the top right of the markup window on your Mac to save the annotations.

Basic File Management

File management is a crucial aspect of computing that involves organizing, storing, and handling your files efficiently. Whether you're working on a personal project, managing a business, or just using a computer for everyday tasks, effective file management can save time, prevent data loss, and streamline workflows.

Files are typically organized into folders (sometimes called directories). These can be nested, allowing for a hierarchical structure. Folders allow you to group related files together, making it easier to locate and manage them.

Using consistent naming conventions can make it easier to locate files later. For example, "Invoice_June_2023.pdf" is more descriptive than "Doc1.pdf".

On a Mac, your files are primarily stored in your home folder. If you use iCloud Drive, files and folders stored in iCloud will also appear in the Finder sidebar.

Let's take a look at the basic folder structure on a Mac:

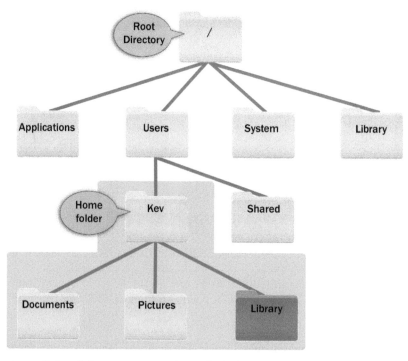

The top of the drive structure is called the root directory or folder. All other files, folders/directories are created in the root directory.

The **Applications** folder contains apps, such as Mail, Calendar, Safari and any others you install. Apps in this folder also appear in Launchpad.

The **Users** folder contains the home folders of all the users on your Mac. The home folder is where you save all your files, photos, documents, music and so on.

System is a folder that contains all the system files and folders required to run MacOS. This is a folder you don't normally have to worry about and should keep clear of unless you know what you're doing.

The system **Library** folder contains files necessary for MacOS to run properly and includes global settings and settings. The Library folder inside a user's home folder stores system, and individual settings for that user.

Creating Folders

You can create folders to keep your files organised. To create a folder, in Finder, click on the location in the sidebar where you want to create the folder, eg in 'documents'. Right click, then select 'new folder'.

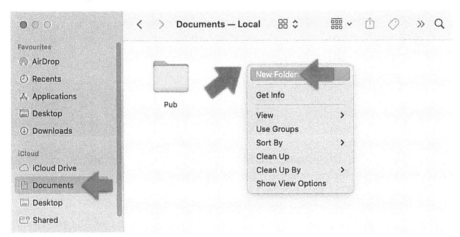

Give the folder a meaningful name.

Smart Folders

Smart folders can be quite useful for keeping track of files. Smart folders allow you to create search parameters and save them as a folder. So for example, you could create a folder that displays the files you worked on in the last 30 days, or show all your photos, documents, and so on.

First, open finder. Select a location to search, eg iCloud Drive.

To create a smart folder, open your finder app and click the 'file' menu. From the menu select 'new smart folder'.

Along the top of the smart folder window, select where you want to search for files. We're searching iCloud Drive so click 'iCloud Drive'.

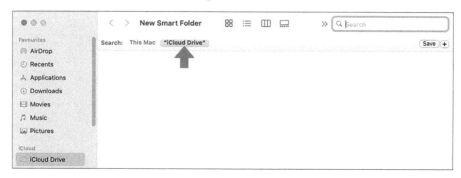

If you want to search your whole mac, select 'this mac'.

Now we need to create the search criteria for our smart folder. Click the '+' icon on the right.

In this example, I want to show all the documents I've worked on in the last 30 days. Click the 'any' field and select 'document'.

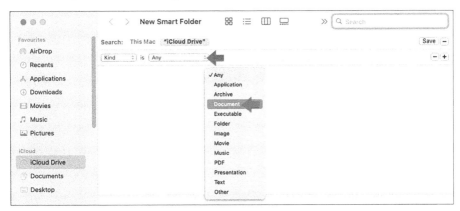

You'll see a list of documents appear in the window. Now we need to add another criteria. We wanted a smart folder to show all documents we worked on in the last 30 days. So, click the '+' icon on the right.

Select the 'last opened date' and from the drop down select 'last modified'. In the next field set it to 'within last'. In the next field enter the number of days: 30. In the last field, set it to 'days'.

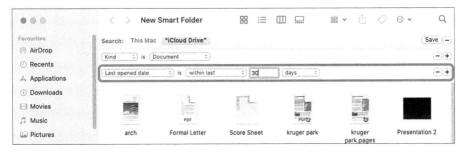

Click 'save' on the top right.

Give your smart folder a meaningful name in the 'save as' field. Save it in 'saved searches', and make sure 'add to sidebar' is ticked. Click 'save'.

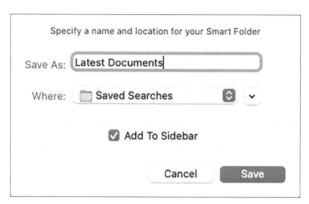

Your smart folder will appear on your finder's sidebar.

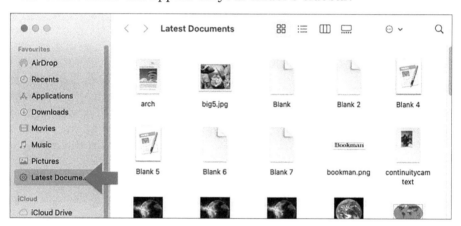

Try creating smart folders with some other criteria using the same procedure as above.

Copying Files

To copy a file to a folder or drive use copy and paste. First, select the files you want to copy - hold down the command key if you want to select multiple files.

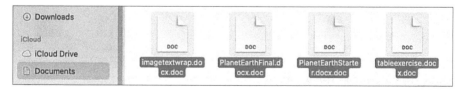

Press **Command C** on your keyboard to copy the files.

Click on the location or folder you want to copy the files to. Eg my external drive called 'data'.

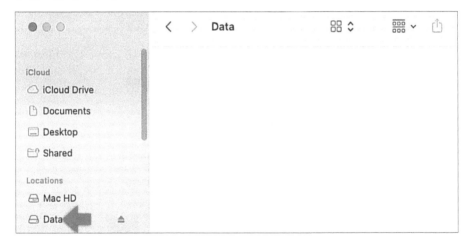

Press **Command V** to paste the files in. You'll see the files copy over.

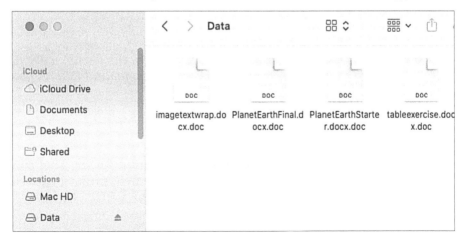

Moving Files

To move files, you can use drag and drop. To do this, select the files you want to move - hold the command key to select multiple files.

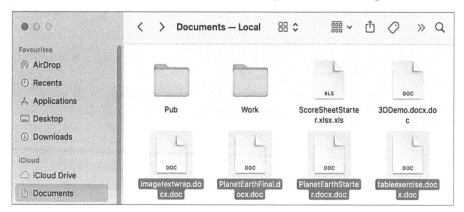

Click and drag the selection to the folder you want to move the files to.

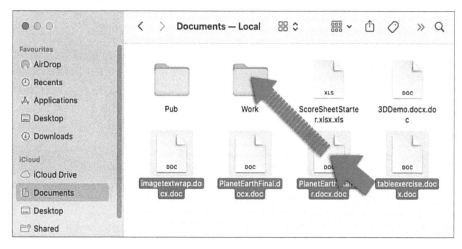

Note if you drag a file to another drive, this will copy the file not move it. To move the file to another drive, hold down the command key as you drag the file.

Compress Files

You can compress files into zip archives right within finder. This can be useful if you intend to send a lot of files over email, messaging or if you're making multiple files available for download.

You can also unzip them later.

Zip

To compress files, select them in finder - hold down the command key to select multiple files. Then right click on the selection, from the popup menu select 'compress items'.

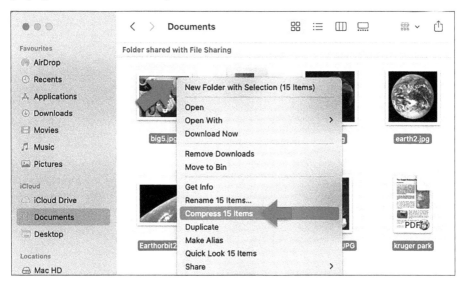

You'll see a new file appear called **archive.zip**. This is the file that will contain all the files you selected. You can rename and send this file.

Unzip

To unzip a compressed file. Double click on the zip file in finder. The files will extract into a folder with the same name as the zip file.

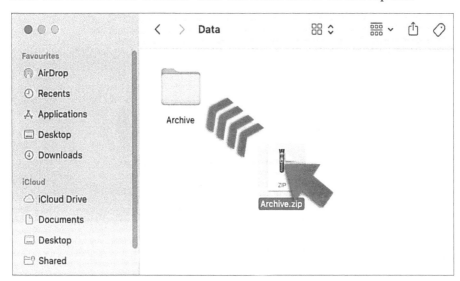

External Drives

When you plug in a USB flash drive or an external hard drive like the one below, an icon will appear on your desktop.

Double click this icon to open the drive in finder.

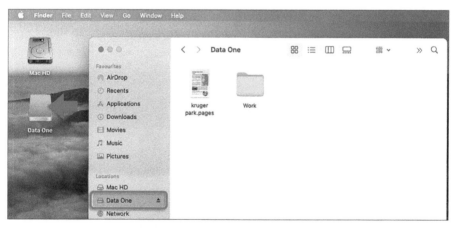

Note before unplugging the drive, it is good practice to eject the drive by clicking on the eject icon next to the drive name in finder.

Accessing Data CDs, DVDs & BluRays

Macs no longer include DVD or CD drives. If you want to listen to a CD, watch a DVD or access files on disc, you'll need to buy an external USB DVD drive.

Plug the DVD drive into a spare USB port and insert your disc. An icon will appear on your desktop. Double click on the icon to open the disc contents in finder.

Notice the DVD/CD drive is selected under 'devices' on the left hand panel of the finder window.

In the main finder window, you'll see all the files and folders contained on the disc. Double click on any of these to open them up.

To eject your disc. Click the eject icon next to the DVD/CD drive on the left hand panel in finder.

Networking

You can share files across your home network. This is useful if you are sharing resources such as documents with other people who are connected to your network and is ideal for transferring larger files.

Sharing Files on a Network

To set up file sharing, open your system settings.

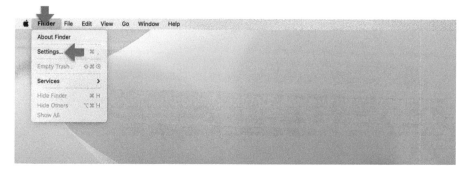

Select 'general' from the list on the left, then click on 'sharing'.

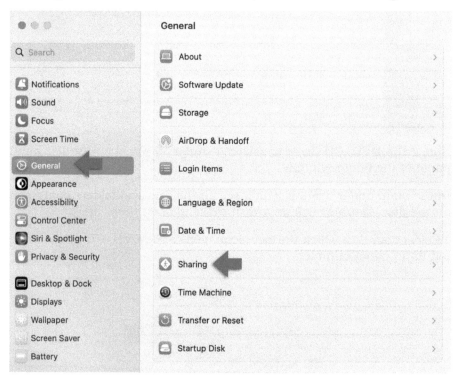

On the right hand side turn on file sharing. Then click on the 'i' icon.

Remember the 'computer name'. In this example it's 'mac'. You'll need it when connecting to this machine later on.

Now, select the folder you want to share. Under 'shared folders', click the plus sign and select a folder on your mac you want to share.

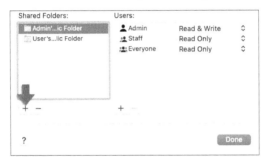

Select the folder you want to share. Click 'add'.

Select the folder you just added, then select the users to whom you want to grant access. Under 'users' click the plus sign.

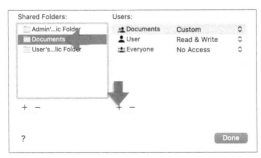

Select the name of the person to whom you want to grant access.

Next select what access rights you want to give them: read only or read & write. Click the selector next to the name to change this. If you want anyone to be able to access the folder, set 'everyone' to 'read & write' or 'read only'.

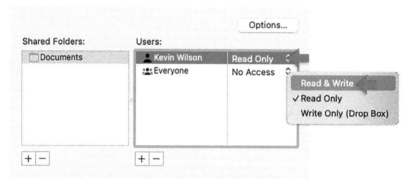

If you are going to connect to this folder from a windows or linux machine, you'll need to enable SMB support. To do this, click options.

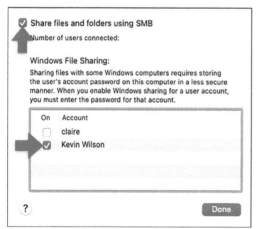
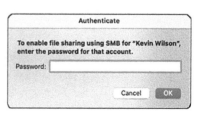

Connect to a Shared Folder on Another Computer

You can connect to shared resources on a network or the internet. You can connect to another computer running Windows 10, Windows Server, Linux or MacOS. To start, open finder from the dock then click the 'go' menu at the top of the screen, select 'connect to server'.

To connect to a shared folder located on a linux or windows computer, you'll need to use the SMB protocol.

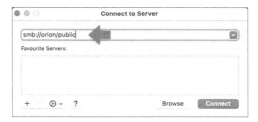

For example...

```
smb://orion/public
```

Where 'orion' is the server or computer name and 'public' is the shared folder on that server or computer. Click the plus sign on the left hand side to add the server address you just entered to the 'favorite server' list. Click 'connect' to connect. You may be prompted for a username and password - this will be the username that you use to log into the server or computer you're trying to connect to, and will probably be different from the username and password you used to log onto your mac.

You can also connect to FTP servers using the same method, except use ftp:// instead followed by your FTP username, then server name.

```
ftp://kevwils@ftp.myftpserver.com
```

You'll be prompted for your username and password for that server. You can usually obtain this from your internet service provider.

153

iCloud Drive

iCloud Drive is Apple's cloud storage service for devices running iOS, iPadOS, MacOS, and Windows 10. This feature allows users to save photos, videos, Keynote, Pages, Numbers files, and music to the cloud.

Using iCloud Drive

Once you have signed in with your Apple ID on your Mac, you will find iCloud Drive on the side panel in your finder app.

To start using iCloud drive, you can save documents from any of your Applications. For example, say you are working on a document in Pages, you can save it in the 'documents' section of iCloud drive as shown below.

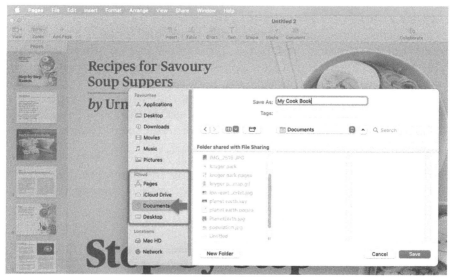

Now if I want to carry on with my document I can get my 'documents' folder on my iPad/iPhone. Select 'icloud drive' from the panel on the left, then tap 'documents'.

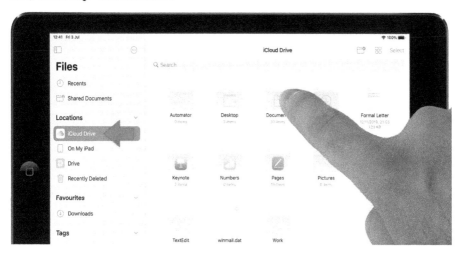

The document was saved in the 'documents' folder. If you tap in the 'documents' folder you will find your saved document.

Tap on the file icon to open it up. Note, you'll need the same app on your iPad as you used on your Mac to edit the documents. In this example, I used Pages word processor installed on Mac and iPad. You can download the apps from the app store if you need them.

iCloud Drive File Sharing

Any file in iCloud Drive can now be shared with another person through a new link feature. The link option will give direct access to specific files and folders while keeping the rest of your iCloud Drive private.

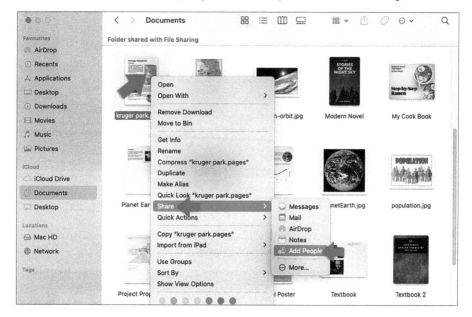

Select how you want to share the link with the other person. In this example I'm going to send it via email. Click 'add people', to grant permission to a person to view your file.

Click 'mail' to share by email, then adjust the options below. Set 'who can access' to anyone with a link. If you just want the person you're sharing with to see the file, leave this setting on its default.

Enter the person's email address in the 'to' field, add a subject if you wish. In the message body, you'll see an icon representing the shared file. Just above the icon, type a message.

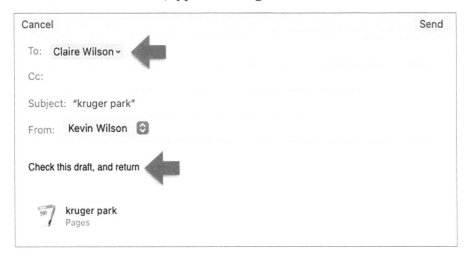

Click 'send' when you're done.

When the other person checks their email, they can click on the link in the email to see your file.

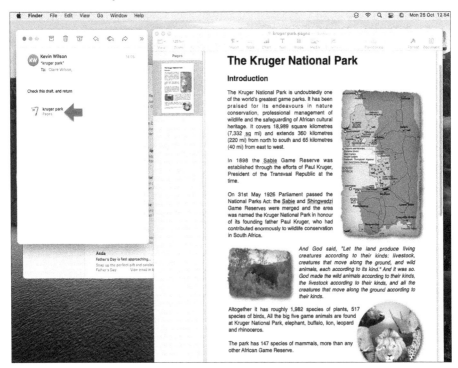

If the other person is on a Windows machine, they can click the link to download.

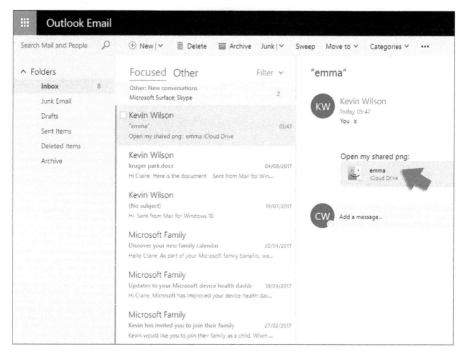

Click 'download a copy' from the prompt.

Managing App Windows

When working on your Mac it's best to arrange the windows on your desktop, especially when you're using more than one application at a time. For example, you could be browsing the web and writing a document at the same time- perhaps you're researching something, you could have the Pages App open and your web browser next to it on the screen.

Moving a Window

To move a window, move your mouse pointer to the title bar at the top of the window.

Now click and drag the window to your desired position on the screen.

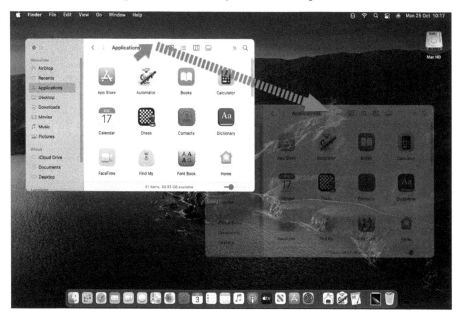

Release your mouse button. You can move the windows to anywhere on the desktop.

Resizing a Window

To resize a window, move your mouse pointer to the bottom right corner
of the window - your pointer should turn into a double edged arrow.

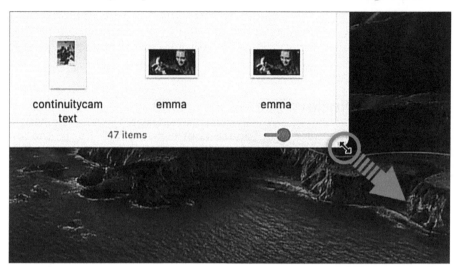

The double edged arrow means you can resize the window. Now click
and drag the edge of the window until it is the size you want.

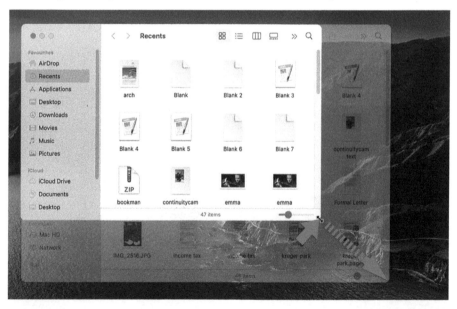

You can drag any edge of the window - left, bottom or right edge, but
I find using the corner allows you to freely resize the window much
more easily.

Minimise, Maximise & Close a Window

On the top left hand side of every window, you'll see three little icons. These three icons appear on all apps that run in a window.

Lets take a closer look at an example. Here's the finder window.

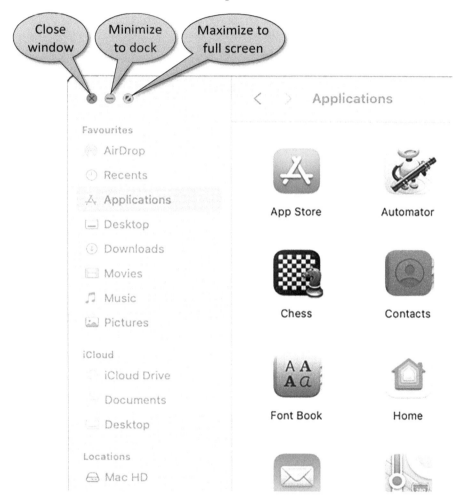

Use the first icon to close the window. Note that this doesn't close the app fully.

The second icon will minimise the window to the space on the right hand side of the dock.

The third icon will maximise the window so it fills the entire screen, or if the window is already maximised, using the same icon, restore the window to its original size.

Stage Manager

Stage Manager allows you to organize your open windows on your desktop. When you open an app it will display prominently in the center of your screen - this is called the stage. When you open another app, the app that was already open will minimise to a thumbnail sidebar on the left hand side. To switch to any of the other apps, just click on the thumbnail on the sidebar.

Stage manager is turned off by default. To turn it on, go up to the control center on the top right of your screen. Click on 'stage manager'

You can also drag and drop files from one app to another. For example, here I want to add a photograph to my Pages document. To do this, click and drag the photo to the app on the sidebar. Hold your mouse button on the app on the sidebar, you'll see it flash then appear full screen.

While still holding your down the mouse button, move the photo into position. Release your mouse button.

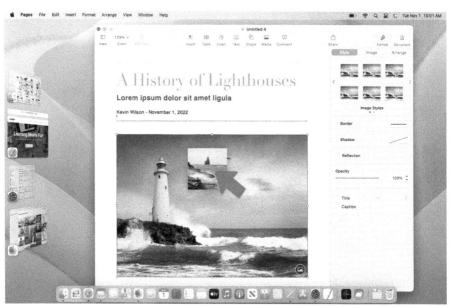

You can also group apps together. This allows you to create workspaces of apps that you use for a particular task. When you have an app open on the stage, you can drag another app off the sidebar. The app will join the app that's already on the stage. To remove an app, just drag it back to the sidebar.

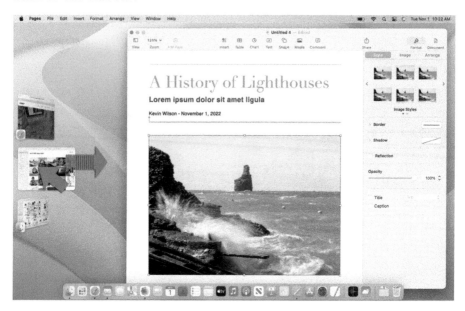

Any grouped apps will appear on the sidebar with the app windows overlapping.

If you need to tweak the settings of stage manager, you can do this through the system settings app. Open the system settings app, then select 'dock & desktop' from the list on the left hand side. Scroll down to the 'stage manager' section, click on 'customize'.

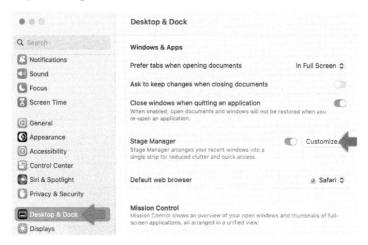

Here, you can adjust the settings. Enabling 'recent applications' shows or hides the sidebar - thumbnails remain hidden until you move your mouse to the left edge of the screen.

Enabling 'desktop items' allows you to show or hide the icons on your desktop. When this setting is disabled, the icons will remain hidden until you click on the desktop

If 'show windows from an application' is set to 'all at once', the app on the stage will show all of its open windows at the same time. If it is set to 'one at a time', the app on the stage will show one window at a time. Its other windows are in the app's thumbnail. .

Spotlight Search

Spotlight is a search engine that allows you to locate anything on your Mac, iCloud or the web. If you look in the top right hand corner of the screen, you'll see what looks like a magnifying glass. Click the icon and type in what you're searching for.

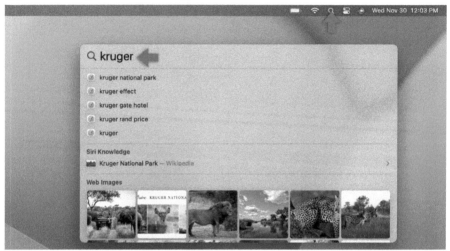

You'll see a list of top hits which are the closest matches to your search query and a list of suggestions. Click on any of these to select.

Spotlight can also give you definitions of words, convert currencies, temperatures, measurements, and make calculations. Just type them into the search field.

To customise the search parameters, open system settings click 'siri & spotlight'. Scroll down to 'search results'. Select the apps, categories and file types you want to appear in the search results.

To exclude results, select 'spotlight privacy' on the bottom right. Click the '+' icon in the popup window, select an app or location to exclude.

Notification Centre

Notification Centre is a side panel that shows alerts from apps such as new email, new messages, reminders, calendar events and system alerts. As well as an assortment of widgets.

To open notification centre, click the date & clock on the top right.

In notification centre you'll see alerts and notifications from applications at the top, and widgets underneath.

You can add widgets for local weather, calendar, clock and so on. To change or add widgets click 'edit widgets'. See page 171 for more info.

Notifications

At the top of notification centre you'll see your alerts and messages, such as new email, new tweets, new events, current song etc.

There are three types of notifications: banners, alerts, and badges.

Banners

These are displayed for a short period in the upper right corner of the screen for a few seconds, then slide off to the right. Click banner to open app.

The application's icon is displayed on the left side of the banner, while the message from the application will be displayed on the right side.

Alerts

Same as banners, except an alert has a call to action on the right hand side and will not disappear from the screen until the user takes action. Click the action button on the bottom right of the alert to open the app.

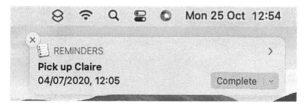

Badges

These are red notification icons that are displayed on the application's icon. They indicate the number of items available for the application.

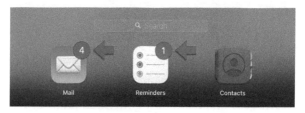

Notification Settings

Open the system settings. Select the Apple menu on the top left, then click 'system settings'.

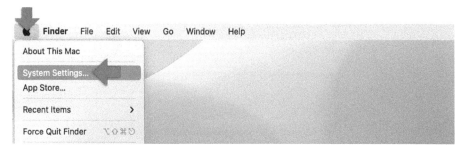

From the list on the left, select 'notifications'. Here at the top you can set how the alerts and notifications appear on your screen when an event happens. You can show previews of the notification when your mac is locked or on the lock screen. You can also allow notifications when your mac is in sleep mode or when you are sharing your display. Just set the switches next to the setting on or off. These are the default settings for all notifications

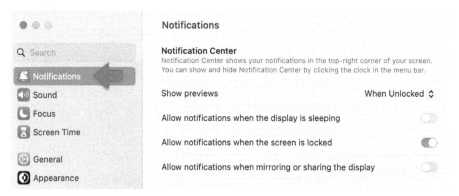

If you want to change the notification settings for a particular app, select an app from the list at the bottom. For example, email notifications.

This will show you configure the notification settings for that app. You can allow/disallow notifications for the selected app - just turn off the switch to disallow notifications. You can also change the alert style of the notification (banners and alerts).

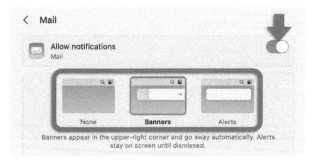

To change the alert style, select either 'none, 'banners' or 'alerts'.

- 'None' turns off the notification so it doesn't appear on the screen.
- 'Banners' appear on the screen and disappear after a while.
- 'Alerts' stay on the screen until you dismiss them.

You can choose whether to show the app's notifications on the lock screen, notification center, or show the notification badge on the app's icon.

Under show previews, you can set when you want the notification previews to appear:

- 'Default' uses the setting selected in the 'show previews' pop-up menu at the top of the notifications settings window.
- 'Always' shows notification previews (even in the login window).
- 'When unlocked' shows previews only when you're logged in to your account.
- 'Never' turns off notification previews.

'Notification grouping' specifies how notifications for a particular app or websites are grouped together in notification centre - eg by app.

Editing Widgets

You can add more widgets by clicking 'edit widgets' at the bottom of the notification center panel.

You'll see the widgets gallery appear. Scroll down the list on the left hand side. For example, I'm going to add the world clock widget, so I'd select 'clock'. In the main window, select the widget you want to add, then drag and drop the widget onto the notification centre on the right.

If you want to remove a widget, just click on the '-' icon on the top left of the widgets listed in notification center down the right hand side.

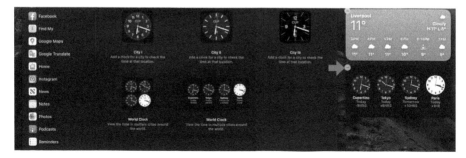

You can also rearrange the widgets listed on notification center, just click and drag the widget into position

Click 'done' when you're finished.

171

Control Centre

The control centre allows you to control common settings such as WiFi, Bluetooth, AirDrop, music, volume control and screen brightness without having to go into the settings app.

To open control centre, click the control icon on the top right of your screen.

Here, you can control your display brightness, volume, as well as WiFi, Bluetooth and AirDrop. Just click on the icons to adjust.

You can drag and pin your most used items from control centre to the top of your menu bar for easy one-click access.

Add controls for the apps and features you use most, such as fast user switching, battery status and accessibility features. To do this, open the system settings. Select the Apple menu on the top left, then click 'system settings'. From the system settings window, select 'control center'.

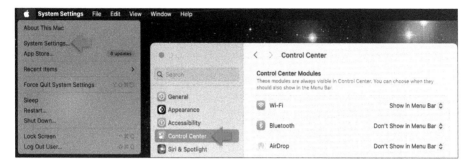

Scroll down to 'other modules'. Click the toggle switch next to the module add to control centre.

To remove an item, just toggle the switch to off.

Handoff

Handoff is a continuity feature that allows you to start something on one device such as your iPhone or iPad, then seamlessly pick up and continue on another such as your Mac.

First, you'll need to enable Handoff on your devices. To enable Handoff on your iPhone, open the settings app from your home screen. Tap 'General', then 'Handoff'. Tap the switch to set 'Handoff' to 'on'.

Now enable your Bluetooth. Go to the settings app, select 'Bluetooth'. Tap the switch to set it to 'on'.

To enable it on your Mac, go to the System Settings in the Apple menu. Tap 'Bluetooth' and turn it on.

Select 'General' from the list on the left, then click 'airdrop and handoff'. Click the check box next to "Allow Handoff between this Mac and your iCloud Devices".

Now for this demo, I'm going to start typing an email message on my iPhone. When you bring your iPhone near your Mac, you'll see the icon of the app you're using, appear on the right hand side of the dock.

Click on this icon on the dock to continue using the app. In this demo, you'll see the email open up on your Mac.

Here, you'll be able to continue from where you left off.

Universal Control

Universal Control allows you to use your keyboard, mouse across all your Apple devices such as an iPad or another Mac. You can also drag and drop files, documents or photos across your devices. This feature is only available on the newer iPads and Macs.

In this demo, I'm going to use my iMac and Macbook Pro, as you can see in the image below. See page 90 for info on how to set up this feature.

Moving Between Devices

Here on my desk I have my iMac and my Macbook Pro. I'm going to use the mouse and keyboard connected to my iMac to move between both devices.

To do this, move the mouse pointer off the edge of the screen. If you have 'push through the edge of the display' setting enabled (see page 90), then you'll see a purple marker. Push your mouse through to the other Mac.

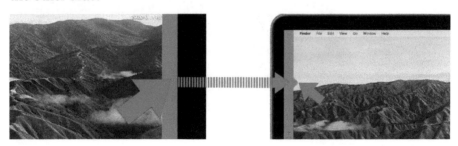

If you disabled the 'push through the edge of the display' setting (see page 90), then your mouse pointer will seamlessly move to the other Mac.

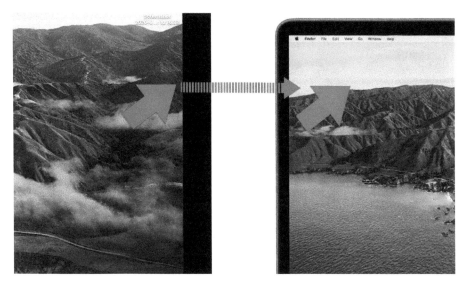

If you move your mouse pointer over to an iPad, the mouse pointer will turn into a dot.

Moving Files

To move files, simply click and drag the files off the edge of the screen to the other Mac.

You can also drag and drop files from and iPad to a Mac. Useful if you want to use Apple Pencil to create a design on your iPad and then drop it into a project you are building on your Mac. Just use the mouse to move the pointer over to the iPad, then click and drag the file into the project on your Mac.

Universal Clipboard

This is another interesting feature that allows you to cut, copy and paste with your clipboard across all your Apple Devices; iPhone, iPad as well as your Mac. This works when all your devices are logged in with your Apple id.

In the demonstration below, I have copied a paragraph from a Pages document on the Macbook Pro, and pasted it into an email on my iPhone.

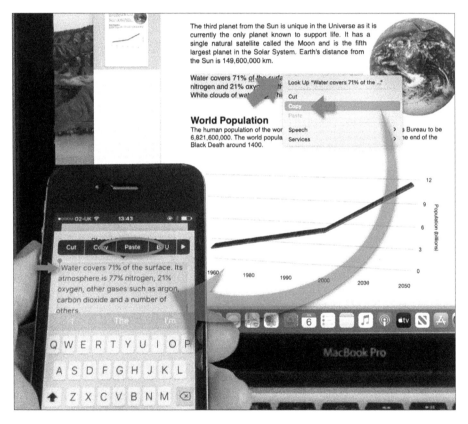

To do this, highlight the text from an application on your Mac, right click and click copy.

On your iPad or iPhone, go into the application you are going to paste the text into, tap and hold your finger in the position you want the text to appear, and tap paste from the menu that appears.

Universal Clipboard also works the other way around, if you wanted to copy some text from your phone and paste into a document on your Mac.

Shortcuts

Shortcuts was originally introduced in iOS 12 on the iPad/iPhone, and introduced in MacOS Monterey.

You can also create sharing shortcuts such as sending a message through email, Messages, or AirDrop, to a group of people, or a quick notes to people you communicate with often. You can also create shortcuts for working with files, such as creating folders, marking up documents, or text editing and batch image editing among many others.

Getting Started

You'll find the shortcuts app on the dock, or in the applications folder in finder.

Shortcuts

Lets take a look at the shortcuts app

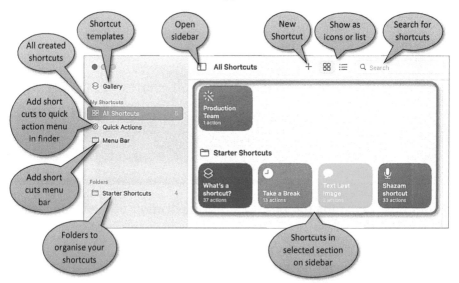

On the sidebar at the top, you'll see the gallery, which is a library of shortcuts, grouped into sections based on their functionality.

Creating Shortcuts

Select 'all shortcuts' from the sidebar on the left, then click the + icon on the top right of the screen.

Using the search bar on the top right, type in the action/app you want to use to execute your shortcut. You can also select one from the list on the right. In this demo, I want to create a shortcut that will send an email to my production team, so I can send files and updates to them without having to add the email addresses each time. In this case, I would select 'send email' from the actions.

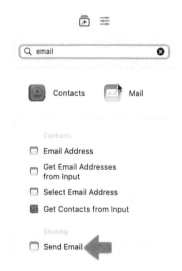

Click and drag the action onto the canvas as shown below.

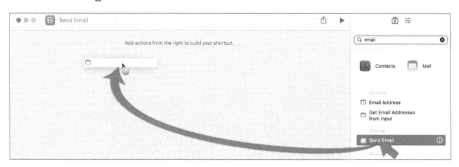

Now we need to add all the email addresses.

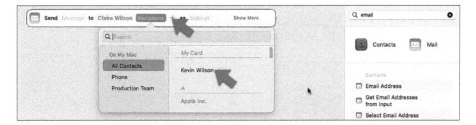

Give the shortcut a meaningful name.

Select the settings icon on the right hand side.

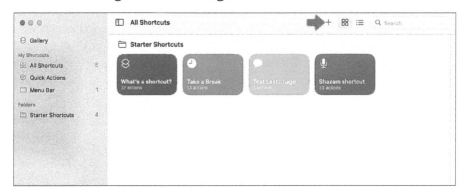

Now add the shortcut to the menus you want. Add it to the settings icon on the top right of the menu bar, or on the share menu in finder.

Shortcut Gallery

The shortcut gallery contains pre-built shortcuts you can use and customise to your needs. To view the gallery, select 'gallery' from the sidebar on the left hand side.

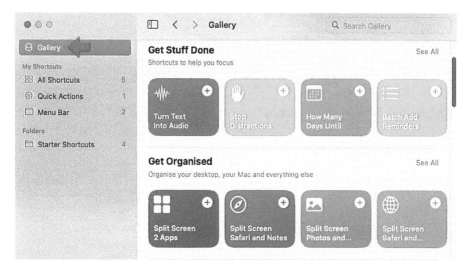

You'll find basic shortcuts for creating a note, reminder, or sending a photo to someone. As well as shortcuts for sharing files on mail, or social media, and ones that work with Siri.

First use the search field on the top right window to find a shortcut, or select one from the categories on screen.

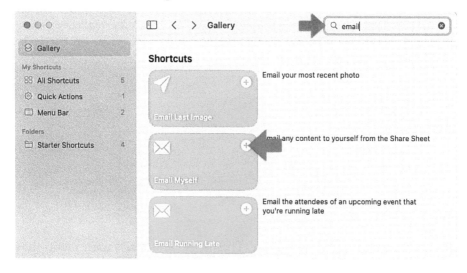

Click the '+' icon on the top right of the shortcut to open it up.

Customise any settings if prompted. In this example, I need to supply an email address. Click on 'add shortcut'.

Now, select 'all shortcuts' from the side panel on the left. You'll see the shortcut you've just created. Right click on the shortcut, select 'open' from the popup menu.

In the left hand pane, you'll see all the steps the shortcut will go through when executed. Check the steps. In this case we're sending an email, so make sure the email address is correct. Over on the right hand side, click the 'settings' icon.

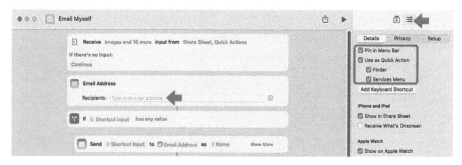

Pin the shortcut to the menu bar. This is the shortcuts menu icon that appears on the top right of the screen next to the clock/calendar. You can also add the action to the quick action menu in finder.

Running Shortcuts

To run your shortcuts, on the top right of the screen, you'll see the shortcuts icon. Select a shortcut from the drop down menu.

You can also run shortcuts from finder, if you've added the shortcut to the quick actions menu. This is useful for shortcuts that are written to manipulate or send files. Right click on the file you want to run the shortcut on... eg email myself a photo. Go down to 'quick settings', select the shortcut from the menu.

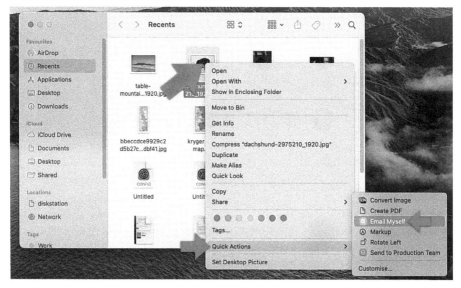

The last place you can run a shortcut from, is the services menu.

Focus Mode

Focus mode helps remove distractions on your screen while you are working on something. You can filter notifications, or turn on Do Not Disturb to turn off all notifications. You can also choose from presets for work, personal time, driving, or you can customise your own.

To configure your focus modes, open system settings.

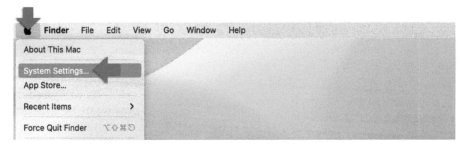

Select 'notifications & focus' from the list on the left hand side. You'll see a list of focus modes listed under 'focus'.

You can click on any of these to change the settings. At the top you can add any people or apps you want to allow messages, calls and notifications from. Just click 'allowed people', then 'add', then select the people from your address book or type in their contact number or email.

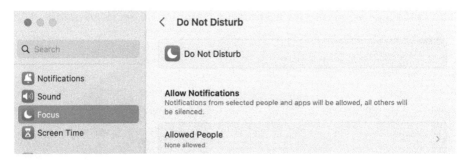

Do the same for allowed apps. Click 'allowed apps', then 'add', then select the apps you want to allow

Underneath you'll see the time the focus mode will be in force. To change the settings click on the schedule.

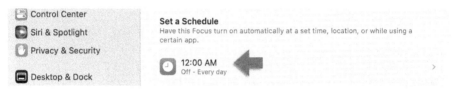

Then edit the settings. Click 'done' when you're finished.

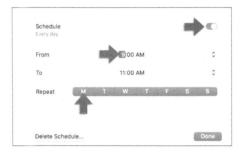

To add a new schedule click 'add schedule'.

Select when you want the schedule to start: a particular time, location, or when you launch a particular app.

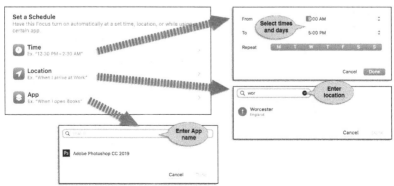

Creating a Focus Mode

To create a new focus mode, click 'add focus'.

Select 'custom'.

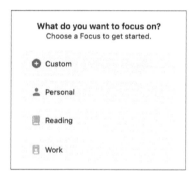

Give the focus mode a meaningful name, eg 'study'. Then select a color and an appropriate icon. This helps to identify the focus mode.

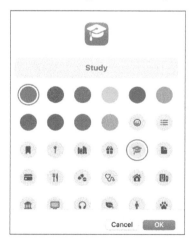

Next, we need to customise the focus mode. Under 'Allowed People', you need to add any contacts you want to allow notifications to appear for.

To do this click 'allowed people'. Select a contact from the list and click the 'add'. If you don't want to receive any notifications from anyone, don't add anyone to the list. Click 'done'.

Add the apps you want to see notifications from, eg email. To do this click 'allowed apps'. Select an app from the list then click 'add'. If you want to silence all apps, then don't select any from the list.

Click 'done'.

Under 'Set a schedule', you can set a time or location this focus mode is automatically enabled. You can also set the focus mode to turn on when you use a specific app. To set this up, click 'add schedule' on the bottom right of the section.

Select one of the options from the popup menu.

'Time' allows you to select a time and day this focus mode is enabled.

'Location' turns on the focus mode when you reach a particular location. Eg a university if you're studying.

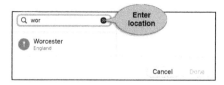

'App' allows you to automatically enable this focus mode when you start a particular app or apps.

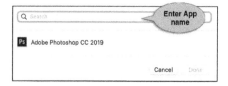

Manually Enable a Focus Mode

To open focus mode, select the 'control center' icon from the top right of the screen. Select 'focus'.

Select a focus mode from the list.

You'll see a small icon appear at the top of the screen. Click to view details.

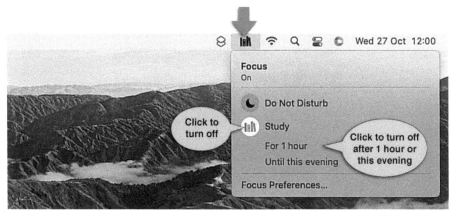

Using Siri

Siri has finally made it to the Mac and works pretty much as she does on the iPhone.

You can find Siri on the top right hand side of your screen. Or hold down command space on your keyboard for two seconds.

Try some of the following phrases...

See what Siri does.

Voice Control

You can give voice commands to your mac. To do this, first you will need to enable the feature. Go to system settings.

Select 'accessibility' from the list on the left. Then click 'voice control'.

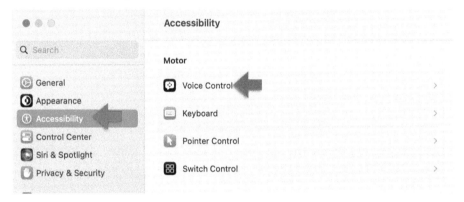

Click the switch at the top to enable voice control. When you enable this, a microphone indicator will appear on the screen.

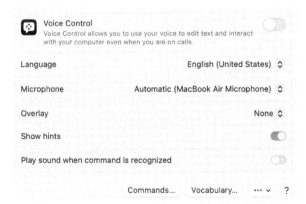

Try saying "open safari", or "scroll to the top". To pause voice control say "go to sleep" or click 'sleep' on the microphone indicator. To resume say or click 'wake up' on the microphone indicator.

To see all the commands you can give, click 'commands' in the voice control settings.

Voice Dictation

Instead of typing text, you can actually dictate the work using a microphone. Dictation converts your spoken words into text.

First you'll need to enable dictation. To do this, open the system settings.

Select 'keyboard' from the list on the left. Scroll down to 'dictation'. Click the check box to enable dictation.

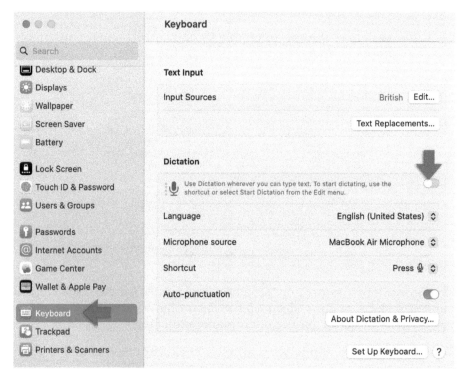

Where it says 'short cut', you can specify the keyboard shortcut you want to use to start dictation. The default is usually F5 on a macbook, or you can change it to double press the fn key.

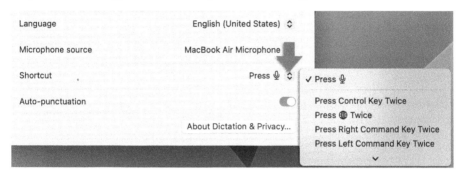

In your app eg 'Pages' or 'notes', press F5. You'll see a mic icon appear next to your document. Now you can begin dictating your notes.

As well as entering text by dictation, you can also add punctuation. To enter a punctuation mark or symbol, just speak its name.

To insert a question mark say "question mark"
To insert a period mark to end a sentence say "period" or "full stop"
To insert a comma, say "comma".

You can also move your cursor to enter text in different parts of your document. Try these...

"Move forward one paragraph" or "move up one line"
"Select next word".
"Select next paragraph."

You can format text. For example, if I wanted to enter a word or sentence in bold text, speak the word or sentence, then immediately after say "bold that". Use "italicalise that", for italic, and "underline that" to underline the text.

To see all the voice commands, open system settings, select 'accessibility', click 'voice control' on the left hand side, then click 'commands'.

Using Apple Pay on your Mac

To be able to use Apple Pay on your Mac, you will need to use the Safari Web Browser and have an Apple device such as your iPhone near by. On participating websites, you will see "pay with Apple Pay Button". When you click on this button, you will see an authentication prompt on your nearby iPhone or Apple Watch. This uses the continuity feature.

Browse your favourite shopping site and, when you're ready to buy, click on the Apple Pay button.

Once you click the Apple Pay button on the website, a notification will pop up on your iPhone asking you to authorise the transaction. You can do this by using Touch ID or Face ID on your iPhone. If you're using a macbook with a fingerprint scanner, tap the touch sensor to authorise the transaction.

You'll only see the Apple Pay logos on participating websites and only if you have your iPhone set up and in the vicinity of your Mac.

Auto Unlock

You can automatically unlock your Mac using another Apple Device such as Apple Watch.

Open your Macbook's lid or tap a key while wearing your Apple Watch to unlock your Mac from sleep mode.

Auto Unlock only works when waking your Mac from sleep. If you restart your Mac or start it up from Shut Down, then you will need to enter a password to unlock.

First you need to enable 'two factor authentication'. To do this, open your web browser and head over to...

```
Appleid.Apple.com
```

...and enter your Apple ID and password.

Click 'edit' under the security section, then 'get started' under 'two step verification' and follow the on screen prompts.

Now, go to system settings, select 'touch id & password' from the list on the left.

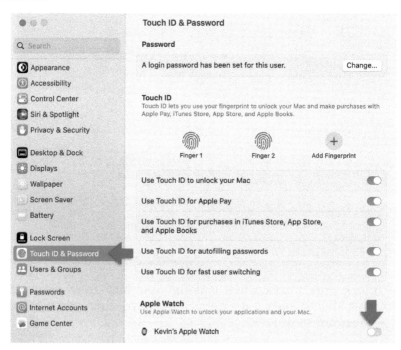

You'll see your Apple Watch listed at the bottom of the screen. Turn on the switch next to your watch. Enter your mac password if prompted.

Once set up, you can wake and unlock your Mac simply by opening up the lid, or tapping a key while wearing your watch.

The Mac Keyboard

The Mac keyboard is not much different from a standard computer keyboard, although there are a few keys to take note of. These are highlighted below.

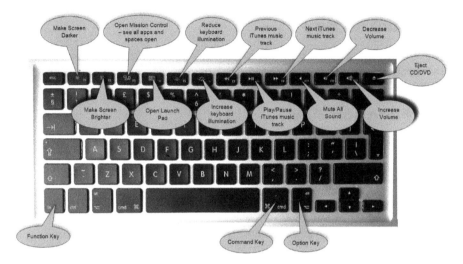

Macs have a few special keys that allow you to carry out certain operations on your mac.

The Command Key

This is equivalent to the control key on a PC, and allows you to use keyboard shortcuts for various commands available on the menu in different applications. For example, to undo something press Command-Z, to save press Command-S to print press Command-P and so on.

The Option Key

Also known as the Alt Key, allows you to select which drive to boot from when your Mac starts. Useful if you need to boot your mac from a start-up disk.

The Control Key

This key allows you to use the right click option on your mouse. Hold down control and click the mouse button.

The Function Key

This key is used to perform special functions with the 'F' keys along the top on a MacBook keyboard.

Executing Keyboard Shortcuts

Hold down one of the keys above, then tap the letter corresponding to the command you want to execute, as shown below.

Useful Keyboard Shortcuts

Use the command key on your keyboard to execute these commands.

Using the command key, you can execute several commands common to most applications

⌘ +	P = Print
	Q = Quit
X = Cut	W = Close Window
Z = Undo	C = Copy
A = Select All	S = Save
H = Hide	V = Paste
F = Find	O = Open Window
G = Find Next	E = Eject
M = Minimize	N = New
- = Zoom Out	+ = Zoom In

If you're having some trouble with an application, you can force it to quit using the combo: command option escape

⌘ + ⌥ + ↻

Select the application from the popup window and click 'force quit'.

MacOS Startup Keys

When your Mac starts up, you can hit certain keys to use different tools. This is particularly useful if your Mac encounters problems or you want to re-install MacOS - eg, hold down option key to select boot device.

When your Mac restarts, quickly hold down the keyboard combo until you see the Apple logo.

Keyboard Combo	Command
Shift ⇧	Start up in safe mode with minimal drivers.
Option ⌥	Open start up manager. Allows you to select boot device.
C	Start up from a bootable CD, DVD, or USB thumb drive
D	Run Apple Hardware Test.
Option D	Run Apple Hardware Test over the Internet.
Option N	Start up from a NetBoot server using an image stored on MacOS Server.
Command R	Start up in Recovery Mode using local recovery partition.
Command Option R	Start up in Recovery Mode using recovery data from Apple's Servers.
Command Option P R	Reset NVRAM. Hold keys until you hear startup sound.
T	Start up in target disk mode, allows your mac to be used as if it was an external hard drive.

Use both the shift, command and option keys to execute these commands.

Command Key   Option Key

Making Gestures

If you have a Macbook with a trackpad, you can use a number of finger gestures to operate certain features of MacOS.

One Finger Point and Tap

You can move your mouse pointer across the screen by using one finger on the trackpad. Tap your finger on the pad to select an icon and is the equivalent of your left mouse click.

Right Click

Tap with two fingers on the trackpad. You can also hold down the control key and tap with one finger.

Two Finger Scroll

You can scroll down web pages and documents using two fingers on the track pad.

Two Finger Rotate

You can rotate things on the screen by using your forefinger and thumb on the trackpad making a twisting action with your wrist. This works well when viewing photographs or browsing a map.

Two Finger Swipe

Swiping two fingers across the trackpad swipes between pages in a document, book or on a website.

Four Finger Open Launchpad

Use your thumb and three fingers on the trackpad and draw your fingers and thumb together will open Launchpad where you can select an app to open.

Magic Mouse

A Bluetooth wireless mouse with multi gesture support. We'll take a look at these gestures below.

Left Click

Primary select button to click or double click on an icon

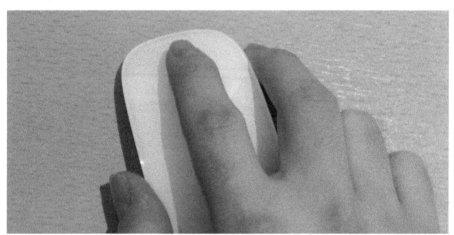

Right Click

Secondary click or right mouse button click to reveal context menus. Click with two fingers on your mouse. You can also hold down the control key and click your mouse button.

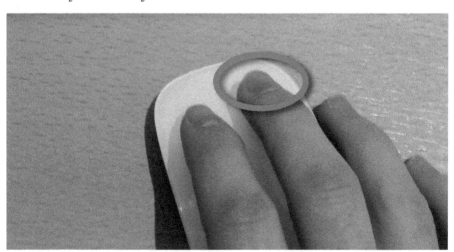

Scrolling

Scroll vertically or horizontally around a page, image, document, etc. Hold your mouse still then run your finger over the surface of the mouse - up and down, left and right to scroll pages

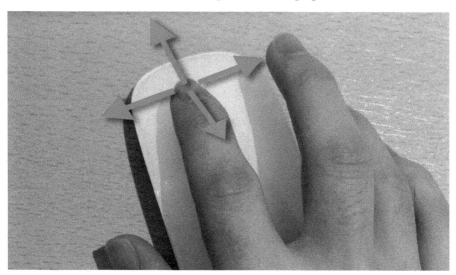

Swipe

Hold your mouse still, then use two fingers to swipe left and right across the surface of the mouse to move a page forward or backward when reading a document or website.

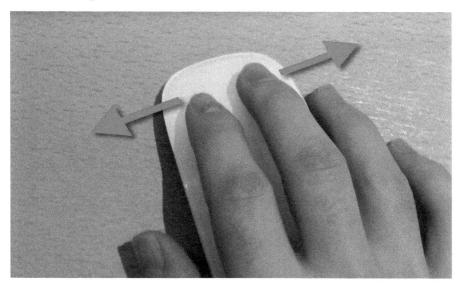

Find your Mouse Pointer

If you have lost your mouse pointer somewhere on the screen you can wiggle your finger backwards and forwards across your track-pad .

Wiggle your mouse and your cursor will grow to a larger size making it easier to find.

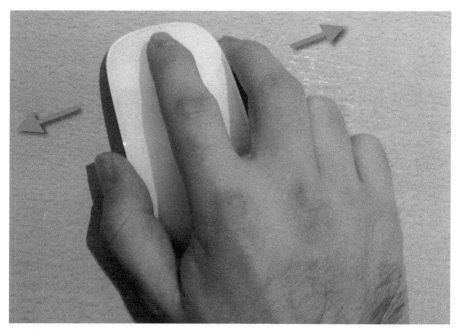

Taking Screenshots

You can capture a screenshot of the entire screen, or just a portion of it. You can either save the screenshot as a file on the desktop or to the clipboard, where you can paste into another app.

Command-Shift-3 captures the whole screen and saves it as a PNG file on the desktop.

Command-Control-Shift-3 captures the whole screen and saves to your clipboard.

Command-Shift-4 captures a selected portion of the screen and saves it as a PNG file on the desktop.

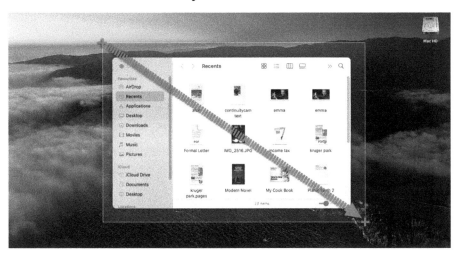

Command-Control-Shift-4 captures a selected portion of the screen and saves it to your clipboard.

Command-Shift-5 opens up the on-screen capture controls.

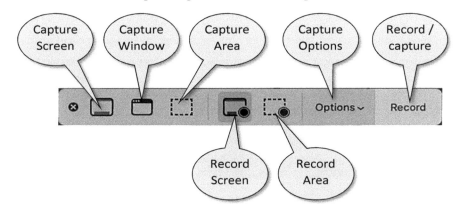

Select 'capture screen' to capture the full screen, select 'capture window' then click the window you want to capture, select 'capture area' then click and drag the box around the area of the screen you want. Click 'capture'. Your screenshot or recording will appear on your desktop.

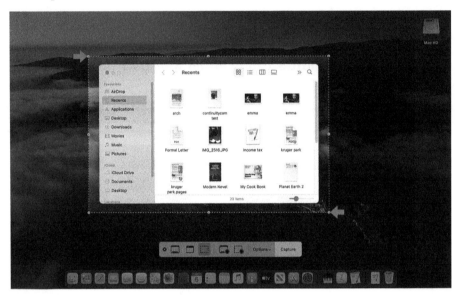

Screen Recording

Press **Command-Shift-5.** Click 'record screen' icon. Click 'options' to change save location, timer, microphone or show/hide mouse pointer etc.

Click the stop icon on the top right of your screen to stop recording.

Your recording will appear as an MP4 video file on your desktop.

210

Split Screen Mode

You can arrange your windows side by side. Open the two apps you want to arrange side by side, eg: Pages & Safari. Left click and hold your mouse button down on the app's green maximize button on the top-left hand side.

Select 'tile window to left of screen'.

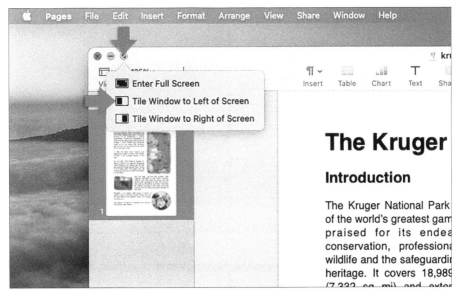

Select the other window to arrange them side by side...

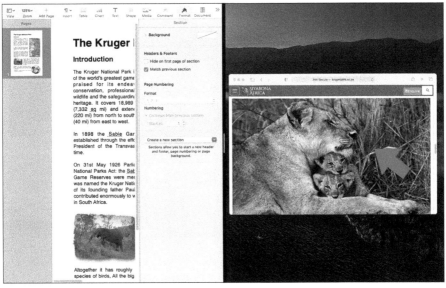

Chapter 3: Getting Around Your Mac

Split Screen opens in full screen mode, so you wont see the Dock or Menu Bar.

Move your mouse pointer to the top edge of the screen to reveal the Menu Bar.

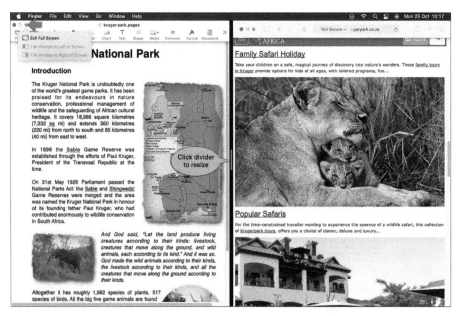

Click the green maximise button again to return to desktop view. Do this with both apps to return them to normal mode.

Keychain

Keychain is your password manager. Keychain allows you to save passwords so you don't have to remember them when you access an account on a website, or when you check your email, or connect to a network server. When you sign into these services for the first time you'll be given the option to save the password.

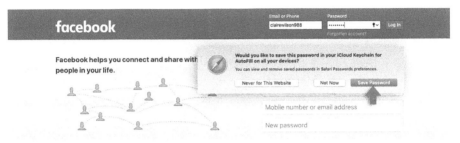

Or in MacOS, you can select the option to save your password.

You'll find all your saved passwords on your keychain app. To open the app, select 'launchpad' from the dock.

Select 'other'.

Click 'keychain access' to start the app.

Lets take a look at the keychain app. Along the top of the app window you can add a new password, or change, view and update password information.

Underneath you can filter the password list to view all, passwords only, passwords for secure notes, certificates, and PassKeys. This bar will filter out the password list at the bottom of the window.

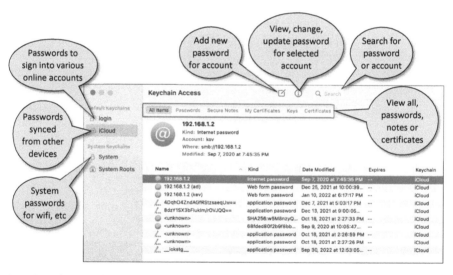

On the 'keychains' panel along the left hand side, you'll see some keychains. Here, under 'logon' you'll see sites or services for which have saved passwords for - this could be a server on a network, a website such as facebook, or the mail app.

Under 'icloud' you'll see sites or services whose passwords have synced from other devices such as an iPhone or iPad.

Under 'system' you'll see WiFi networks, servers and other system passwords that you've saved. System Roots: This is where system certificates are stored

Certificates and Keys are used to ensure encrypted communication with websites and services.

On the middle pane you'll see a list of sites/services for which you have passwords saved for on the keychain that is selected in the left hand 'keychains' panel. Use the tabs along the top: 'all items', 'passwords', 'secure notes', 'my certificates', 'keys' and 'certificates' to filter out the services in the list. For example, if you want to see passwords, select 'passwords'.

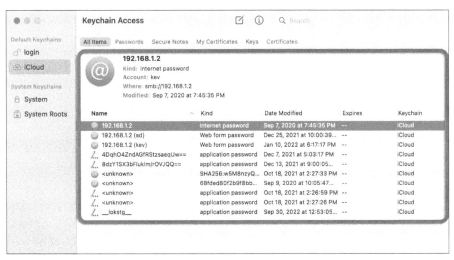

You can double click on a service in the list to view. On the attributes tab you can change password or account username.

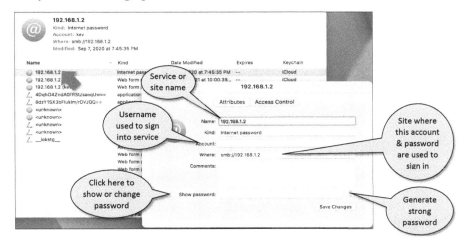

You can also click the 'key' icon next to 'show password' to generate a strong password. You'll still need to change the password on the actual site.

The 'access control' tab allows you to grant access to the password for the service or site named in the attributes tab.

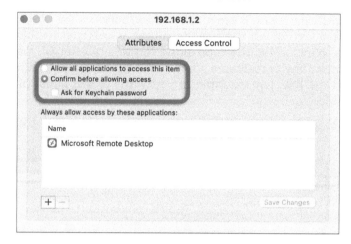

For example, if you select 'allow all applications to access this item' you won't be prompted to unlock the password to access the site or service.

If you select 'confirm before allowing access', and 'ask for keychain password' for an item, you will need to type the password to unlock the keychain before you can access the password to login to that site or service (named in the attributes tab).

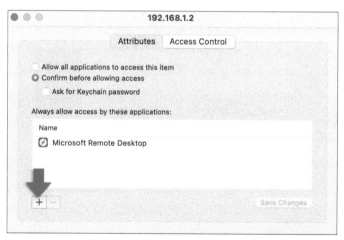

You can add apps in the section underneath that always have access to this particular password. Just click the '+' icon then select an app.

Here, I've added 'microsoft remote desktop' meaning this app will always have access to this username and password.

PassKeys

PassKeys are intended to serve as an alternative to traditional passwords, utilizing biometric identification methods such as Touch ID on a Mac or Face ID an iPhone. These PassKeys are stored and synchronized through iCloud Keychain.

For each website or account, a PassKey is generated that contains a distinct cryptographic key pair - a private key which remains securely stored on the user's device, and a public key which is shared with the website or app. If a Mac or Magic Keyboard is equipped with a fingerprint scanner, users can authenticate using Touch ID. Alternatively, an iPhone can be used for authentication by scanning a QR code or verifying with Face ID.

It's important to note that for PassKeys to work, individual apps and websites must integrate support for this feature. In instances where PassKeys are not supported, the traditional password prompt will appear. At the time of writing only a limited number of websites, such as Google, Microsoft, PayPal, iCloud, and eBay have implemented PassKeys, but more are anticipated to adopt this feature in the near future. For websites that have adopted PassKeys, users will notice the absence of the usual password prompt. Instead, they will be prompted for Touch ID or Face ID authentication.

To use PassKeys you need to make sure iCloud Keychain is set up on your iCloud account. To do this open the system settings on your mac, then click your name at the top left of the window. Click iCloud.

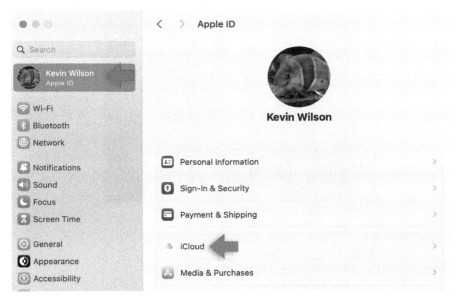

Turn on 'password & keychain' if it isn't already. Follow the on-screen instructions if prompted.

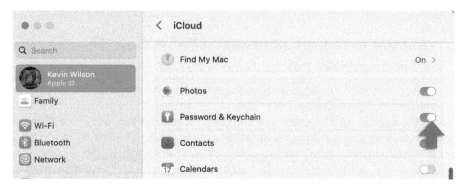

Create a PassKey for a New Account

Navigate to an app or website that offers PassKey support. Go to the sign-up page. Fill in your registration details as you normally would and complete the sign-up process.

Safari will prompt you to save a PassKey for the account

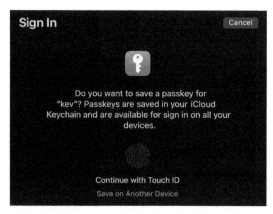

You can choose how you want to sign in:

- **Touch ID on your Mac**
- Scan a QR code with your iPhone or iPad
- External security key

Create a PassKey for Existing Account

To create a PassKey for an existing account, sign in to the account with your password as normal. You will usually see an option to add a PassKey when you sign in. Follow the on screen prompts. Here in the example below, I've signed into eBay.

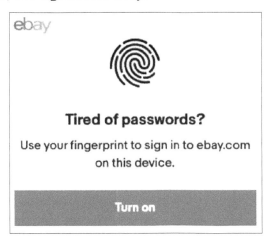

If you don't see a prompt, open the settings app, then select 'passwords' from the list on the left.

Click the 'info icon' for the website. Then click 'change password on website'.

You may need to search security, password or sign in options in the account settings on the website. This will depend on the website or app you're using, so check with their customer support if you're having problems.

Sign in with a PassKey

On the account sign-in page, enter your account name, then click the account/user name field. Select your account from the list of suggestions.

You'll see a security prompt asking you how you want to sign in.

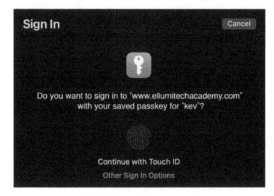

If you have Touch ID on your Mac, place your finger on the Touch ID sensor.

If you don't have a Touch ID sensor on your Mac, click 'other sign in options', then select 'iPhone, iPad or Android device' to authenticate.

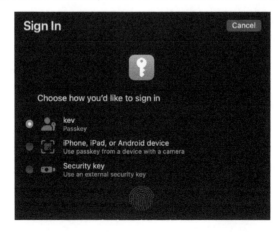

Open the camera app on your phone then scan the QR code.

Tap 'sign in with PassKey'.

For websites that support PassKeys, the login process becomes seamless, prompting users for biometric verification rather than a password. This approach not only increases security by reducing risks associated with password breaches but also simplifies the authentication process, eliminating the need to remember and manage multiple passwords.

For a detailed list and to stay updated on the latest integrations, you might want to visit the first two websites mentioned below:

www.passkeys.io/who-supports-passkeys

passkeys.directory

4

Using MacOS Applications

MacOS comes with a lot of apps pre-installed. In this chapter we'll take a look at the various apps installed on your Mac as well as:

- Launching Your Applications
- Killing Unresponsive Apps
- App Store
- App Tabs
- Maps
- Apple Books
- Notes
- Calendar
- Image Capture
- Photobooth
- DVDs & BluRays
- Voice Memos
- News
- Terminal
- Pages App
- Keynote App
- Numbers App
- Dictionary App
- Sticky Notes App
- Preview App

To help you better understand this section, take a look at the video resources. Open your web browser and navigate to the following sites:

elluminetpress.com/mac-apps

Launching Your Applications

You can find applications on the dock at the bottom of your screen.

You can also find apps by hitting the Launch Pad icon on the dock.

If there are apps you use a lot, you can drag them from launch pad to the dock.

The next time you need the application just click on the icon on the dock.

Chapter 4: Using Applications

You can also launch applications from the 'applications' folder in your finder window. Click the finder icon on the dock, then click the 'applications' folder.

If the application you launched is one you use quite often, but is not permanently on the dock, you can easily add it. To do this, right click on the icon, go to options, and from the slideout click 'keep in dock'.

This will keep the application's icon in the dock whether it is running or not.

Killing Unresponsive Apps

Sometimes apps lock up and freeze and there is no way to close the app using conventional means.

Press **CMD - OPTION - ESC**, as shown below...

From the popup window, select the app you want to shut down, then click 'force quit'.

App Store

The App Store allows you to browse and download apps developed for your Mac. You'll find the icon on your launchpad or dock.

You can also access the app store from the Apple menu on the very top left of the screen.

Once you launch app store, you'll see the main screen. Here you can type in the name of the app you are looking for in the search field on the top left of the screen, or click the 'categories' icon to browse categories such as reference, productivity and entertainment listed down the panel on the left hand side.

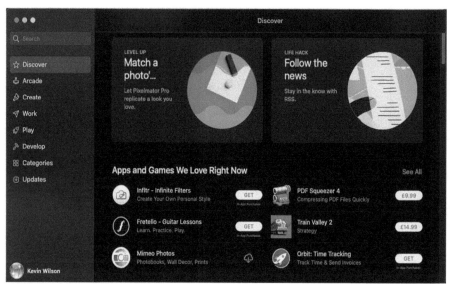

To buy or download anything, just click the price - or click 'get' if it's free.

The buttons will change to 'buy app', or 'install' if it's free. Click on the icon again to confirm the download.

Sign in with your Apple ID email and password if prompted.

The app will download. Once the install is complete, you will find your new app in Launchpad or in the applications folder in Finder.

App Tabs

The tabs feature allows you to open multiple application windows as tabs in the same window.

You can merge all your open windows using the 'merge all windows' command. To do this click the 'window' menu at the top of your screen. Select 'merge all windows'.

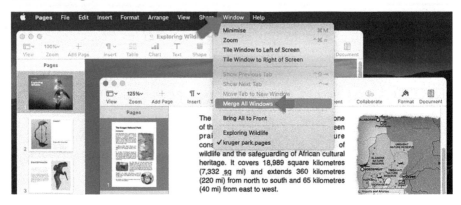

This will merge all the open windows of the same application into one tabbed window.

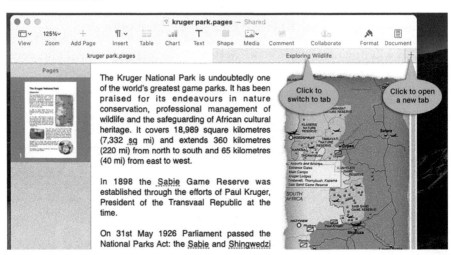

Click the tabs to switch between the tabbed windows, click the + sign on the right hand side to open a new tab.

Maps

With the Maps app, you can explore cities, places of interest, as well as finding directions to a particular destination.

You'll find the maps app icon either on your dock or on launchpad.

Exploring Places

To find a place, click in the search field on the top left, then enter an address, name of a shop or location you're looking for.

You'll see a list of matching places appear down the left hand side. If your location is found on the map, you'll see an orange pin appear with the place name. Click a location's pin on the map for more info.

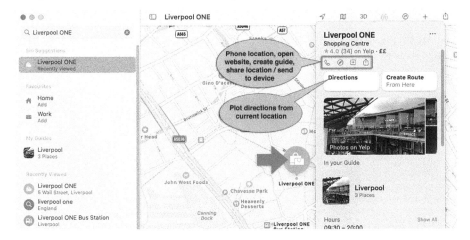

You can use the four icons at the top of the info sheet to place a call to the location's customer service line, open the location's website, create a guide, and share the location with someone or send it to your iPhone or iPad.

You can also plot a route from your current location. Click 'directions'.

Share a Location

To share a location with someone, click the location's pin on the map. Click the 'share' icon, go down to 'share', then select the app you want to use to share the location with. Eg you can send the location using mail, messages, airdrop, or you can add the location to your notes or reminders.

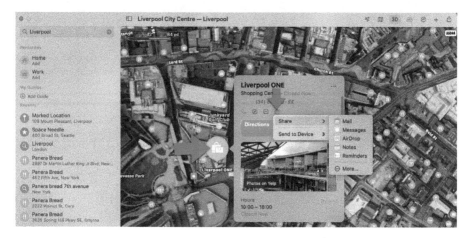

If you're sending the location using mail, messages or airdrop, select the person you want to send the location to.

Share a Map

To share a map, click the 'share' icon in the top-right corner of the info window.

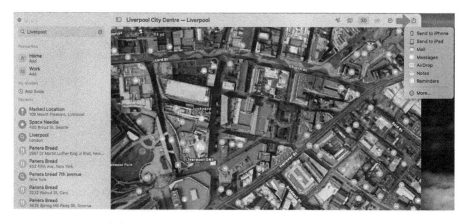

From the drop down menu, select the app you want to share the map with. If you're sending the location using mail, messages or airdrop, select the person you want to send the location to.

230

Favourites

Click the location's pin, then click the three dots icon on the top right of the location's info card.

You'll see your favourite locations appear on the sidebar. Click a favourite on your sidebar to revisit.

Drop a Pin

Right click on the position on the map where you would like to drop a pin. Select 'drop pin'

Chapter 4: Using Applications

Guides

The Guides feature is intended to provide expert recommendations for the best places to visit in a city, such as places to eat, shop, and places of interest to explore. Useful if you're visiting a city and want to find out where to eat, shop, or what to do. There are only a few cities such as Los Angeles, San Francisco, New York and Seattle that include this feature at the moment, but more will be added soon.

To view a guide on a city, type the city name into the search at the top left of the screen. Select the city name from the search results. If the city has guides you'll see them appear at the top of the info card for that city. Click 'see more' to view the whole list.

Click on any of the guides to view more information and see the location on the map

Select an attraction and you'll see the location appear on the map with an info card.

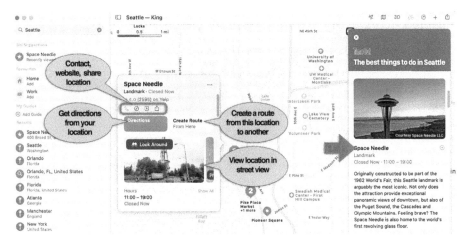

You can also create your own guides and share them with friends, family and colleagues.

To add a location to your own guide, click the three dots icon on the top right of the info card. Select the guide you want to add the location to. If you're creating a new guide, click 'new guide'.

Rename your guide. Right click the guide in the left hand pane, then select 'edit guide'. Type in a new name

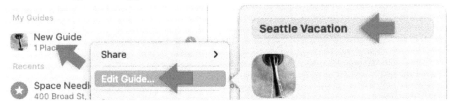

Public Transport Routes

You can also check public transport in the local area. To do this click the maps icon on the top right, select 'public transport' from the menu.

You'll see bus and train routes appear on the map. Click on a bus or train station to see what services are running and when your next bus or train is due.

Find your service from the list. You'll see the route numbers and the times when they're due. Click on the route number to see the full route.

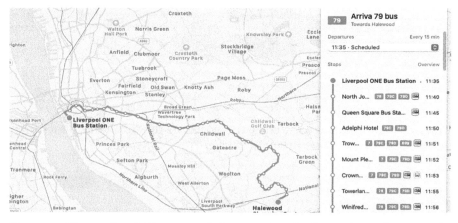

Here you'll see the full route of the service, indicated on the map in blue.

Driving Directions

You can type the name of the city or venue you are looking for in the search field at top centre of the screen. You can also enter postal/zip codes to find specific areas.

Click 'directions' icon on the top right of the screen.

Select the 'car' icon to plot driving directions. Type in your location and your destination in to the fields shown below.

Sometimes the maps app will come up with more than one route. These will be listed down the right hand side. Click on the route you want to take. Click the small right arrow to expand the route to show turn-by-turn directions.

You'll see the route shown in blue on the map.

To send the map to your iPhone or iPad, click the share icon on the top right, then from the drop down menu, select your device.

Walking Directions

Walking directions are useful if you're trying to find your way to a shop or location in a city.

Click 'directions' icon on the top right of the screen.

Select the 'person' icon to plot walking directions. Type in your location and your destination in to the fields shown below.

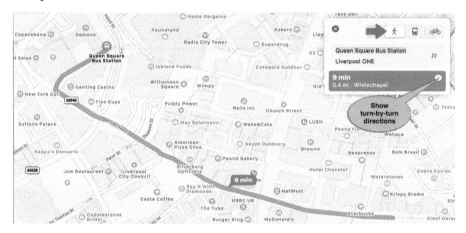

Click the small right arrow next to your route to show turn-by-turn directions.

Useful to transfer to your iPhone when walking around the location.

Look Around

To take a closer look at a place, click the binocular icon on the top right

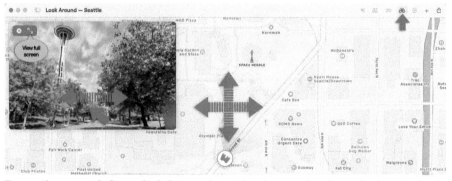

Drag the map left and right or drag the image in the window to look around.

Explore in 3D

Using the satellite map, you can view cities in 3D. Type the name of the city into the search field on the top left of the screen.

Select the maps icon, then 'satellite' from the selections.

Click '3D' on the bottom right hand side. Use the '+' & '-' icons on the bottom right to zoom in and out of your map. Click and drag your mouse to move the map around the screen.

Look Inside

Apple has started adding indoor features to their maps app. This includes interior layouts and maps of airports, shopping malls and other venues. Just click 'look inside' link.

Not all locations have this feature yet.

Interactive Globe

With the interactive globe of the earth, you can explore mountain ranges, deserts, rain forests, and oceans. This feature only works on Macs with the M1/M2 chip.

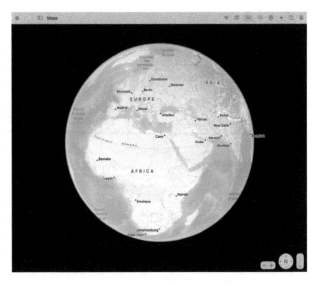

To view the globe, zoom all the way out of your map. If you're using a mouse, run your finger down over the scroll wheel. If you're using a macbook pinch two fingers together on your trackpad.

To rotate the earth, click and drag the globe with your mouse or drag two fingers over the trackpad.

To zoom into a location, scroll up using the scroll wheel on your mouse, or use two fingers on the trackpad and spread them apart.

Here, I've zoomed into San Francisco. To see the city in 3D click '3D' on the toolbar on the top right.

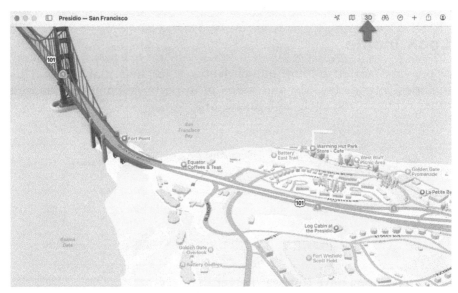

On the bottom right hand corner you'll see some controls. Here, you can zoom in and out of the map, use the compass to rotate the map, or use the slider on the right to adjust the tilt of the map in 3D.

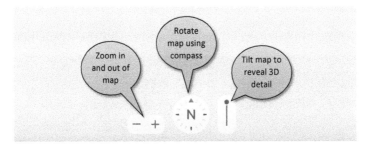

You can click on any of the place names or landmarks to see more information.

You can also change the map. To do this, click the map icon on the top right of the screen. Use 'explore' to explore the cities and see detail, select 'driving' to view driving routes and roads, select 'public transport' to view buses and train routes and stations, select 'satellite' to explore the cities using a real life satellite image.

Apple Books

Formerly known as iBooks, Apple Books allows you to download and read ebooks.

To open Apple Books open launchpad and select the Apple books icon.

Once Apple Books opens, you'll see the main screen. Let's take a look at the different sections. Along the top of your screen you'll see a toolbar, here you can select your library, bookstore, audio book store, and the search field.

To search for more books, click the search field on the top left.

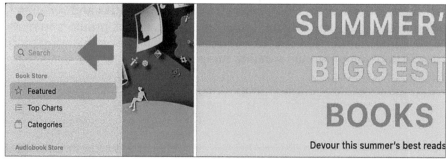

Once you have found a book you want, click on the book cover.

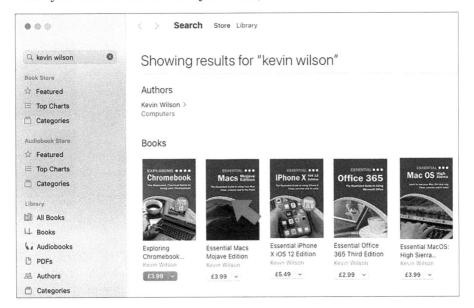

You'll see a description of what the book covers or is about, details about the book such as sample pages, technical stats, reviews and write ups.

Click 'get sample' to see inside the book.

Click the price to buy the book, this will download it and add it to your library.

Enter your Apple ID email address and password if prompted. Click 'buy' on the confirmation dialog box.

Chapter 4: Using Applications

You can find all your books that you have purchased, in your library section. Select 'all books' from the grey panel on the left hand side.

Double click on the book covers to open the books.

Once the books are open, you can 'turn the pages' by swiping two fingers left or right across the trackpad on your macbook. If you are using a mouse, click the left or right arrows on the edge of the screen to turn the page.

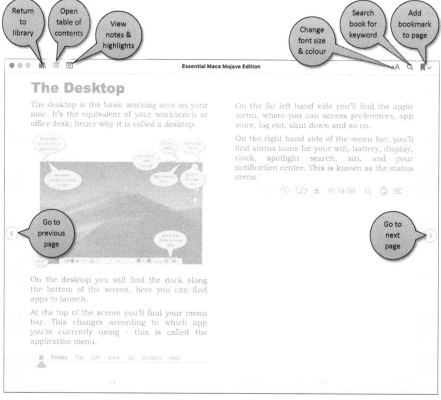

You can also add notes and highlight parts of the book. Click and drag your mouse across the text you want to highlight, then right click on the selection.

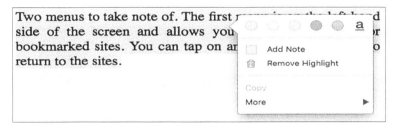

From the popup menu select a color to highlight the text.

To add a note, click 'add note' then type your note into the post-it that appears. To see all your notes click 'view highlight or notes' icon on the tool bar at the top.

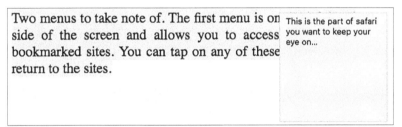

You can also add bookmarks. To do this, on the page you want to bookmark, click the bookmarks icon on the top right of the screen.

To return to a bookmark, click the small down arrow next to the bookmarks icon on the top left. Select your bookmark from the drop down list.

Notes

You can take notes using the notes app. To launch notes, open launchpad and select the notes icon.

When you open the notes app, you'll see the main screen. Here you can see your notes you have created either on your iPad/iPhone or on your Mac - these are listed in the centre pane.

On the right hand pane, you'll be able to edit a note you've selected in the centre pane.

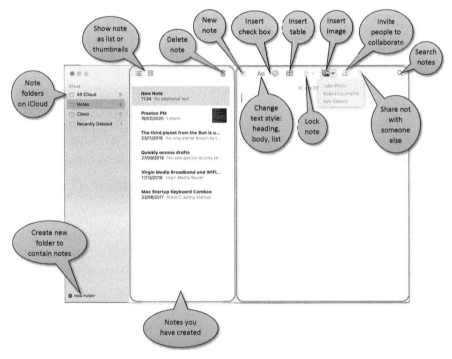

Click on a note in the list to view. Click the 'new note' icon to create a new note. There's an option to pin your most used notes to the top of the notes app for quick access to lists and other frequently used notes. To do this, right click on the note in the list and from the popup menu, click 'pin note'. This will make sure it stays at the top of the list. You can also insert an image - drag and drop from finder, or use your iPhone.

Tables can also be added to individual notes for better organization. Open an existing note or create a new one. Click on the 'insert table icon' on the toolbar.

You can also add check boxes to make 'to do' lists. To do this, open a new note or select one to edit. To add the check box, click the check box icon on the toolbar.

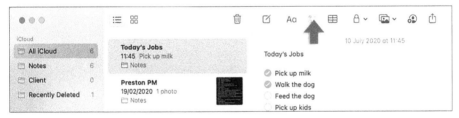

Once you have completed the task, click the circle next to it, to mark the task as complete.

You can also add photos. Select the photo icon from the toolbar. From the drop down menu select 'take photo' to take a photo with your iPhone or iPad, select 'scan documents' to scan a doc with your iPad, or 'add a sketch' to use your pencil on your iPad to create a sketch.

To invite people to collaborate on your note, click the share icon. Then select the name of the person you want to share the note with. You can also share via message and email.

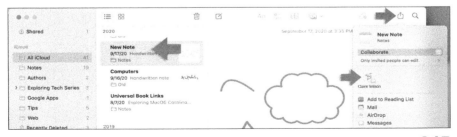

Chapter 4: Using Applications

You can create a quick note using the shortcut on the bottom right corner of the screen.

Click 'new quick note' when the popup appears on the screen.

If the quick note option doesn't work, open the system settings, select 'desktop & dock' from the list on the left. Scroll down to the bottom of the page, click on 'hot corners'.

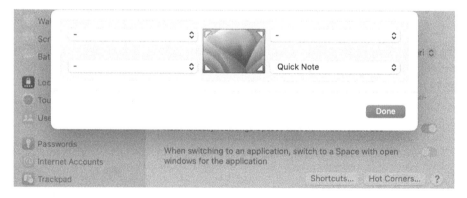

Add 'quick note' to the bottom right corner.

Calendar

This app is useful for scheduling appointments, events, meetings and so on. These can be synced with your iPad or iPhone. To open calendar, select launchpad from the dock, then click the calendar icon.

I find it easiest to view the calendar in month view as shown below.

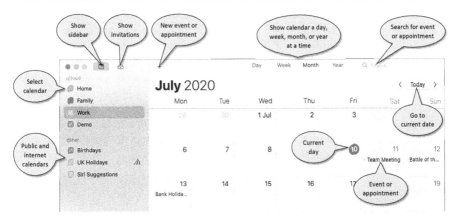

Adding an Event

The quickest way to add a new event is to click on the plus sign, then type in your event, date, time and location.

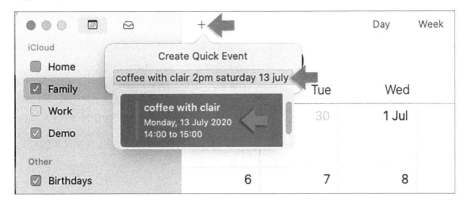

As you can see calendar has interpreted the event and added an entry into your calendar. Click on the suggestion show.

Your appointment will show up on your calendar. Select the calendar from the icon on the left. Eg this is a family event, so I'll add it to the family calendar. If it's a work appointment, select 'work'.

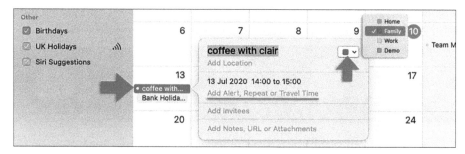

You can also add a location, click 'add location'. If you want to set a reminder, click 'add alert'. If this is a repeating event, click 'repeat', then select the frequency - daily, weekly, monthly etc.

Create a Calendar

You can create calendars to keep your appointments organised. All work appointments go in the 'work' calendar, personal appointments go in 'home, etc. You can also create other calendars. To do this, click the 'file' menu, then select 'new calendar'.

The new calendar will appear in the sidebar on the left, type in a meaningful name.

Export Calendar

Select the calendar you want to export from the side panel. Click the file menu, then select export, then click 'export' on the slideout. In the 'where' field, select the folder you want to save the calendar into.

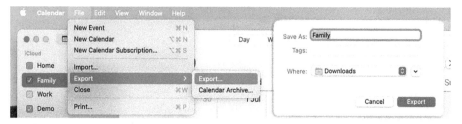

Import Calendar

Click the file menu, then select 'import'. From the popup dialog box, select the calendar file you want to import. Click 'import'.

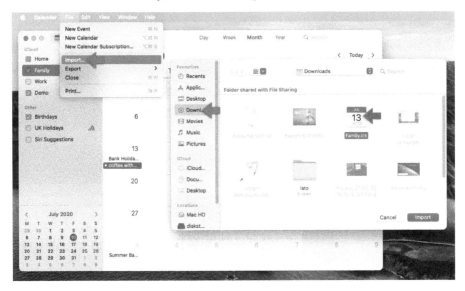

Add an Event from Email

Apple Mail scans your emails for possible events, meaning in some emails informing you of or inviting you to events, you'll see an option to add the event to your calendar. To add to your calendar, tap 'add' circled below/top-right.

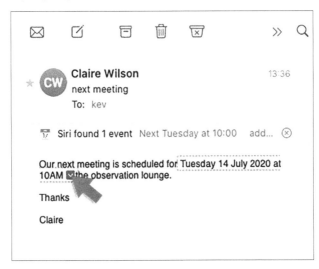

A window will appear detailing the event. Edit the title if necessary, select the calendar to add the event to eg 'work'.

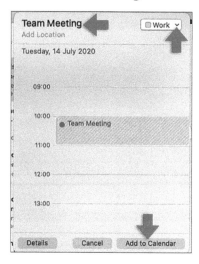

Click 'details' if you need to add reminders etc,. Click 'add to calendar' to add event.

Subscribing to Public Calendar

To add a public calendar go to the file menu and select 'new calendar subscription'.

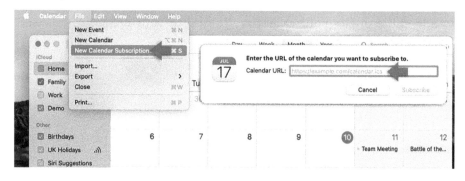

Then give it an appropriate name and enter the address as shown above. Some sample addresses are below. These are public holidays. The first is public holidays in the UK, the second public holidays in the US.

```
webcal://ical.mac.com/ical/UK32Holidays.ics
```

```
webcal://ical.mac.com/ical/US32Holidays.ics
```

Sharing Calendars & Creating Public Calendars

You can share calendars with friends, family and colleagues. This is useful if you have events or appointments that people in a team or group need to know about.

To share a calendar, right click on the calendar in the sidebar you want to share. From the pop up menu, select 'share calendar'.

Select the people you want to share your calendar with. Start typing the person's name, then select the contact from the suggestions that appear. Do this with all the names you want to add.

If you want to make the calendar public, that is anyone with a link can view it, click the check box next to 'public calendar'. You'll see a URL appear. This is the link people will use to view the calendar. Click the icon next to the link to share it with people via email or social media.

Image Capture

Image capture is useful for importing images from scanners and some cameras. You can find the image capture app in finder/applications and on your launchpad.

Down the left hand side of the window you will see a list of your installed devices; cameras and scanners. Click on the device name to select it.

Along the bottom, select the directory you want to save the scanned image to, then select the scan size. To start the scan, click 'scan' on the right hand side.

If you need to change resolution, scan name or image format (png or jpg), select 'show details'. Use 72dpi for screen and 300dpi for printing.

Photobooth

This is probably the most entertaining app that comes pre-installed on a Mac. I had the kids entertained for hours. You can find photobooth on your launch pad.

Photobooth allows you to use your Mac's on-board camera to make face distorting images; pull a funny face or key out the background and find yourself underwater, on the moon, or a roller coaster.

Click the red camera icon in the middle of the tool bar along the bottom to take a picture.

You can also record video, if you select the video icon on the left hand side.

The fun part is when you get to the effects. Click 'effects' on the right hand side of the screen.

253

Chapter 4: Using Applications

Have a look at the different effects below in the 9x9 grid. You can move around in the frame, or pull a funny face.

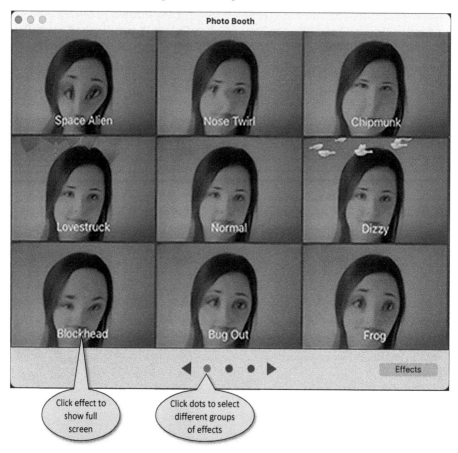

You can select different types of effects, from the distorted mirrors, shown above, to highlight effects or keyed backgrounds.

To do this, click on the dots along the bottom of the window, highlighted above, to browse through the different effects.

Photo Booth is known for its simplicity and is often used for quick selfies, fun projects, and creating memories with friends and family.

Have fun.

DVDs & BluRays

MacOS still has the ability to play DVDs but has a lack of support for BluRay discs. Many of the new Macs no longer have built in DVD drives so you'll need to buy an external USB DVD or BluRay drive.

To play a BluRay, you'll also need to buy a piece of software called *Aiseesoft - BluRay Player*. Go to the following website, then click 'free download':

www.aiseesoft.com/mac-blu-ray-player/

Plug the drive into a spare USB port and insert the disc.

To watch a BluRay, open Aiseesoft BluRay player from launchpad.

To watch a DVD open DVD player. If you're using Mojave, Catalina or Big Sur, DVD player no longer appears on launchpad or the applications folder. To open DVD player, if it doesn't open automatically, click spotlight search on the top right of the screen. Then type:

dvd

From the spotlight search results 'top hits', click 'dvd player'.

Once DVD player has started, your DVD will begin and will usually go to the DVD menu.

Lets take a look at the control panel at the bottom of the movie window.

Select the play movie option on your DVD menu to begin your movie.

Press **ctrl - cmd - F** on your keyboard to view in full screen mode. Press they key combo again to exit full screen mode.

To skip chapters in full screen mode, move your mouse pointer and you'll see a control bar appear on the bottom.

Here, you can also return to the menu, adjust volume, skip/play/ pause or stop movie.

Voice Memos

You can record audio using your Mac's built in mic or a bluetooth external mic. You can record voice memos, meetings, and lectures.

You'll find the voice memo app on your launch pad.

Lets take a look at the main screen. Here you can see your previous recordings listed down the left hand side. Any recording you select here will appear in the panel on the right hand side of the screen.

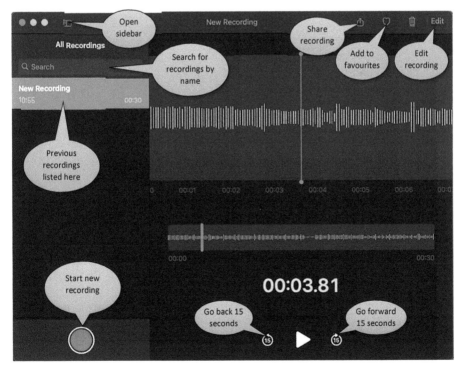

Click the play button in the panel on the right to playback the recording.

Recording Memos

To record a memo, simply click the red record button on the bottom left of the screen.

The memo app will start recording. You'll see a wave form appear in the middle of the screen to indicate the app is picking up audio.

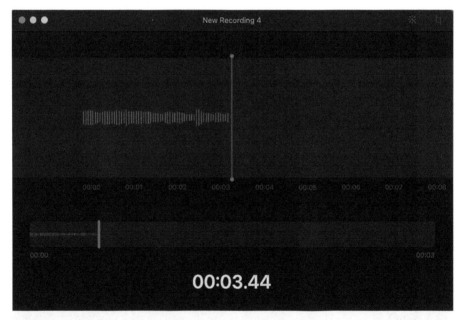

To pause a recording temporarily, click the pause icon on the left. To stop the recording, click 'done'.

Your memo will appear in the list on the left hand side of the main screen.

258

Renaming Memos

The first thing you should do with a new voice memo recording is give it a meaningful name. The last thing you want is every memo called 'new recording.

To demonstrate this, we'll rename the voice memo we just recorded. Select the voice memo from the list on the left hand side.

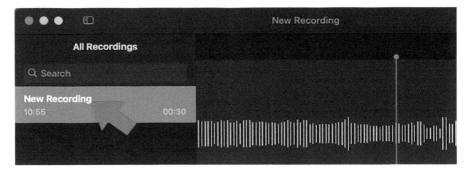

Select the file menu on the to left. From the file menu, select 'rename'.

Delete the default text, then type in a meaningful name for the recording. Hit enter on the on screen keyboard to confirm the name.

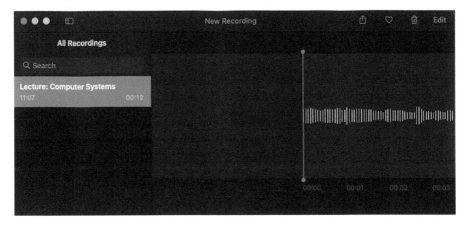

Trim a Memo

You can trim the beginning and the ends of the memo voice recording. To do this, select the recording you want to trim from the list on the left hand side of the main screen. Then click edit on the top right of the grey panel on the right hand side.

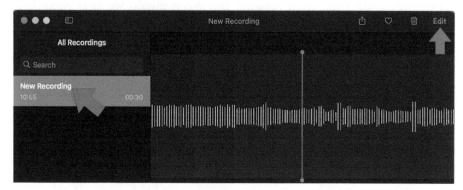

Click the trim icon on the top right

Now to trim the beginning and ends of the clip, drag the yellow handles along the track until you get to the start and end points you want.

Click 'trim' when you're done.

260

News

The news app collects breaking stories from around the world and locally into one app, based on the topics you are interested in. You'll find the news app on your launch pad.

When you first start the app, you'll see a list of top stories, trending stories, and stories recommended for you. Scroll down the page, click on a story to read the details.

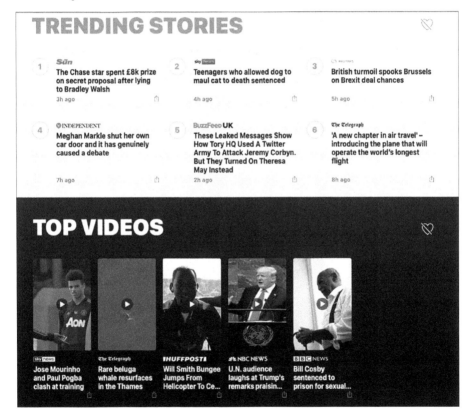

To open the side panel, tap the icon on the top left of the screen

Chapter 4: Using Applications

From here you can select different news sources, magazines, newspapers and websites.

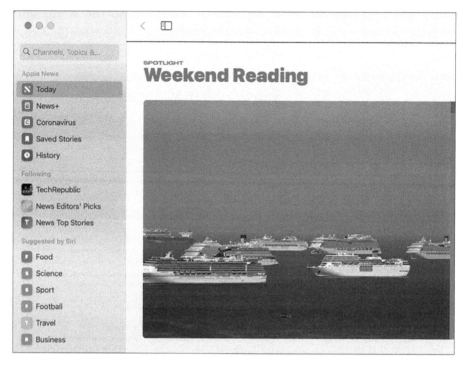

You can also search for specific channels. To do this, enter your search into the search field on the top left of the side panel.

FreeForm

FreeForm an app that allows you to collaborate with friends and co-workers on a single electronic whiteboard via FaceTime. If you have an iPad running iPadOS 16 with Apple Pencil, you can add freehand drawings and illustrations. You can also add, text, videos, and images as well as view contributions made by others or make edits.

You'll find the FreeForm app on your launchpad. Once FreeForm opens, you'll land on the main screen.

Add Sticky Note

To add a sticky note, click the icon on the toolbar. Double click the note, type in your text. Use the popup toolbar to format the text.

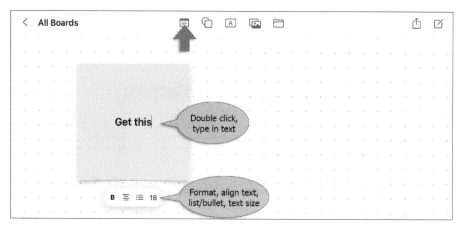

Add Shape

To add a shape, click the shape icon on the toolbar, select a shape from the drop down menu.

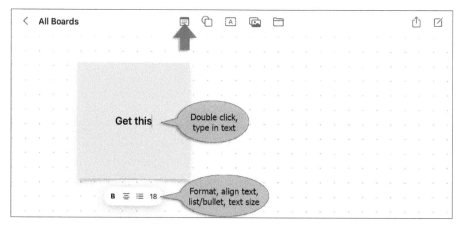

Add Textbox

To add a textbox, click the icon on the toolbar.

You'll see the textbox appear on the board. Click in the text box, you'll see a popup toolbar appear. Here, you can format the text, align text, create bullet/numbered lists, change the font size, and font color. If you click the three dots icon to the right, you can see all the fonts and colors available.

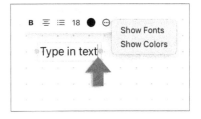

Add Image

To add a photograph or diagram, click the image icon on the toolbar. From the drop down menu, select where you want to get your image from. You can capture an image from your iPhone/iPad if you have one nearby, or you can insert a photo from your photos app library

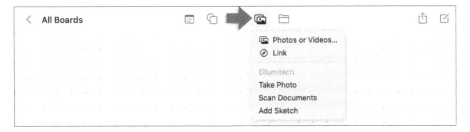

Add a File or Document

To add a file, click the file icon on the toolbar. From the popup window, navigate to, and select the file you want to add.

Share Board

If you want to share your board with other people so you can collaborate on a project, click on the share icon on the right hand side of the toolbar.

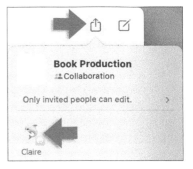

From the drop down menu, select the people you want to share the board with.

You can send them a link via message or email.

Clock

The clock app is now available on the Mac where you can set the local time as well as in different time zones around the world. You can also set an alarm at a specific time. You'll find the clock app on launch pad.

Along the top of the window, you'll see some tabs. Here, on the 'world clock' tab you can set various clocks for cities around the world, you can set an 'alarm' to sound at a specific time, or you can use 'stop watch to time something, or set a 'timer' to sound an alarm after a specific amount of time.

World Clock

Click the 'world clock' tab, you'll see any you've added marked on the map, as well as a clock with the time underneath. To set a new clock, click the '+' icon on the top right.

Type in the city or country name into the search bar. Click on the city.

You'll see your clock appear on the map.

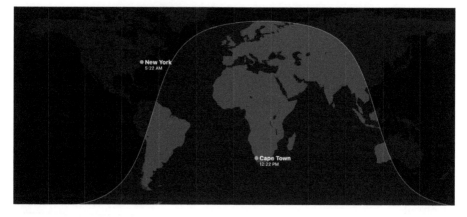

Also in the section at the bottom. To delete any clocks, hover your mouse over the clock, then click the 'x' on the top left.

Alarm

To set an alarm, select 'alarm' from the tabs along the top of the window. Click the '+' icon on the top right.

Enter the time you want the alarm to sound. Set which days you want the alarm to work, give it a meaningful name, then select the sound you want from the drop down menu. Click 'save' when you're done.

You'll see a list of all your alarms listed. Use the switch to turn them on or off. To delete any alarms, hover your mouse over the clock, then click the 'x' on the top left.

Stopwatch

To time how long something takes such as an event, select 'stopwatch' from the tabs along the top. Click 'start' to start the watch. To set a lap, if you're timing an event, click the 'lap' button. Tap 'stop' to end.

Timer

The Timer is used for counting down from a specified amount of time. For example, in the kitchen, a timer can be used to ensure that food is cooked or baked for the precise amount of time, eg 15 minutes.

To set a countdown timer, select 'timer' from the tabs along the top. Enter the hours, minutes, and seconds.

Select a sound from the 'when timer ends' drop down menu. Click 'start' to begin the countdown.

Weather

The weather app is now available on the mac and includes animations, detailed maps, and forecasts for various locations. You can also see weather warnings, air quality and so on. You'll find the weather app on launch pad.

You'll see a weather report for your current location.

To get a weather report on another location, type the name of the country or city into the search field on the top right of the screen. Select the closest match.

To add the location to your sidebar, click 'add' on the top right.

Open the sidebar, click the 'sidebar' icon on the top left.

Here you can add various locations of interest.

Terminal

The terminal app provides text-based access to your Mac using a command-line interface allowing you to type in commands.

Opening Terminal

You'll find the terminal app in the 'utilities' folder in launchpad.

Click the terminal icon to start the app.

Here at the command prompt you type in commands...

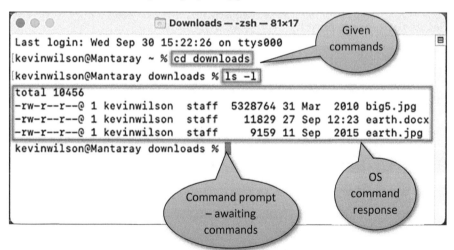

All commands have three parts: the command name, flags, and arguments. The command name always comes first. The flags indicate a specific function of the command given, the arguments indicate the file, folder or process the command is working on.

```
command_name -flags [arguments]
```

Giving Commands

To give a command, type at the command prompt. For example to list the files in a directory. Type

```
ls -l
```

ls is the command, **-l** is a flag which returns a detailed list of the files.

Here are some common commands to try:

Command	Description
ls	List files and directories
ls -a	List all files and directories
ls -l	Detailed list of files and directories
mkdir <dir-name>	Create directory
cd <dir-name>	Change to directory
cd /	Change to root directory
cd ~	Change to home-directory
cd ..	Change to parent directory
find <name>	Find file <name> (use *)
pwd	Display the path of the current dir
cp <file> <destination>	Copy file to destination
mv <file> <destination>	Move file to destination
rm <file>	Delete file
rmdir <dir>	Delete directory
more <file>	Displays file a page at a time
head <file>	Displays first few lines of file
tail <file>	Displays last few lines of file
grep 'keyword' <file>	Search file for keyword
zip -r <archive> *	Zip files & folders in current directory
zip <archive-name> <files>	Compress files into zip archive
unzip <file-name>	Uncompress zipped file
nano <file-name>	Text editor
tree	Display directory tree

To create a folder use **mkdir**

```
mkdir documents
```

To copy a file use the **cp** command

```
cp earth.doc documents
```

This copies the file earth document to the documents folder.

271

Pages App

Pages is a desktop publishing and word-processing package that allows you to create all sorts of documents from letters to flyers

If you don't have these applications on your Mac, you can download them from the App Store.

Getting Started

To launch Pages, click the icon on your Launchpad.

Once Pages has opened, you can open a saved document, or click 'new document' to open a new one.

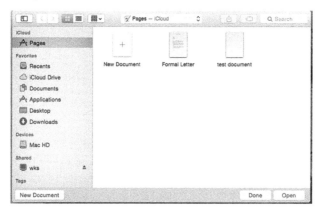

Double click on a template from the options, or select 'blank' to start from scratch.

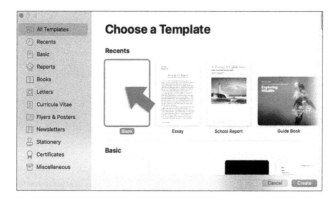

Once you have selected the template to use you will see the main work screen. Select the 'document' icon on the far right to edit document settings such as document margins, paper size, page orientation, sections - page numbering and bookmarks. Select 'format' to edit text styles, change font, text alignment etc.

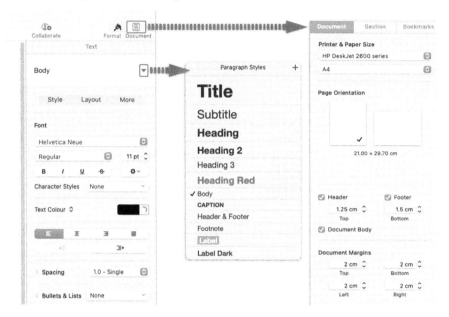

Let's take a closer look at the main editing screen.

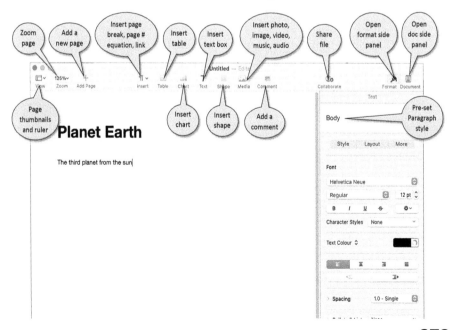

Formatting Text

To format text, select the text with your mouse. For example, I'm going to change the text 'planet earth' to a heading

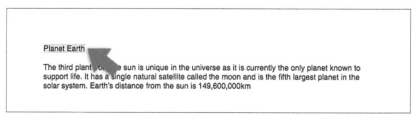

Highlight your text with the mouse as shown above then click the 'format' icon on the top right. Select the small down arrow on the right hand side of the screen and click title from the menu that appears.

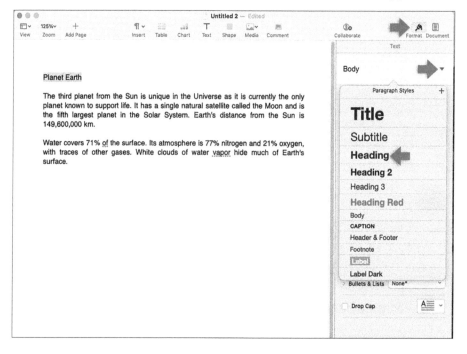

Formatting your document means laying it out in a style that is easy to read and looks attractive. This could involve changing fonts, making text bigger for headings, changing color of text, adding graphics and photographs, etc.

For each document template you choose from the Template Chooser there are a number of pre-set paragraph styles. These are to help you format your document consistently, eg so all headings are the same font, size and color.

Adding a Picture

The easiest way to add a picture is to find it in your finder window, then click and drag it into your document.

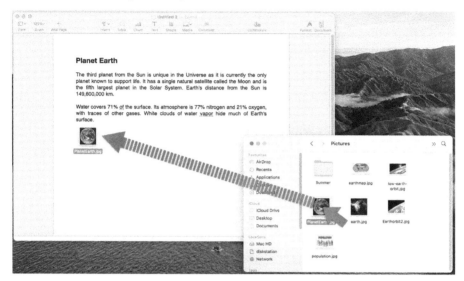

It might be helpful to position your finder window next to your document window as shown in the figure above.

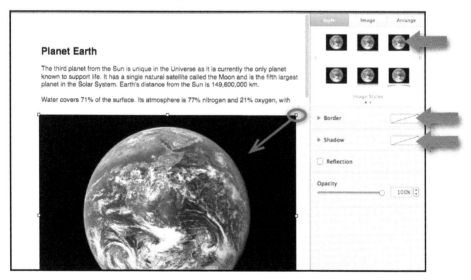

You can resize your image by clicking the resize handles, circled above, and dragging them. You can change the styles by adding borders and shadows by experimenting with the options in the style tab on the right hand side of the screen.

Instant Alpha

If you look at the image we just added, you'll see it has a black background. To get rid of this you can use 'instant alpha'. First select your image.

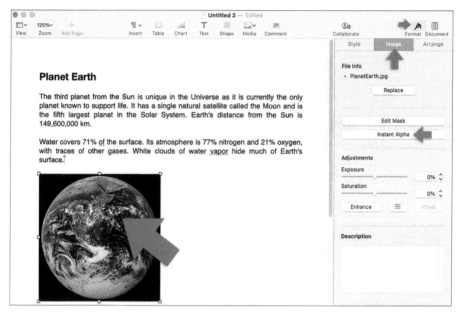

Click the 'format' icon on the top right then select the 'image' tab.

Click and drag your mouse in the black area around the image. This is the bit we want to get rid of. To remove any similar colors that are not initially deleted. On the image click your mouse on the area of the image and drag it slightly until it changes to grey. Click 'done'.

276

Saving

You can either save your work on your iCloud Drive or your local documents on your mac. Go to the file menu and select save...

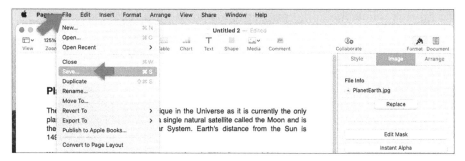

Give your document a name, then select the small down arrow to expand all the options.

Down the left hand side of the screen you will see some destinations where you can save your file. Select 'icloud drive', then select a folder on icloud drive, eg 'documents'.

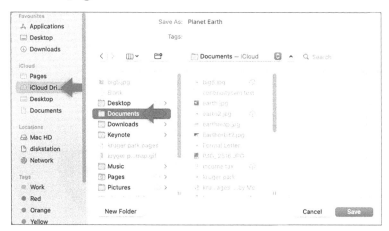

The advantage of saving to your iCloud Drive is you can access and edit the documents you have just been working on, on your iPhone or iPad. Or even another mac.

Sharing and Collaboration

You can share your document with other people and invite friends and colleagues to collaborate and contribute to your document.

To do this, click the collaboration icon on the top right.

Select the app you want to share the document with. Eg send an email link, click the email icon. Set the permissions, use 'make changes' if you want the person to contribute.

Enter the person's email address, click 'send'.

When the other person opens the document, you'll see their changes indicated with a marker.

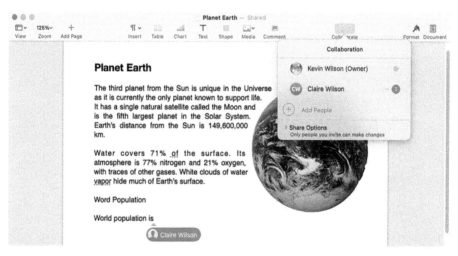

To change any settings, click the collaboration icon.

Keynote App

Keynote allows you to create multimedia presentations. If you don't have these applications on your Mac, you can download them from the App Store.

Getting Started

To launch Keynote, click the icon on your Launchpad.

Once keynote has loaded, you can select a saved file to open.

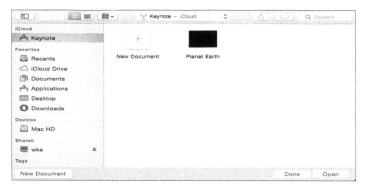

If you want to create a new presentation, click 'new document' on the bottom left hand side of the window. From here you can select from a variety of pre-designed templates with different themes, fonts and colors.

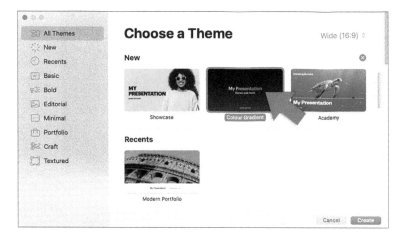

Chapter 4: Using Applications

Once you have selected a template you will see the main screen as shown below. This is where you can start building your presentation.

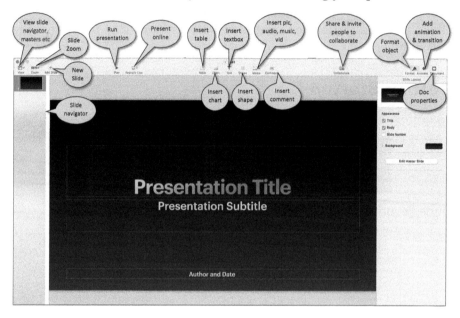

Editing a Slide

Double click in the heading field shown above and enter a heading eg 'Planet Earth'.

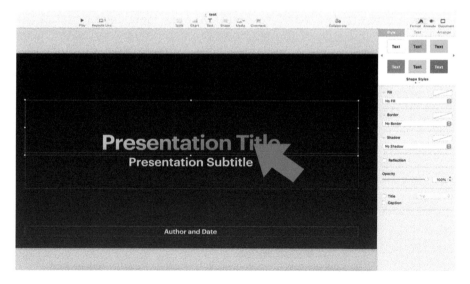

You can click and drag the heading wherever you like.

Adding a New Slide

Click the new slide button located on the bottom left of the screen. Select a slide layout from the options that appear.

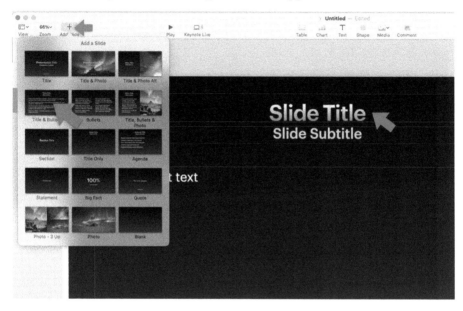

Add some text by double clicking on the text box that appears in the slide.

Adding Media

The easiest way to add images and media to your slides is to find them in your finder window then drag and drop them onto the slides where the image is to appear.

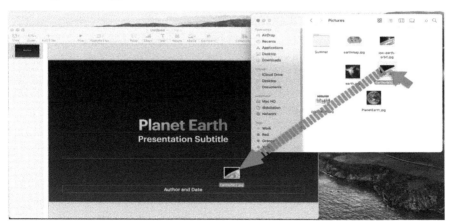

Browse through, select the one you want, then drag and drop the image onto the slide. If you want photographs, you can drag and drop them from your photos app in the same manner as above.

It helps to drag your photos app window over to the right, as shown above so you can see your slide underneath.

You can insert videos and audio clips in the same way.

Animations

Animations allow you to make objects such as text or photographs appear in sequence or with an effect...

Select the object to animate. In this case, I want the bullet points to appear one by one.

Select the animate icon located on the top right corner of your screen

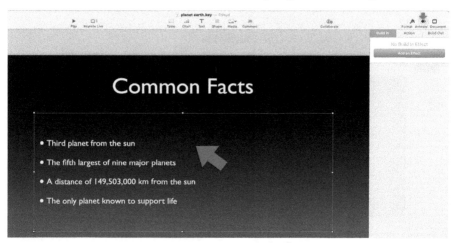

Select 'built in', then click 'add an effect'. Select an effect from the effects drop down menu, eg 'fly in'.

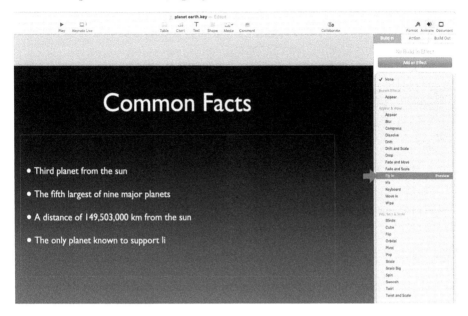

Then specify that you want the bullet points to appear one by one. Click the box under 'delivery' and select 'by bullet' from the drop down menu.

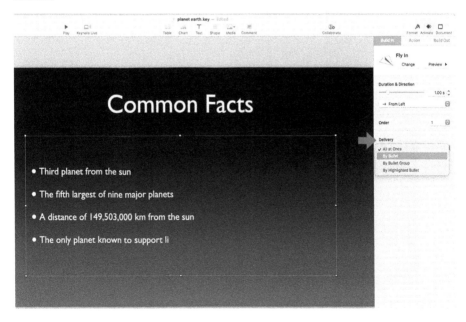

To see what the effect looks like, click 'preview'.

Slide Transitions

You can add transitions between slides. To do this, select the slide you want.

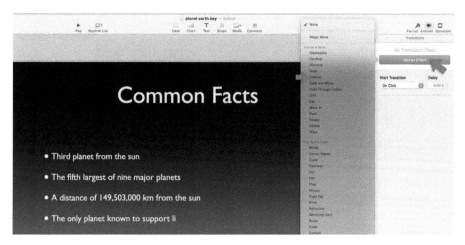

Select the 'animate' icon from the top right then click 'add effect'.

Formatting Text Boxes

Click text box to add shown below. Select the 'format' icon on the top right, then select the 'style' tab.

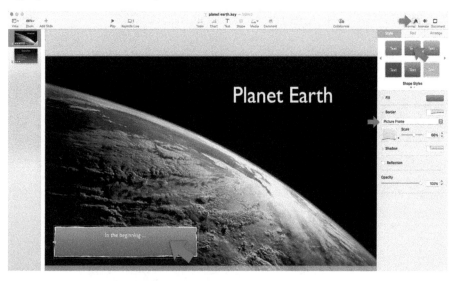

Now you can select a style, change the fill color, border, opacity and reflection effects.

Enter some text into your textbox, and drag it into position on your slide.

You can format your text box by adding borders, changing fonts, changing the background color, etc To format the border and fill click your text box and on the right hand side of the screen select style.

Formatting Text Inside Textboxes

To change the formatting of the text, for example to change the color of the text or make it bold.

First select your text in the text box you want to change then click the text icon on the right hand side of your screen as shown below.

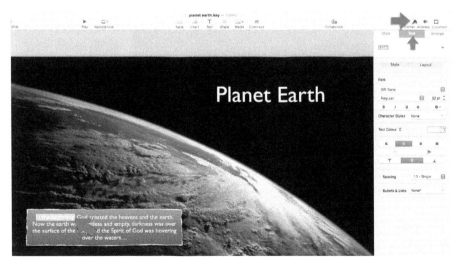

From here you can change the font, the font color, size etc

Adding Styles to Textboxes

To change the background color (also called fill color) or add a nice border around the box click on your text box then select the format icon located on the top right of your screen

If you look down the right hand side you will see sections: 'Fill' allows you to change the background color of the text box. 'Border' allows you to add fancy borders such as picture frames and colored line borders. 'Shadow' allows you to add a drop shadow effect as if the text box is casting a shadow onto the slide.

To change the background color of the textbox, click 'fill' and select a color.

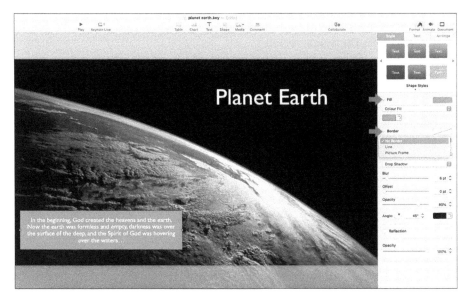

Also if you want to add a border, under the border section click where it says 'no border' as shown above and change it to 'picture frame'.

Click the 'choose frame style' button circled above and select a picture frame style from the menu that appears.

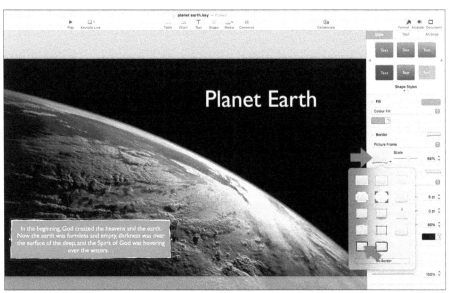

Change the size by moving the scale slider.

Saving

You can save your work onto your documents on your local mac or onto your iCloud Drive as with Pages. To do this, click the 'file' menu on the top left, then select 'save'.

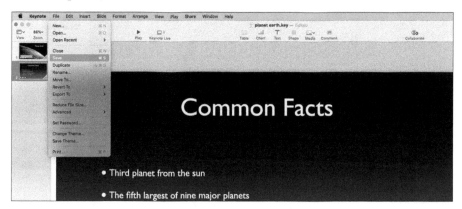

Give your document a name, then select the small down arrow to expand all the options.

Down the left hand side of the screen you will see some destinations where you can save your file. Select 'icloud drive', then select a folder on icloud drive, eg 'documents'.

Numbers App

The Numbers App allows you to create spreadsheets to present and analyse data. If you don't have these applications on your Mac, you can download them from the App Store.

Getting Started

To launch Numbers, click the icon on your Launchpad.

Once Numbers has loaded, you can select a saved file to open. Or to create a new spreadsheet, click 'new document' on the bottom left hand side of the window.

From here you can select from a variety of pre-designed templates with different themes, fonts and colors.

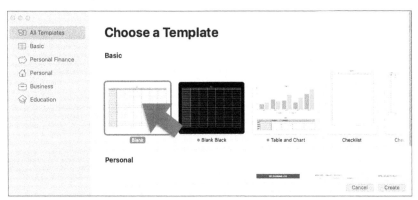

For this example use a blank sheet

289

Chapter 4: Using Applications

Once you have selected a template you will see the main screen as shown below.

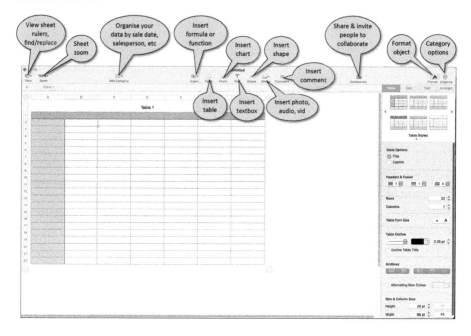

Along the top of the screen you'll see your toolbar. Here you can insert functions, images, tables and charts.

The 'format' icon on the right hand side opens up the sidebar and contains the tools needed to format text, rows, columns and the cells on your spreadsheet. The sidebar is split into tabs: table, cell, text, arrange, as shown below.

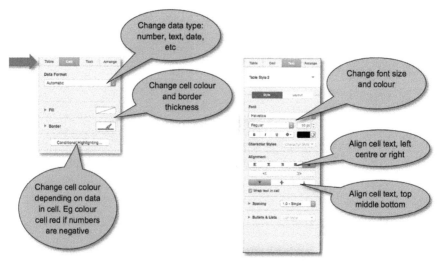

Building a Spreadsheet

To begin building your spreadsheet, enter the data into the cells. In this example we are going to build a basic invoice.

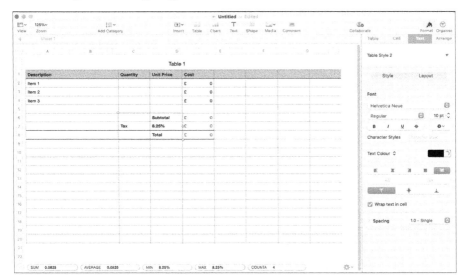

Entering Data

Enter the header cells into the grey row at the top of your spreadsheet. Then enter the rest of the data as shown below.

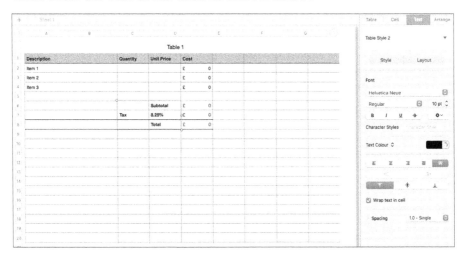

Change the total cells at the bottom to bold text. To do this, highlight them with your mouse, from the 'text' tab on the right hand side of your screen, click 'bold'.

291

Changing Data Types

Next highlight all the cells that will contain the prices for items, and make them a currency data type. Change it to Pound Sterling or US Dollar.

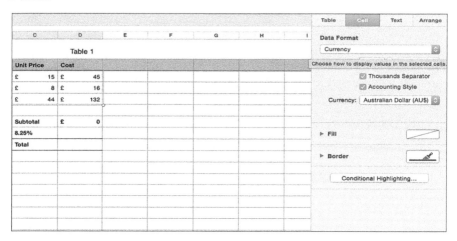

Do this by highlighting your cells as shown above, then from the cell tab on the right hand side, click in the dropdown box under 'data format' and select currency. Further down the tab you can change it to a specific currency depending on which country you are in.

Adding Formulas

Enter a formula to calculate the cost of each item. In the first cell under the heading 'cost' hit your equals sign to begin your formula. Click the cell under quantity, press the asterisk (*) then click the cell under unit price. This means you want to multiply the values in these two cells together.

Description	Quantity	Unit Price	Cost	
Item 1			= B2 ▾ × C2 ▾	✗ ✓
Item 2			£ 0	
Item 3			£ 0	
		Subtotal	£ 0	
	Tax	8.25%	£ 0	
		Total	£ 0	

Cost = Quantity * Unit Price.

Adding Functions

Now add a function to work out the total cost. For this one use the sum function to add all the values together.

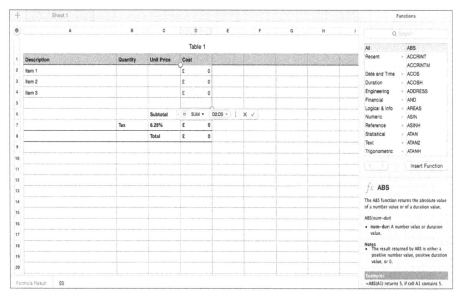

Click in the cell next to subtotal and click the function icon on the tool bar at the top of the screen.

Select 'sum' from the drop down menu. The function will automatically highlight the values to add up.

If it doesn't click where it says D2:D5 this is the cells it will add up. Now select new the cells you want to add.

Saving

You can save your work onto your documents on your local mac or onto your iCloud Drive as with Pages. To do this, click the 'file' menu on the top left, then select 'save'.

Down the left hand side of the screen you will see some destinations where you can save your file. Take note of Documents under favourites - this is on your mac. Also take note of iCloud at the top, this saves onto your iCloud Drive.

The advantage of saving to your iCloud Drive is you can access and edit the documents you have just been working on, on your iPhone or iPad. Or even another mac.

Dictionary

With the dictionary app you can get definitions of words and phrases from a variety of sources. You'll find the app on launchpad.

Type the word in the field on the top right, select a source from the bar underneath.

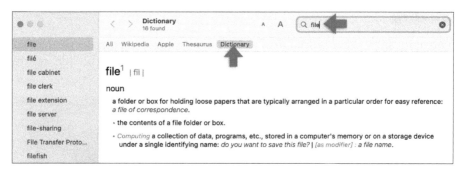

In the main window, you'll see the definition of the word. On the sidebar on the left, you'll see variations of the word you typed into the search field.

Stickies

You can keep notes, lists and pictures in sticky notes on your desktop. To do this open launch pad, select 'other', then click on 'stickies'.

In the Stickies app, click on the file menu, then select 'new note'.

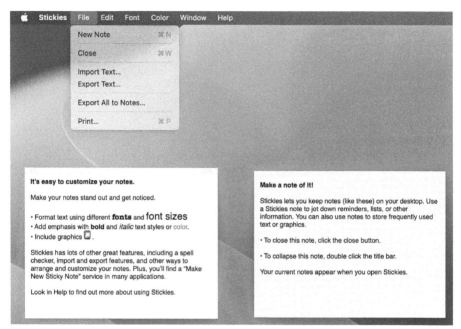

You'll see your new note pop up on the desktop.

To change the color, click on the note then select the 'color' menu on the top of the screen. Select a color from the drop down.

To add a list: Press option-tab, type in your item, press return. To end the list, press return twice.

Increase list level, click at the beginning of a line in the list, then press tab. To decrease list level, click a line in the list, then press shift-tab.

Preview App

The Preview app is a versatile tool that comes pre-installed on all Mac computers. It allows users to view various types of files, including PDFs, documents and images.

Preview supports a wide range of image formats, including JPEG, PNG, TIFF, GIF, and more. You can view individual images or browse through a collection in a folder. You can adjust the color, size, and orientation of images. Basic editing tools like cropping, rotating, and adjusting color levels are available.

You can open PDF files, navigate through the pages, zoom in and out, and use bookmarks. You'll also find some basic editing tools that allow you to add text, shapes, arrows, and other annotations to PDFs. This is particularly useful for highlighting or making notes on documents. Preview allows you to add your signature to PDFs. You can create a digital signature using your trackpad or by scanning a handwritten one.

Tools

You'll find the preview app in the applications folder in finder or on launchpad. Preview will also open if you double click on an image or a PDF when you haven't got any other image editor or Acrobat Reader installed.

Info/Inspector: Shows general file information, keywords, and annotations about the open file.

Zoom In/Out: These are magnifying glass icons, one with a "+" and the other with a "-". They allow you to zoom in or out of the image, respectively.

Share: Allows you to share currently opened image with someone else.

Highlight: Allows you to annotate PDFs and add notes.

Rotate: Allows you to rotate the image counter clockwise.

Markup: This reveals a set of tools for annotating and editing the image and includes tools for drawing shapes, adding text.

Form Filling & Signature: This icon opens a toolbar that allows you to fill out PDF forms, and create signatures

Adjust

When previewing images, you can adjust the colors. To do this, go to the 'tools' menu, select 'adjust color'. You'll be able to use the sliders in the side panel to adjust the image.

Resize

If you need to adjust the size of the image, go to the 'tools' menu, select 'adjust size'. Enter the sizes of the image. Click 'ok' when you're done.

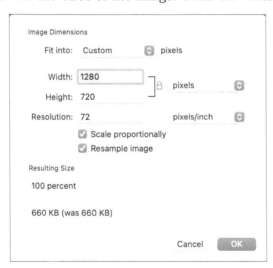

If you want to write on or markup an image or PDF, click the markup icon. See page 135 for more information.

Digitally Sign a Document

MacOS includes a signature creation feature in the preview app. You can import an image of your handwritten signature and use it to sign any documents you need to.

First, sign your name on a blank sheet of white paper using a black marker.

Hit launch pad and open the preview app, click the 'tools' menu, go down to 'annotate', then 'signature. From the slideout select 'manage signatures'.

Select 'camera'.

Now hold the signature you wrote down on your sheet of paper up to the camera.

Make sure your signature fills the whole window on the screen. Click 'done'.

Now open the PDF document you want to sign, click the markup icon on the top right of the toolbar and select 'the signature icon.

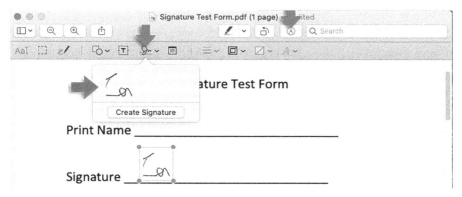

Click your signature. You might need to drag your signature into place.

5

Internet, Email & Comms

Your mac has a wealth of communication apps. MacOS has Safari for browsing the web, an email app to keep track of all your email correspondence. Plus an app for video chat called FaceTime.

You can also use iMessage which is similar to the message app on your iPhone/iPad as well as AirDrop for sharing files and mac phone which syncs with your iPhone to allow you to answer calls right from your Mac.

In this chapter, we'll take a look at:

- Using Safari to Browse the World Wide Web
- Apple Mail
- Contacts
- FaceTime
- Group FaceTime
- SharePlay
- Message App
- Air Drop
- Mac Phone

To help you better understand this section, take a look at the video resources. Open your web browser and navigate to the following site:

elluminetpress.com/mac-comms

Using Safari to Browse the Web

The tab bar at the top of the screen has been redesigned giving it a more streamlined look while taking up less screen space. Website tabs now appear along the top bar, this is called compact mode. You can also create tab groups which allow you to group website tabs together, helping you organise your workflow and browsing experience.

Launching Safari

You will find Safari's icon either on the dock at the bottom of the screen or on your launchpad

Click the icon to start the app. You'll land on Safari's customisable start page. Let's take a look around the screen. Along the top, you'll see your navigation bar. Here, you can open the sidebar, type in a Google search or enter a website address. Over on the right, you can share the current page, or open a new tab.

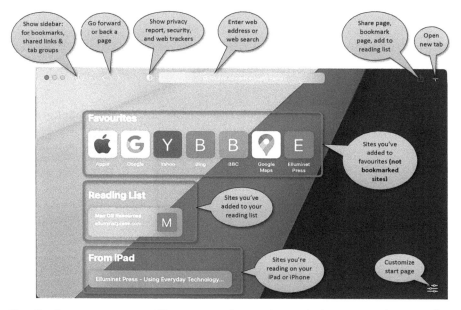

On the home page, you'll see your favourite websites, any sites you've added to a reading list, frequently visited sites, and any sites you've visited on your iPad/iPhone. To customise, click the customise icon on the bottom right.

Customise your Homepage

Select your customisations from the popup menu. The list of sections on the popup list corresponds to the list of sections on the home page.

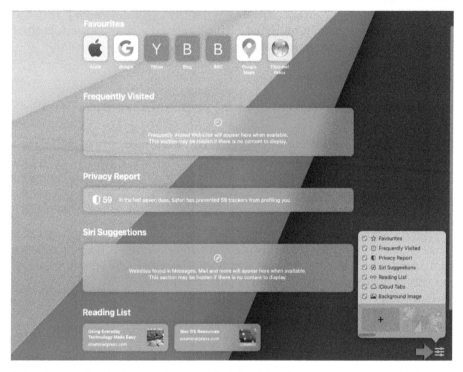

Select the check boxes to enable/disable the sections on the home page.

At the bottom of the popup click the + icon to choose a background image for your safari home page.

You can also scroll along the list to select a pre-installed background.

Using Safari

If for example, I wanted to find Elluminet Press's website, all you need to do is type it into the search bar. You can use a web address (URL) or type in keywords to do a Google search.

You can use this technique for anything you want to find. Just start typing it into the address bar.

Tab Bar

MacOS Monterey introduced a new streamlined tab bar layout to Safari, which takes up less space on the page and changes according to the color scheme of the site you're visiting. This tab bar layout may or may not be turned on by default. To turn it on, click on the safari menu on the top left, then select 'settings'.

Select 'tabs'. At the top of the page, you'll see a 'tab layout' section. Select 'compact' to switch to the streamlined tab bar, or select 'separate' to use the traditional tab bar. If you want to collapse the website tabs into icons, tick 'automatically collapse tab titles...' If you want to allow the tab bar to take on the color scheme of the website, tick 'show color in bar...'

Chapter 5: Internet, Email & Communications

Browsing Tabs

Tabbed browsing allows you to open multiple websites within a single window, using tabs as a navigational feature for switching between open websites. Here is the traditional tab bar

This is the streamlined tab bar.

To open a new browsing tab, click the + icon on the top right of the browser window.

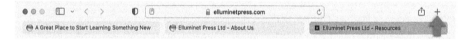

To switch between the tabs, just click on the tab you want to switch to.

To close a tab, just click the small x that appears on the left of the tab.

To open a link in a new tab, hold down the command key while you click the link

Show all Browsing Tabs

To show all open tabs at once, open the sidebar

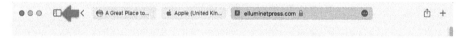

Click the 'show all tabs' link at the top.

Tab Groups

Tab groups were introduced in Monterey. With tab groups, you can organize your tabs and keep them together in groups according to interest. You can also drag your tab groups into an email, note or message.

If you're doing web research, it can involve visiting several websites meaning you can have multiple sites open in tabs at the same time If you're researching multiple things, this can quickly become difficult to track.

This is where group tabs come in. Group tabs allow you to save groups of these tabs together. For example, if you are planning a holiday (or vacation), you could be visiting multiple sites to compare prices for flights and hotels, as well as checking weather forecasts and local activities. You can save all these sites as tabs into a tab group, so you can return to the sites later.

New Tab Group

To save your open tabs into a new tab group, click the sidebar icon.

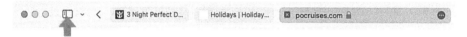

From the sidebar panel click the tab groups icon at the top

Give the tab group a meaningful name.

Add a Site Tab to Tab Group

If you were browsing the web and wanted to add a tab to an existing tab group, right click on the address bar. From the popup menu, go down to 'move to tab group', then select the tab group you want to add the tab to.

Reopen Tab Group

Open the sidebar. At the top of the panel, you'll see your tab groups. Click on the group to reopen.

Bookmarking Pages

Bookmarking pages allows you to save websites you visit frequently so you don't have to search for them or remember the web address. You can just click the site in the bookmarks side bar to revisit the page.

To bookmark the page you're currently on, click the share button on the top right of the browser window.

From the menu, select 'add bookmark'.

Now, under 'add this page to', select where you want to save the site to. Select either 'favourites' or 'bookmarks'.

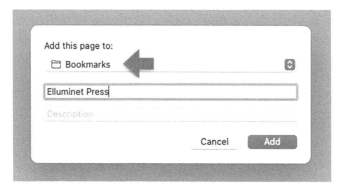

Select 'favourites' to add the site to the favourites section of the 'start page'. Select 'bookmarks' to save the website to the bookmarks side panel, as shown below.

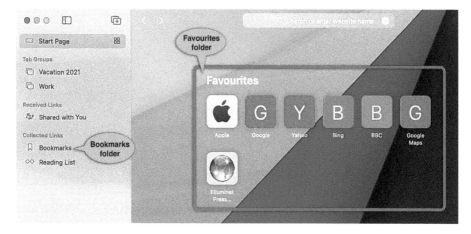

At the bottom of the dialog box, type in a name and description if necessary, then click 'add'.

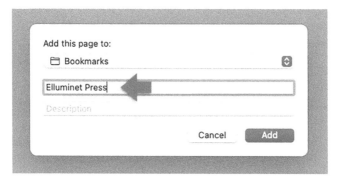

Revisiting Bookmarked & Favourite Sites

If you saved the site to 'favourites', then you'll see the site in the 'favourites' section of the start page. To return to a bookmarked site, click the 'sidebar' icon on the top left of the toolbar to open the panel.

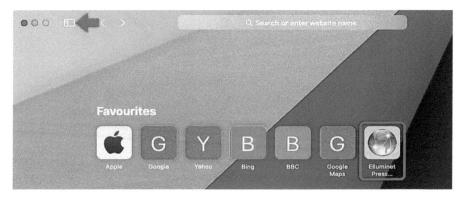

From the sidebar, click on the bookmarks link.

Here you'll see a list of all the sites you have bookmarked. Click the site link to revisit the site.

You might need to expand the folders, do this by clicking the small triangle to the left of each folder, indicated with the small red arrow in the above screen.

Organising Bookmarks

You can also organise your bookmarks into folders. So for example, all my publishing websites I could put into a publishing folder. First, open the sidebar.

Select the bookmarks link.

To create folders right click on the bookmark sidebar, then select 'new folder'. Give the folder a name. In this example, I am naming it 'Publishing'.

Drag and drop your bookmarks into the folders, as illustrated below.

This helps to keep all your bookmarks organised and easy to find. You could have a folder for your work, interests, hobbies or sites you use to book your holidays/vacations.

Reading List

The reading list is where you can queue up a load of websites for reading later, useful when you are not connected to the internet all the time. To add a site to your reading list, click the share button on the top right. From the drop down menu select 'add to reading list'.

To view the sites you've added to your reading list, click the 'sidebar' icon on the top left of your screen.

Select the 'reading list' link from the sidebar, then select your site.

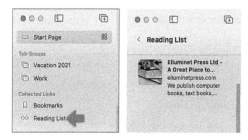

Downloads

Click the downloads icon on the top right of the screen. This icon only appears after you've downloaded something. Click the document to open, click the small magnifying glass icon next to the download to open it in finder.

You'll also find your downloads in the document stack on the bottom right of your dock.

Extensions

Safari extensions customise the way your browser works. You can add extensions to block adverts, and add extra functionality.

To install the extensions, open safari, click the 'safari' menu on the top left, then select 'Safari Extensions. The app store will open up with a list of extensions that are available.

To install any extension click 'get', then click 'install' to add the extension.

Now, you'll need to enable the extension. To do this, click the 'safari' menu, then select 'settings'.

Click the 'extensions' tab.

On the left hand side, click the tick box next to the extension to enable it. Remove the tick to disable it.

To remove the extension select it from the panel on the left, then click 'uninstall'.

Privacy Reports

Safari uses its Intelligent Tracking Prevention to identify and block trackers advertisers use to track your web activity.

To the right of the address bar, you'll see the 'three dots icon'. Click to reveal the menu, then select 'privacy report.

You can also get a privacy tracking report. In safari, click the 'safari' menu, then select 'privacy report'.

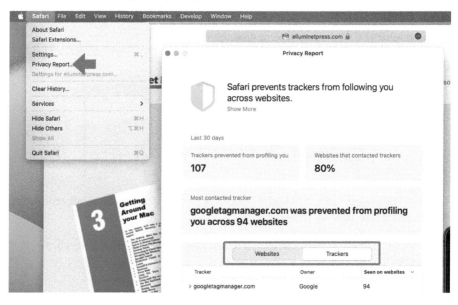

You'll see some stats. Click the 'websites' tab to see all the websites where trackers have been blocked. Select the 'trackers' tab to see a list of all the trackers that have been blocked and who they belong to.

Passwords

When you sign into a website or for the first time, you will receive a prompt asking you whether you want to save your login details.

Sign in, in the normal way - enter your username and password. Once you sign in successfully, Safari will prompt you to save the password.

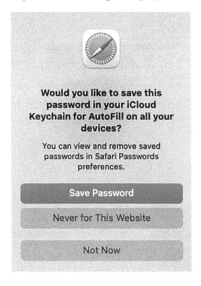

Click 'save password'. This will save your password so you don't have to type it in each time.

To sign in the next time, just click in the username or password field.

Select the username from the drop down list, click 'log in' or 'sign in'.

313

Managing Passwords

You can save passwords to your password list from various different websites so you don't have to remember them all. Top open password manager, click the 'safari' menu, then select 'settings'. Select the 'passwords' tab and enter your Mac password.

Scroll down the list on the left, select the site to view username and password saved for that site. To edit the password details, click 'edit' on the top right.

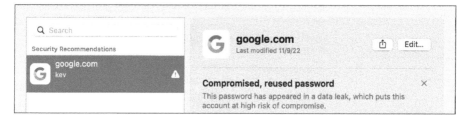

Enter any details you need to change. Remember if you change the password here, it won't change on the website. To change the password on the website, click 'change password on website' then follow the prompts.

To share the password with someone via AirDrop, click the share icon on the top right.

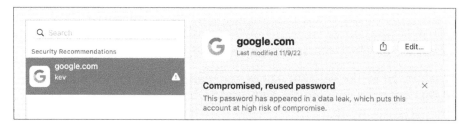

Select the nearby user.

To remove a password, select it from the list on the left, then click the '-' icon on the bottom left. To manually add a site, click'+' icon on the bottom left, then enter the website address, username and password.

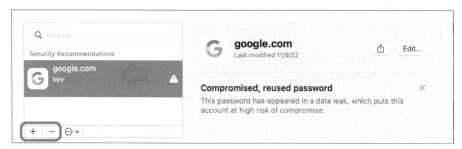

You can also import or export your passwords. To do this, click the icon on the bottom left. Select 'import' to import passwords. To export all your passwords select 'export all passwords'.

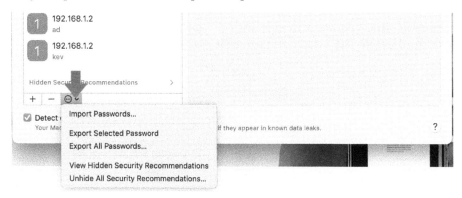

Generate Automatic Strong Passwords

Strong passwords are a must these days. To help you generate good passwords, Safari can automatically generate them for you when you use it to sign up or open an account on any website - whether it's facebook, google, microsoft, yahoo and so on.

To start, go to the website where you want to sign up for an account. In this example I'm going to sign up to GMail.

Fill in the 'create account' form with your details. Click in the password field.

Click 'Use Strong Password'. Safari will automatically generate a strong password for you and save it into your passwords list.

The next time you need to sign into the site, just click in the password field and select the username for that site.

316

Autofill Forms

You can get safari to automatically fill in a form for you using your contact information. To set it up, open the 'safari' menu, and select 'settings'. From the settings window, select the 'autofill' tab.

Next to 'using information from my contacts' click 'edit'. Enter all your contact details.

This will enable you to select them when filling in a from on a website. On the form, click in one of the fields. You'll see a small contacts icon appear on the right hand side of the form.

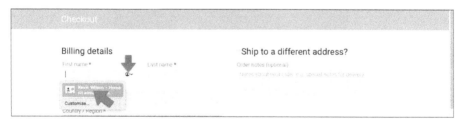

Click the icon, then select your contact from the list.

Billing details		Ship to a different address?
First name *	Last name *	Order notes (optional)
Kevin	Wilson	
Company name (optional)		
Country / Region *		
United Kingdom (UK)		
Street address *		
31 Main Street		

Using a PassKey

Passkeys are designed to replace passwords and rely on biometric identification on your Mac or iPhone such as Touch ID and Face ID. These are synced to your iCloud's Keychain. Passkeys use a unique cryptographic key pair for each website or account, eliminating the need to remember or type in passwords.

On the account sign-in page, enter your account name, then click the account/user name field. Select your account from the list of suggestions.

You'll see a security prompt asking you how you want to sign in.

See page 217 for more information on using PassKeys

Using Profiles

This feature allows you to keep your browsing separate for different activities, such as work and personal. Each profile has its own history, cookies, extensions, Tab Groups, and favorites. This can be particularly useful if you want to maintain a clear distinction between your professional and personal browsing activities.

To set up a profile, launch Safari on your Mac. Then go to the Safari menu and select 'system settings'.

In the window that pops up, click on 'profiles' on the top row. Then click 'start using profiles'.

Give your new profile a name, select a symbol and a color. Select 'create brand-new bookmarks folder', then click 'create profile'.

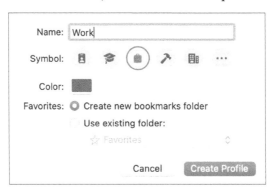

Chapter 5: Internet, Email & Communications

If you need to create additional profiles, click the '+' icon on the bottom left. To delete a profile, select the profile then click the '-' icon.

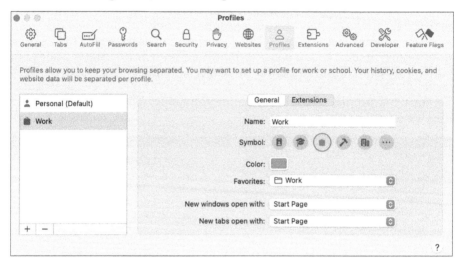

Once you've created your profile, close the settings window. On the top left of the Safari window, you'll see a new icon.

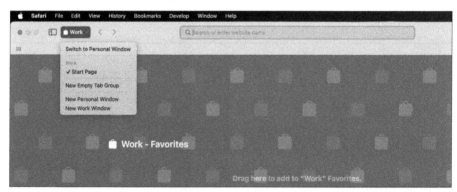

To open a new window in a specific profile, click on the profiles icon on the top left, choose New [Profile Name] Window. For example, if you want a new browser window in your personal profile select 'new personal window'. If you want a new browser window in your work profile, select 'new work window'.

While you're in a browser window within a specific profile, everything you do remains within that profile. This means you can add extensions, and bookmarks, and they won't appear in any other profile.

Have a look at the video demo on the webpage below.

elluminetpress.com/mac-comms

Web Apps

Web apps allow you to use any website as if it were an app. This means you can have an icon for it on your dock. Useful for websites you use all the time such as web based email and many others.

First navigate to the website you want to use as a web app. Click on the 'file' menu, then select the 'add to dock'.

Give the web app a name then click 'add'.

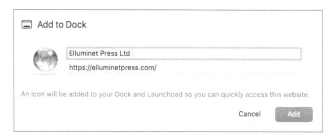

The web app will now appear on your dock. When you launch the web app from the dock, you'll notice that the usual elements of Safari, such as the URL bar, sidebar, new tab button, and other icons aren't visible. This provides a clearer interface, making the web app feel more like a native application rather than just a website in a browser. Additionally, you can control its permissions and clear its data through dedicated sections found in the menu bar.

Apple Mail

Apple Mail, also known as the Mail App, is an email program included with Mac OS.

With Apple Mail, you can include all your email accounts in one app. These are listed in the sidebar down the left hand side of the screen. On the sidebar, you'll also see your mail boxes: inbox, sent, junk and so on for all the email accounts you've added.

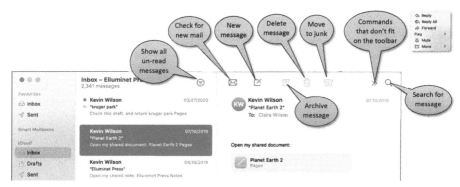

In the middle pane, you'll see a list of email messages in the mail box you've selected from the sidebar. In the example below, 'inbox' is selected from the sidebar and the email messages are listed in the middle pane.

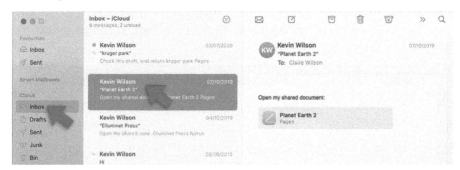

In the far right pane, you'll see a preview of the message you have selected from the middle pane.

To read the message in full, double click the message listed in the middle pane.

Email Threads

An email conversation that spreads across dozens of messages in your inbox is called a thread. Apple Mail organises your email messages by thread. Here in the demo below is an email conversation between Claire and me.

You can see in Claire's inbox below, her email conversation with me. In the reading pane you'll see the email conversation (or thread). To make things easier to explain, I've marked messages Claire has sent in green, and messages I've sent in blue. Notice the latest email is at the bottom of the thread.

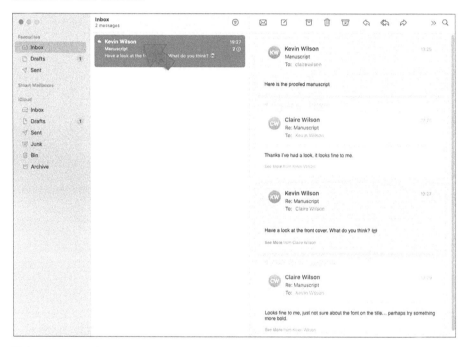

When you select the email conversation in the inbox (indicated above with red arrow) and click 'reply', you'll automatically reply to the latest message in the thread. To reply to a particular message in the thread, hover your mouse over the message, you'll see a small toolbar appear.

Click the 'reply' icon. Or if you want to delete it, click the bin icon.

You can turn this feature off, if you'd rather list all your emails in your inbox as they arrive. To do this, click the 'view' menu on the top left.

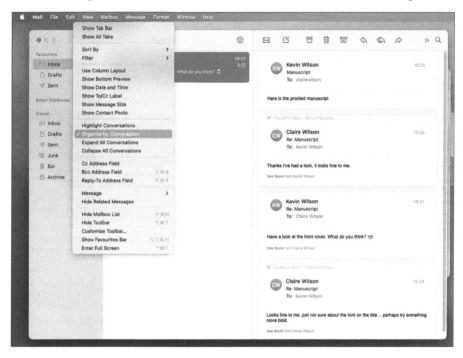

Select 'organise by conversation' to remove the tick.

Show BCC Field

If you want to send messages to multiple recipients, but you don't want everyone to see everyone else's email addresses, you can add the addresses to the BCC field. BCC stands for blind carbon copy and isn't enabled by default. To reveal the field, click the view menu then select 'bcc address field'.

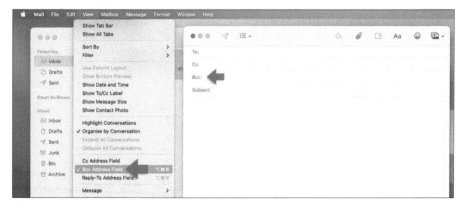

Replying to a Message

To reply to an email, select the email you want from your inbox, then click the 'reply to sender' icon on the top right. If you don't see the icons click the '>>' icon on the right.

Note there are two reply icons. The first icon allows you to only reply to the sender (in the to: field). The second icon allows you to reply to the sender and everyone else the message was sent to - so if the message was sent to multiple recipients in the to:, cc: or bcc: fields.

Type in your message at the top of the window that appears. Here you can craft your reply as you would a new email. See "Writing a New Email" on page 327.

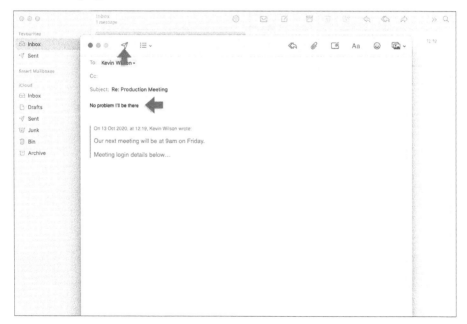

Click the send icon on the top left of the window.

Forward a Message

You can forward a message to another person. To do this, select the email you want to send to someone else, then click the 'forward' icon on the top right. If you don't see the icons click the '>>' icon on the right.

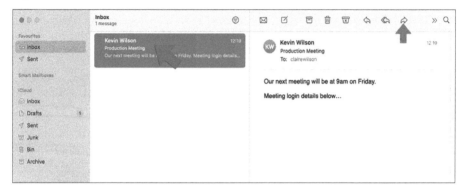

Enter the person's email address in the 'to:' field.

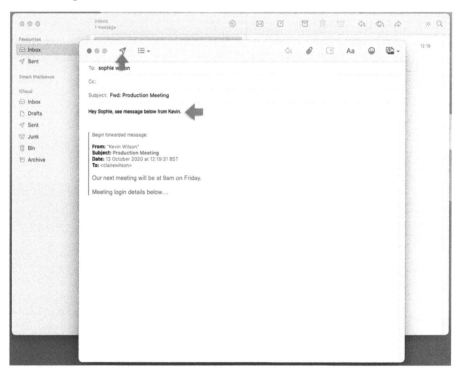

Add a message at the top of the email if you want to.

Click the send icon on the top left of the window to send your message.

Writing a New Email

To send a new email, click the 'new email' icon on the tool bar along the top of the screen. A new blank email window will pop up.

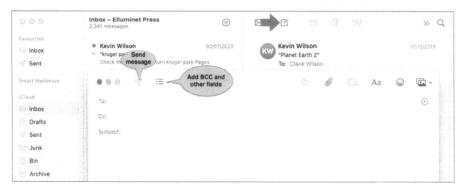

Enter an email address in the 'to' field. If you need to send the message to more than one person, add their email addresses to the CC field. If you don't want everyone else's email address to show up in everyone's copy of the email, enable the BCC field. Type a subject in to the 'subject' field, then type your message in the space underneath.

Formatting your Message

Click the font icon that looks like 'Aa', to reveal the formatting bar.

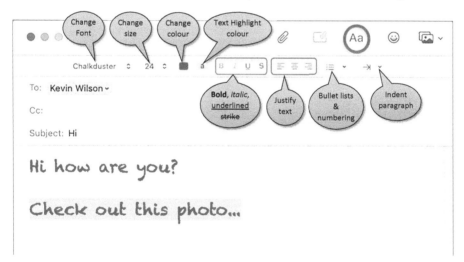

Select the tools from the formatting bar to format your text, change color, size, alignment, and font. Remember to highlight the text you want to format first, if you've already typed it in. To add numbered lists or bullet points, click the 'bullet list & numbering' icon.

Chapter 5: Internet, Email & Communications

Add an Emoji

You can add emojis like the ones you see on iMessage, into your email messages. To do this, click the emoji icon on the toolbar.

From the drop down, select from the categories of emoticons along the bottom, you can choose smilies, animals, fruit, etc. Click the emoji you want to add

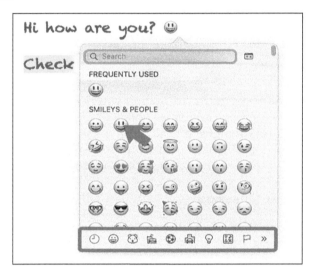

Add Attachment

Click the paper clip icon to add an attachment such as a PDF or word document, or a photo you downloaded. Select the file from the dialog box then click 'choose file'.

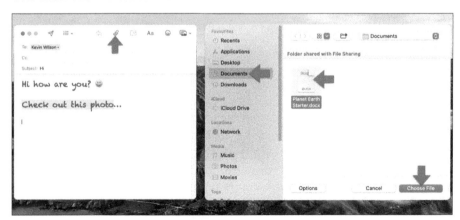

Add Photo from Photos App

If you want to add a photo from your photos app, click the photo icon to pull up your photo albums, as shown above. You can drag and drop any photo into your email to send along.

When you're ready to send your message, tap the send icon on the top left.

Mail Drop

MailDrop allows you to send large files by automatically uploading them to your iCloud drive, and then sending a link to the recipient so they can access the file without clogging up the mail server with large files. MailDrop uses your iCloud to store your files, and because iCloud is built into Mail, this means that anyone running Mail on their own Mac will have the file downloaded automatically, just as though it were an ordinary email.

Mail Drop will automatically upload large attachments to iCloud instead of your email provider ie Gmail, Yahoo, or Exchange etc.

If your recipient also uses Mail on a Mac, they'll be able to download the attachment normally, and if not, they'll get a download link that's accessible for 30 days. These attachments don't count towards your iCloud storage limits, which is great. Smaller attachments are sent as normal.

You can open and compose a new email as normal and attach a file. In this example the file is 161MB which is pretty large for an email attachment.

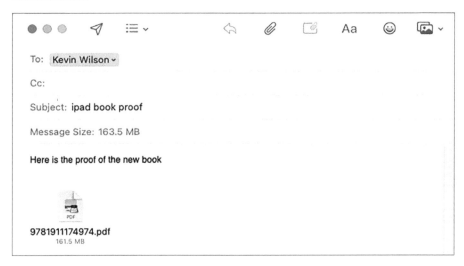

When your recipient receives the email, there will be a link that will allow them to download the attachment. If your recipient using a Mac, then they need to right click on the link then select 'save to downloads folder'. Go to the downloads folder in finder, then double click the file.

If your recipient is using a Windows PC, then they need to click on the attachment link in the email as shown below.

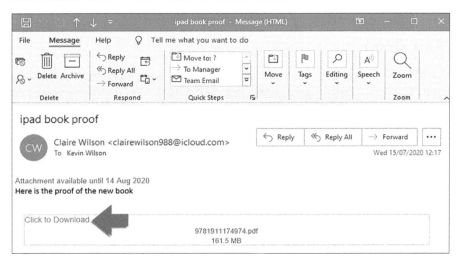

From the 'save as' dialog box select a folder to download the attachment to (eg downloads). This will download the attachment into the downloads folder. From here they can open and read the attachment.

Mail Markup

Markup provides a simple way of adding comments and annotations to file attachments in Mail and mostly works with photos or pdf documents.

If you send someone a photo for example, in an email you can activate markup mode, by clicking on a small pull-down menu that appears in the top-right corner of the image.

You can then annotate your image, type text, draw lines, circles and hand written notes on the image.

Below is an explanation of what all the different icons do.

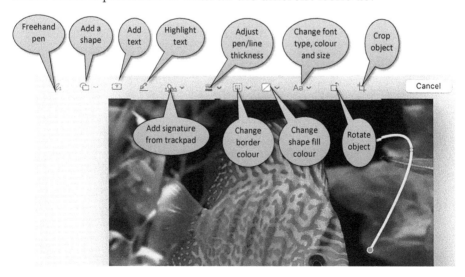

Click the 'freehand pen' icon.

Now you can draw or write on your photograph.

Try some of the other tools such as a shape, add some text. Once you have finished annotating your image click 'done'.

If you don't see the markup pop-up menu, you may need to enable it. To do this, click the Apple menu on the top left of the screen, then select 'system preferences'. Double click 'extensions'.

Click actions, then select the markup checkbox.

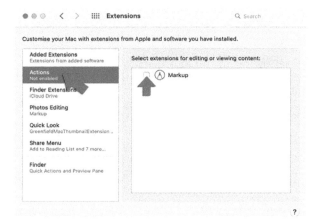

Dealing with Spam & Junk Mail

We all get junk mail - those annoying messages trying to sell you things and just clutter up your inbox with rubbish. Apple Mail has a spam filter where you can filter out these messages.

To enable junk mail filtering, open Apple Mail and go to the 'mail' menu. Select 'settings'.

Select the 'junk mail' tab. Click the tick box next to 'enable junk mail filtering'.

Now occasionally, the junk mail filter will catch legitimate emails, so it's best to move them to the junk mail folder.

To do this, select 'move it to the junk mailbox'. This will keep your inbox clean and move junk to the junk mailbox.

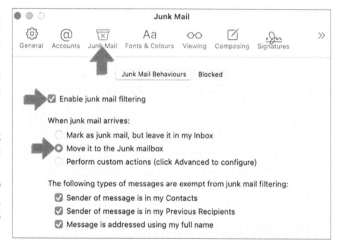

This means that you can check the junk mail box from time to time to check which messages are being filtered and that no important ones have been filtered out.

Schedule Send

In the mail app, write your email as normal, then click the small arrow next to the send icon. To schedule a time, click 'send later'. Emails you choose to send later appear in the 'send later' mailbox in the sidebar.

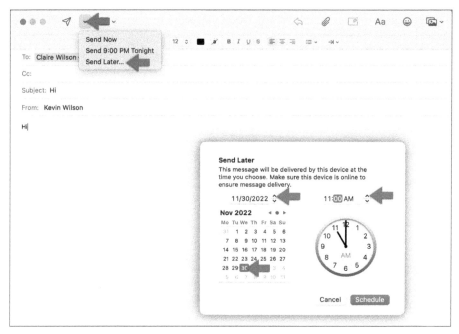

In the popup window, select the date and time from the options, then click 'schedule'. You'll see scheduled emails waiting to be sent in the 'send later' folder on the top left of the screen.

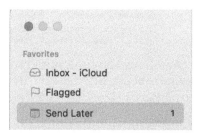

If you want to edit the schedule, select the 'send later' folder on the top left, select the email from the list, then click 'edit' on the top right.

Undo Send

If you've made an error in your email or sent an email by mistake, you can recall the email using the 'undo send' feature.

Once you've sent the email, you'll see an 'undo send' link on the bottom left of the screen. This will stop the email being sent and return you to the email

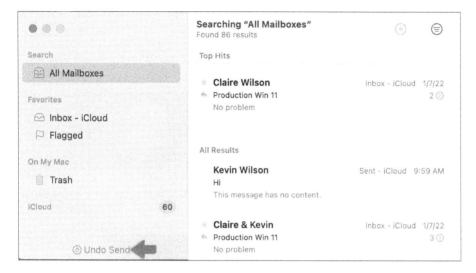

There is limited time in which you can undo a send. The default is 10 seconds. You can change the delay. To change the amount of time, choose open the mail settings, select the 'composing' tab, click the Undo send delay pop-up menu, then choose an option.

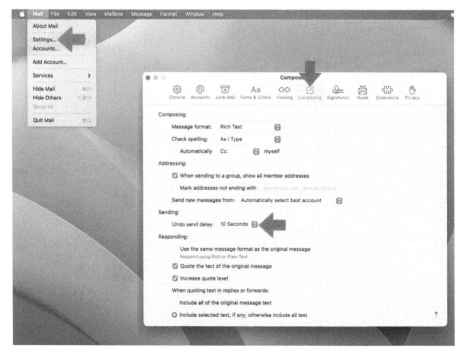

Contacts

This is your address book and stores all your email, phone numbers, and addresses that you can access from the contacts app itself or through your email, FaceTime, or iMessage.

You'll find the contacts app on your dock, or launchpad. Click the icon to open the app.

You can create contacts, add email addresses and phone numbers. These contacts are synced with all your Apple devices; iPhone, iPad etc.

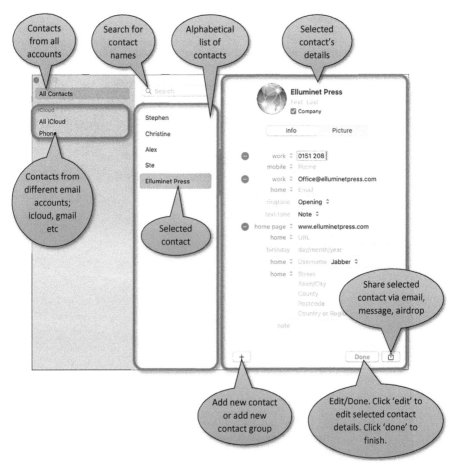

Add a Contact from Scratch

To add a new contact, click the plus sign on the bottom of the contacts window. Select 'new contact' from the drop down menu.

Enter the contact's details - first, last name, phone, email, address and any other information you have in the fields that appear.

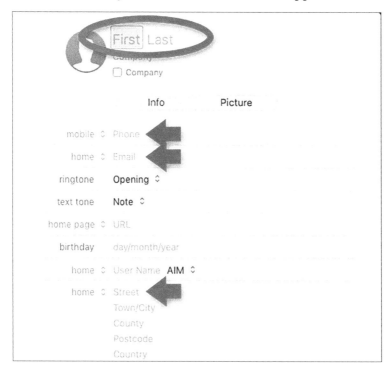

Click 'done' on the bottom right when you're finished.

Creating Groups

Groups make it easier to send an email to several different people. This group can be a team. In this example, I'm going to create a group called 'production team' and will contain a list of email address in my team. To create a group, click the plus sign at the bottom, and from the drop down select 'new group'. An untitled group will appear on the left hand side - type in a name.

Now you can drag and drop your contacts into the group.

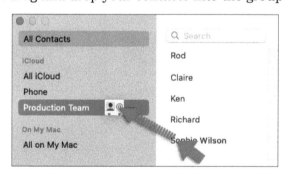

Now when you start a new email, you'll be able to type the group name into the 'to' field, rather than having to add all the email addresses manually.

338

Add Email Contact from Apple Mail

The easiest way to add someone's email address from an email message is to click on the small down-arrow next to the person's name in the email header, as shown below.

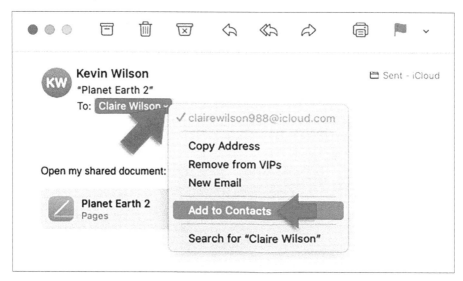

From the popup menu select 'add to contacts'.

This will automatically create an entry in your contacts list with the sender's name and email address from the email you have open.

Take a look at the video demos. Open your web browser and navigate to the following website

www.elluminetpress.com/mac-comms

FaceTime

When you open FaceTime, you will be prompted to sign in if you haven't already done so.

Placing Video Calls

Once FaceTime has opened, you'll see in the main window a preview of your camera. On the left hand side you'll see a darkened panel where you'll find a list of contacts you've called or received calls from.

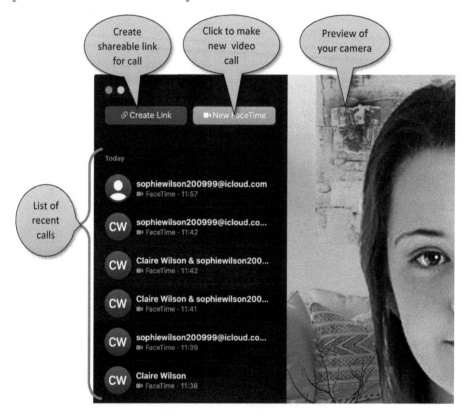

To make another call to the contact, click the camera icon next to their name in the list on the left hand side of the screen. The camera icon will appear when you hover your mouse pointer over the contact.

Wait for them to answer.

Calling Someone New

To call someone new, click 'new FaceTime' on the top of the side panel.

In the field at the top of the popup box, start typing the contact's name. If the name is in your contacts, then it will appear underneath. Click on their name in the list that appears.

Click on the 'FaceTime' button to make a video call.

If you want to place an 'audio' call, click the small down arrow next to 'FaceTime'. Select 'FaceTime audio'.

Wait for the other person to answer...

Create a FaceTime Link

You can create a link to a FaceTime call that you can send to a friend or a group using the Mail or Messages app. You can also use these links to invite people who use Windows or Android.

To do this, click on 'create a link'.

From the drop down, select the app you want to use to share the link, eg mail or messages. I'm going to send this link using mail.

Enter the person's email address, then click the send icon.

Once the other person clicks on the link, they'll be able to join using FaceTime in a web browser.

You'll see the link appear in your side panel. Click to join.

Answering Calls

When a call comes in on your mac, you'll see a notification on the top right with a preview of your camera. *Note, no one will be able to see your camera until you accept the call.*

You'll see the name of the person calling on the left hand side of the notification window. Click 'accept' to receive the call, or 'decline' if you're busy or don't want to talk .

Now in the centre of the screen you'll see an image of the person you're calling. On the bottom right of the screen you'll see a preview of your own camera.

Press *CMD CTRL F* for full screen mode on your Mac.

When you're in a video call, you can access settings in the control center. To do this click the green video icon on the top right of the screen.

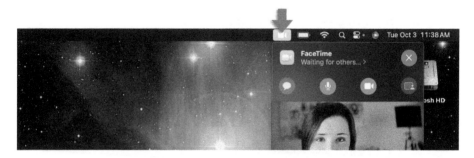

Under the camera effects, you can select portrait mode, studio light and reactions. Portrait mode blurs the background, studio light darkens the background, and reactions allows you to use physical hand gestures to trigger certain visual effects. See the 'video hand reactions' bonus on the website: elluminetpress.com/macos

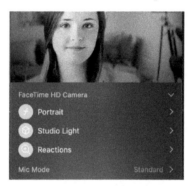

Under mic mode, you can select from 'standard', 'voice isolation', and 'wide spectrum'.

Available on Mac models 2018 and later, spatial audio makes it sound like the people in your video call are in the room with you. Their voices are spread out in your headphones or speakers to make it sound as if they're coming from the direction in which each person is positioned on the screen. Voice isolation mode enhances your voice on a FaceTime call and blocks out background noise. Wide spectrum includes your voice and all the sounds around you.

344

Group FaceTime

To call a group, type the names of the contacts you want to add to your group into the search field on the top left of the screen. Select the names from the drop down menu as they appear.

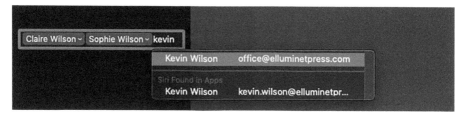

At the bottom you'll see two green buttons. Click 'video' to start a video chat. Click 'audio' to start a voice call.

Now, wait for everyone to answer.

You'll see your camera on the bottom right. Everyone else in the chat will appear in their own window. When a person starts talking their window will highlight.

If you want to add more people, open the sidebar. To do this, click the sidebar icon on the left hand side

Here, you can click 'add people' to invite someone else, or click 'share link' to get a link to send to someone.

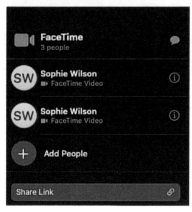

Screen Sharing

Open the app you want to share. To start sharing, tap the green icon on the top right side of the screen. Click the 'share icon'.

Underneath, select what you want to share: a window, the app, or the whole screen.

When you choose to share a "window," you're selecting a specific open window on your computer to share with participants. Sharing an "app" means you're sharing all the windows associated with a specific application. This is the most comprehensive sharing option. When you choose to share "full screen," you're sharing your  entire computer screen with the participants. Everything you see on your screen, including your desktop, taskbar, and all open windows, will be visible to them. For example, I'm going to share Safari, so I selected 'app'.

You'll see a blue marker appear on open apps. Select the app you want to share.

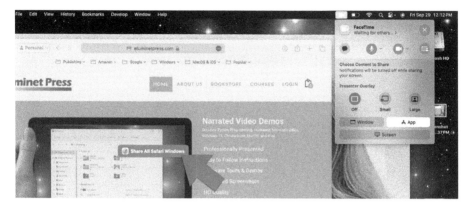

To finish, tap the sharing icon on the top right, click 'stop sharing' at the bottom.

Presenter Overlay

Presenter Overlay keeps you at the forefront while sharing your screen in FaceTime or other video conferencing apps such as Zoom.

Start a FaceTime call and share your screen as in the previous section. Choose a presenter overlay.

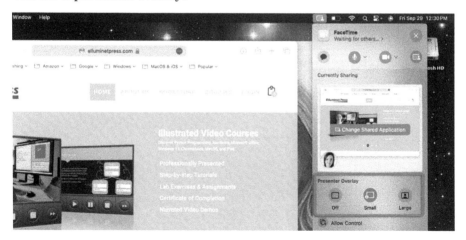

When you choose the "small" option, a more compact thumbnail typically showing your will appear on top of the content you're sharing. The "large" option will display a bigger video feed of yourself with the content behind you. If you use the large option make sure your video background is clear.

Once you've chosen to share your screen or slides, the Presenter Overlay feature will appear on top of the content you're sharing. You'll see a preview on the top right. If you chose the "small" presenter overlay, you'll see it on the bottom left of your screen.

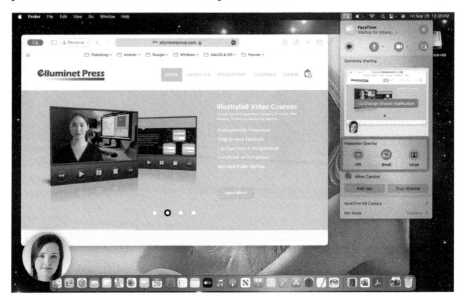

SharePlay

Using the SharePlay feature, you can watch a movie together, or listen to music with your FaceTime contacts as if you were in the same room. You can also share your screen.

Share a Movie or Music

Within a FaceTime call, open an app that supports SharePlay such as the TV app or Music App.

Click 'shareplay'.

The movie will pop up in a window. Maximise the movie window, now you can watch together... You'll still be table to hear everyone. Click the share play icon on the top right to view controls and what is currently playing on shareplay.

Click back on FaceTime to see everyone in the chat group. Here, the girls are enjoying Charlie Brown & Snoopy together.

While FaceTime calls are now accessible to Android and Windows users, the SharePlay feature remains exclusive to iOS, iPadOS, and macOS users.

Third-party services compatible with SharePlay include Hulu, HBO Max, Disney+, TikTok, Paramount+, Pluto TV, Twitch, MasterClass, ESPN+, NBA TV, and more. Notably, as of the last update, Netflix and Spotify have not yet integrated SharePlay support.

Using your iPhone Camera

You can use the camera on your iPhone as a webcam on your Mac during a FaceTime call.

To mount your iPhone, you can get various different stands and mounts.

For example, a mount that sticks on the back of your iPhone and hooks over the top of your macbook, as you can see below on the left.

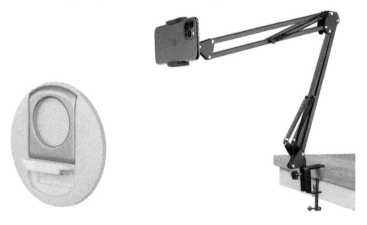

Of if you're using an iMac or a different screen, you can get various different desk mounts that will hold your iPhone. You'll just need to position the mount so it holds your iPhone in the correct place above your screen.

To use your iPhone camera, from FaceTime's 'video' menu, choose your iPhone as the camera and microphone.

If you don't see these options on the menu, open settings, select 'general', turn on 'AirPlay & Handoff. If it's already on, you might need to turn it off, then back on again. Do the same on your iPhone.

The continuity app will open on your iPhone.

You'll notice that the rear camera on your iPhone is now your webcam. Note your iPhone must be in landscape orientation and near your Mac.

Desk View

You can use the camera on your iPhone to view what's on your desk or something else during a FaceTime call with a feature called desk view, useful if you want to demonstrate or show something.

To enable desk view, connect your iPhone camera as demonstrated in the previous section. During a FaceTime call, click on 'desk view' on the top right of the screen.

Use the slider along the bottom of the window to resize the white marker so you can see your desk clearly. You may also need to align your iPhone to make sure everything you want to show is in shot.

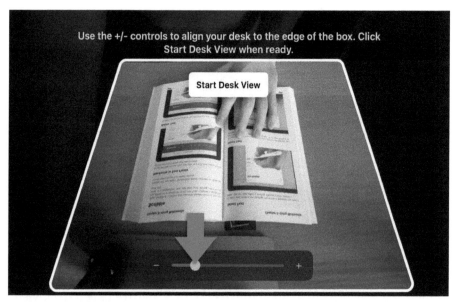

Click 'start desk view' when you're done.

Now you can now show what's on your desk along with your webcam.

To turn off desk view, click the 'desk view' icon on the top right of the chat window then close the desk view window.

Video & Lighting Effects

While using your iPhone as a webcam, you can also use the various video and lighting effects to enhance your call.

You can use effects that include Portrait mode, Centre Stage and Studio Light.

During a call, click on the green video icon on the top right of the menu bar. Down at the bottom you'll see a section for your iPhone camera.

Centre Stage keeps you and anyone else with you in focus and in shot. You can select your main camera, or the ultra wide camera for wide shots - the ultra wide camera will keep you in shot if you move. This appears when using iPhone as camera

Portrait mode automatically blurs the background and keeps the focus on you. Useful for removing distractions.

Studio Light darkens the background keeping the light and focus on you. Useful for removing distractions.

Reactions allows you to use physical hand gestures to trigger certain visual effects. See the 'video hand reactions' bonus on the website. elluminetpress.com/macos

Handoff a Call to iPhone

During a FaceTime call on your mac, you can move the call to another device signed in with the same Apple ID, for example your iPhone. On your iPhone's screen, tap the notification on the top left, then tap 'switch' to transfer the call to your Mac.

If you're on a FaceTime call on your iPhone, tap the notification to switch the call, or tap the Video Handoff button at the top left of the screen, then tap the Switch button.

The call will move to the new device.

Message App

The Messages app allows you to send media rich text messages to other iPhones, iPads and Macs. You can find the Messages App on your Dock at the bottom of the screen.

You can send a new message by clicking on the new message icon, then in the new message window click the + sign to add your recipients.

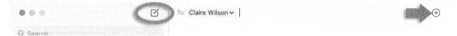

From the drop down, select the contact from the list.

Sending New Messages

The message window will open up. Type your message in field at the bottom of the screen. You'll see a message transcript in the main window.

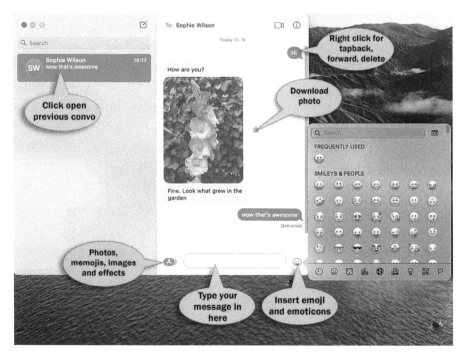

Click on the smiley face on the right hand side of the message field to add your emojis.

In the demo below, you can see the user on the left, is using Messages App on an iPhone, and is in conversation with the user on the Mac.

Sending Files

You can send files in your messages. To do this, click and drag a file, photo, or video from the desktop or finder directly into the message window.

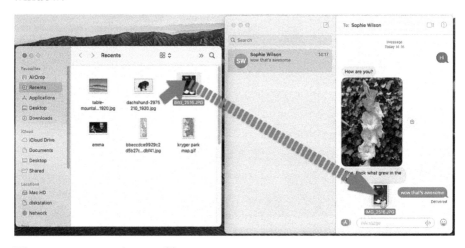

Hit return to send your file.

Edit Message

Select a conversation from the list on the left if you haven't already done so. Hold down control on your keyboard, then click on the message you want to edit.

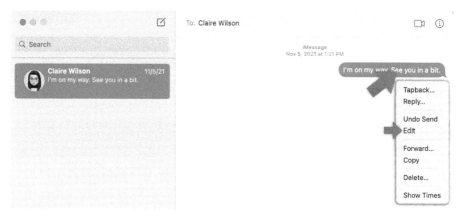

Make any changes, then press 'enter' on your keyboard.

Undo Send

Select a conversation from the list on the left if you haven't already done so. Hold down control on your keyboard, then click on the message you want to undo.

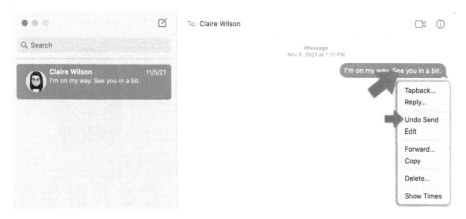

Right click on the message or attachment, then choose 'undo send'.

Currently these two features are only available for iMessage conversations with other iPhone/Mac users. Text messages to other platforms don't allow you to undo, or edit after being sent.

Memojis

Memojis are customised animated stickers designed to look like a cartoon version of you. They can also be other animals and characters known as animojis.

You can create and send Memojis. To do this, click on the icon to the left of the text field. Select 'Memoji Stickers'.

To send, select any of the Memojis. Press enter to confirm.

To create a Memoji, click the '+' icon on the top left.

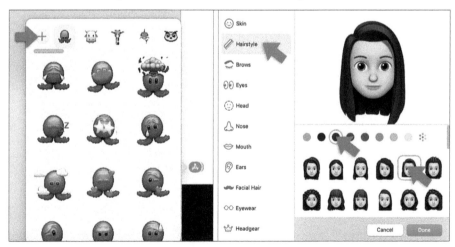

Run through the features listed down the left hand side of the window to create your Memoji. Click 'done'.

Message Effects

You add various effects to your messages such as fireworks, balloons, confetti, and lasers.

To send a message with an effect, type in your message, then click the icon on the left of the message box. Select 'message effects' from the drop down menu.

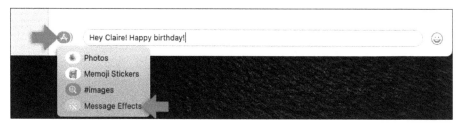

Select an effect from the options along the bottom of the window.

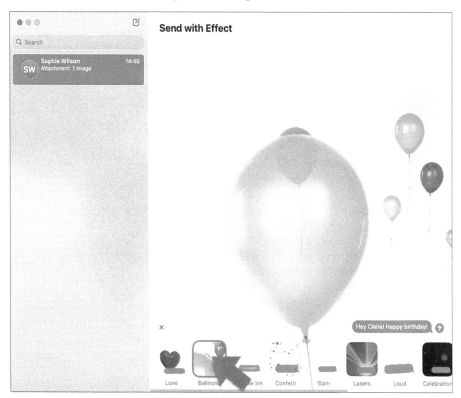

Press enter to send the message.

Try some of the other effects.

Air Drop

AirDrop is a service that enables users to transfer files to another supported devices ie Mac computer and iPad or iPhone without using email or a USB stick or external hard drive.

From Finder

You can AirDrop a file from finder to any nearby device. To do this, open finder and navigate to the file you want to share.

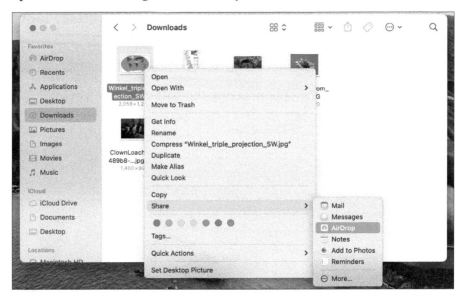

Right click on the file, go down to 'share' then select 'AirDrop' from the slide out menu.

Your Mac will detect nearby devices with AirDrop enabled. Click the one you want to send the file to.

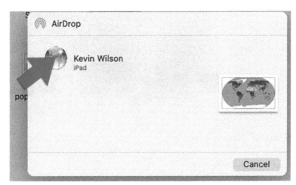

On the device, you'll see the file pop up.

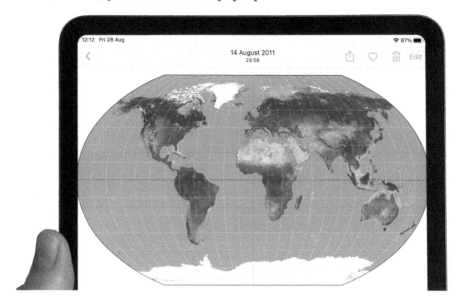

In Safari

To AirDrop a webpage from safari, navigate to the page you want to share, then click the 'share' icon on the top right. Select 'AirDrop' from the slideout menu.

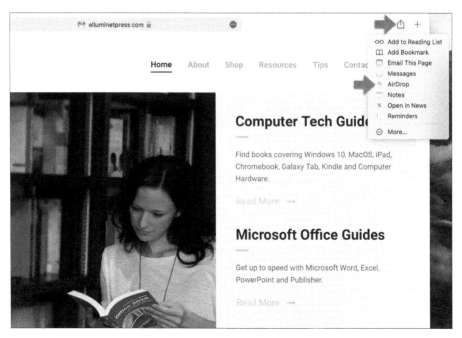

Select the device you want to share the page with.

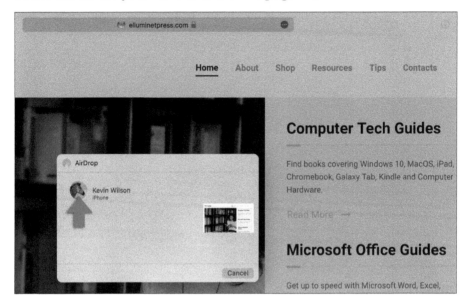

If you have trouble sending/receiving, make sure the person you're sharing with is in your contacts, or set AirDrop sharing to receive from anyone. You'll find the AirDrop settings on control center.

Select 'everyone'.

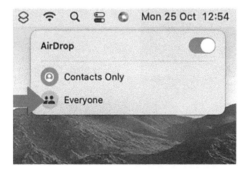

Mac Phone

You can answer calls on your Mac if you have an iPhone. For this feature to work, you'll need to be connected to the same WiFi network, and signed in with the same iCloud account on both your Mac and iPhone. Then you'll need to enable the feature. On your iPhone, open the settings app and select 'phone'.

Turn on 'Calls on Other Devices'. You'll see the other Apple devices you'll receive your iPhone calls on.

Now, on your Mac, open the FaceTime app. Go to the FaceTime menu on the top left, select 'settings'. In the 'general tab', make sure 'Calls from iPhone' is selected.

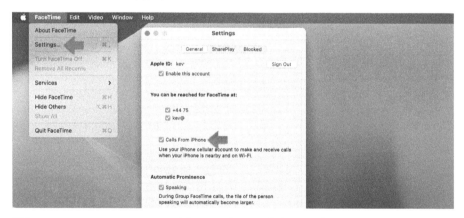

Whenever you are on your Mac and your iPhone rings, you can pick up the call. You'll see a notification appear on the top right of the screen.

Click 'accept' to answer the call.

6

Using Multimedia Apps

Photos has more features that are similar to the Photos app on the iPad and iPhone borrowing some of the same style of operation.

You can import photos from your iPhone and sync them with your Photos library as well as import them from a digital camera.

You can create some very nice looking photo books, greetings cards and slide shows all with your own photographs.

Photos also has features such as intelligent scene detection, face, place and object recognition and will automatically categorise your photos allowing you to search using people's names, place names, and objects.

There is also a 'memories' feature, that will automatically group your photos into slideshows for you to enjoy and share with your friends.

To help you better understand this section, take a look at the video resources. Open your web browser and navigate to the following site:

elluminetpress.com/mac-mm

Photos App

The Photo App is a great way to store, view and manipulate your photographs. You can create albums and slide shows, you can email a photo to a friend, post them onto Facebook, you can even put together your own album send it to Apple and they will print you out a copy and post it to you, these are great for family albums or wedding albums and other special occasions.

To open the Photos App, click the icon on the dock.

Once the app opens, you'll see all the photos that are on your Mac. Along the top of the window you'll see a toolbar.

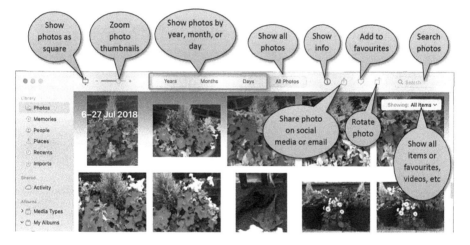

Down the left hand side you'll see the sidebar. Under the library section, you'll be able to select 'photos' to view all the photos on your mac.

Select 'people' to view photos featuring people. The Photos App scans your photos for faces and creates a 'people album' for each person it finds.

Select 'places' to view a map showing the different places your photos were taken.

You'll also be able to see photos you've most recently added ('recents'), and photos you've imported from a digital camera ('imports').

Further down the sidebar you'll also see any albums you've created.

Importing your Photos

Most digital cameras connect to your computer using a USB cable, as shown below.

Open photos from launch pad and connect your camera. Photos will detect the camera connected and open up the import screen.

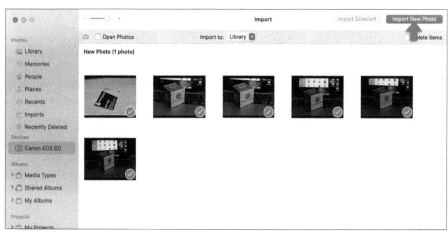

I found it best to delete them off the camera once imported into the Photo library. This means I have a clean camera for the next time I want to take photographs.

To do this, click the tick box next to 'delete items after import'. This helps eliminate duplicate photographs in the library.

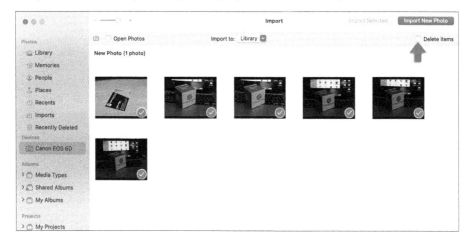

Now select 'imports' from the 'photos' section of the sidebar on the left hand side of the screen.

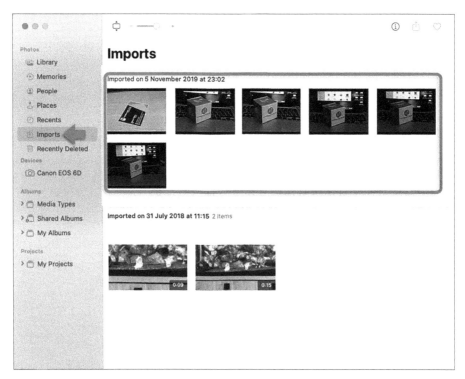

Scroll down, you should now be able to see all the photos you have just imported.

Manipulating & Adjusting Photos

A common problem I have come across, when taking photographs with a pocket digital camera, is sometimes photos can come out a bit dark.

To edit the photo, double click on it. Click 'edit' on the top right of the screen.

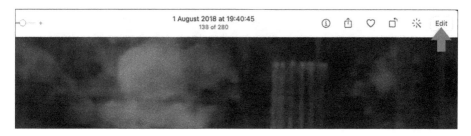

Select 'adjust' from the three options at the top of the screen.

Down the right hand side of the screen, you'll see a list of operations you can perform on your photograph.

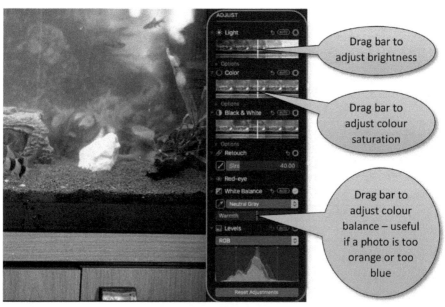

For example, to change the brightness of the image, select 'adjust' from three options on the top, centre of the screen.

Under the adjustments on the right hand side, you'll see one called 'light'. Underneath you'll see a gradient going from a dark image to a light image and a slider somewhere in the middle. Click and drag this slider toward the light, to lighten the image.

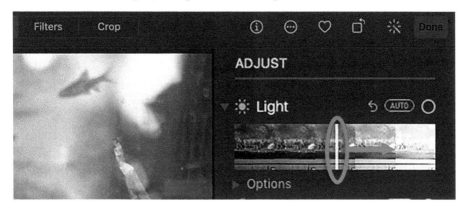

Under the 'light' adjustment, select 'options'. Here, you can adjust the exposure - how bright the image is, you can adjust highlights - the bright areas, shadows - the dark areas, and contrast. To adjust drag the blue sliders left and right.

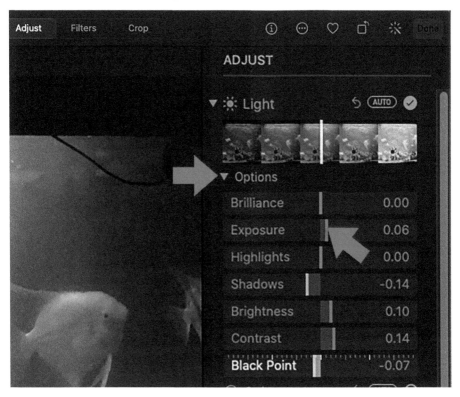

You can do the same for the 'color'; saturate and desaturate the colors. You can also click 'auto' on these adjustments and photos app will make a guess.

If you scroll further down the adjustment controls, you'll see some more advanced features.

You can change the white balance, this is good for adjusting photos that have a distinctive orange or blue tone to them.

Neutral gray is usually one to use, however if you are adjusting a portrait of someone, click this box and change it to 'skin tone'.

If you scroll further down the adjustment options, you'll see some more advanced features.

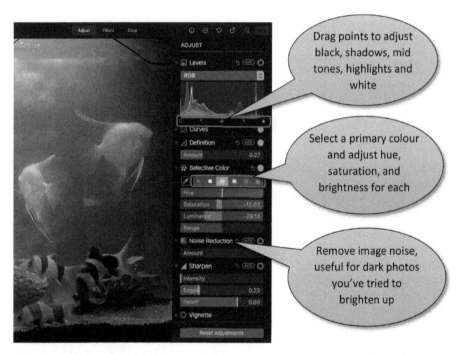

Click and drag the sliders underneath the names of the effects to adjust the photograph.

Adding Filters

Filters give your photograph a predefined look, such as changing your photo to a sepia or black and white look; make the colors more vivid, warm or dramatic.

Double click on your image and select 'edit' from the top right.

Select 'filters' from the options on the top centre of the screen.

Down the right hand side you'll see some filters. Click on the icons to apply the filter.

Click 'done' to save.

Creating Folders and Albums

The photos app allows you to organize your photos into albums (shown in green). You can in turn organise all your albums into folders (shown in blue).

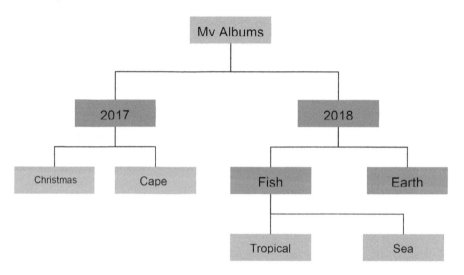

To create a blank folder or album, hover your mouse pointer over 'my albums'. Click the '+' sign that appears. From the popup menu select 'folder' to create a new folder.

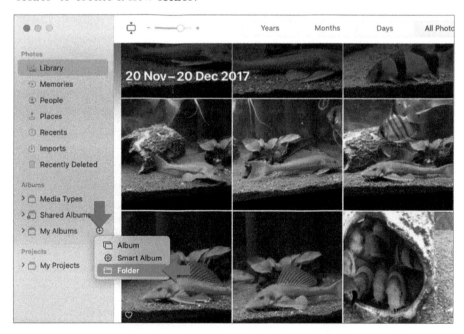

I'm going to create a folder called '2017' to store my albums from that year. So type in '2017'.

Now, you can't create albums within albums, but you can organize your albums into folders.

Inside the '2017' folder, I'm going to create an album called 'cape'. Hover your mouse over the '2017' folder, click the '+' icon that appears. Select 'album' from the popup menu.

Type in the album name. Eg 'Cape'.

Follow the same procedure to create other albums and folders as needed.

Adding Photos to Albums

To add photos to your albums. Select 'library' from the 'photos' section of the side panel on the left hand side. Then select 'all photos' from the toolbar on the top of the window.

Select the photos you want to add - hold down the cmd key on your keyboard to select multiple photos. Click and drag the photos into the albums on the left hand panel under the 'albums' section of the side panel.

Places

Photos App will tag your photos and record where your photo was taken, this is called geo tagging. If you have GPS and location services set on your iPhone, the photos app will tag the photographs with the location.

Select 'places' from the sidebar on the left hand side of your screen.

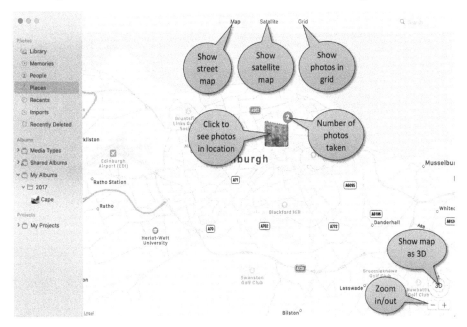

Here you'll see a map with markers on the map containing photos taken at that location. You can view on a street map or a satellite map, click the options on the toolbar at the top to change the map.

Double click on the marker to view all the photos taken in that location.

Double click photo to see larger or edit. Click the back arrow on the top left to go back.

You can also assign locations if your camera hasn't got a geo tagging feature. Select your images, right click on the selection and click 'get into'.

Click on 'assign a location' and type in the name of the city or location the photo was taken. Select the closest match from the drop down menu of suggested locations.

Now when you select 'locations' from the sidebar on the main screen, you'll see your photos appear across the world map according to the locations they were taken in.

Faces

The faces feature scans your photographs for recognisable faces and will show them as thumbnails on the people section. The Photos App will take a while to scan all your photos, so you'll need to wait for it to finish.

Once the Photos App has finished scanning all your photos, you'll notice a marker on each person's face when you open a photo. The Photos App will try to match the face with people in your contacts list. If there is no match you'll see an 'un named' marker.

Click on the marker and enter the person's name - select the closest match from the list that appears, if not press enter. This will train the Photos App to recognise these people in all your photos and any new ones that you take.

Do this for all your 'un named' photos.

Chapter 6: Using Multimedia

To see all your named photos, click 'people' on the side panel on the left hand side of your screen.

Double click on the thumbnail photo of the person to see all photos of them in your collection. Click 'show more' on the top right. Click a photo to see it full size.

To manually tag a face, open a photo from your photos library, then click the 'i' icon on the top right.

From the info panel, click 'add faces'.

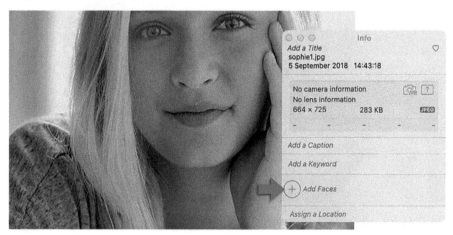

You'll see a circular marker appear on top of the photo. Click and drag the small resize handle to resize the marker.

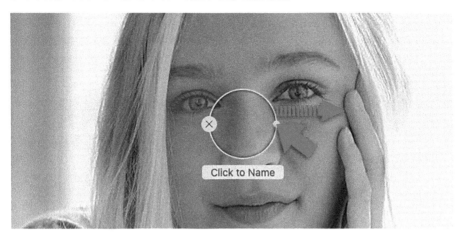

Click and drag it over the person's face.

The Photos App will attempt to identify this person in other photographs, so you don't need to tag multiple photos of the same person.

Chapter 6: Using Multimedia

Memories

Memories are short slide show movies Photos App automatically creates, based on the time and place they were taken. You can add music and transitions between the photos to spice up your memories.

Create your Own Memory

To create your own memories, go to the 'Photos' tab and select all the photos you want to appear in your memory. You can select multiple photos by holding down the cmd key on your keyboard while selecting your photos.

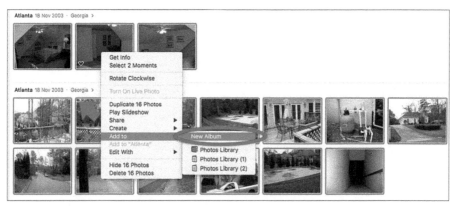

Right click on your selection, click 'add to' and select 'new album' from the slideout. Give the album a name, I'm going to call mine 'Thanks'. Your albums will show up under the albums section on the left hand side of the screen.

380

At the top of your album, click 'Show as Memory'.

Scroll right to the bottom of the page and click 'add to memories'.

Now when you go back to your memories section, you'll see your album has been added to your memories.

Right click on the image and select 'play slideshow'. Select a theme from the popup panel on the right hand side.

Click the 'music' tab, select a theme. If you want to include a track from your music library, click 'theme songs', change it to 'music'. Select the track you want from your library.

Once you have done that, click 'play slideshow'.

Smart Search

The smart search feature scans and analyses your photos to determine what objects the images contain. It will attempt to identify places, objects, animals, faces and will tag them accordingly.

This makes finding and grouping your photos so much easier. Type keywords into the search field on the top right of the screen.

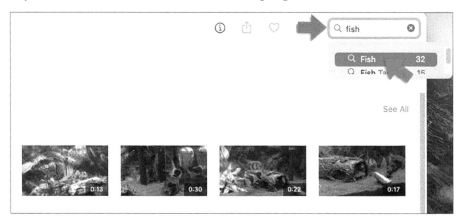

From the drop down, select a keyword. Type in another keyword or select another from the list to narrow your search.

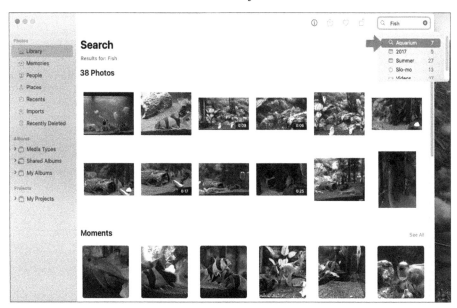

You'll see a thumbnail list of all the photos that match the keywords you entered.

Sharing Photos

You can share your photos with your friends and family from within the Photos App. To do this, select the photos you want to share.

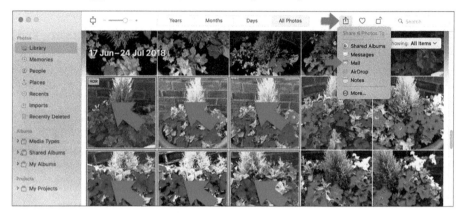

Click the share icon on the top right of the toolbar, then select the app you want to use to share the photos. I'm going to use email in this example. You can also use messages or AirDrop.

Enter the names of the people you want to share the photos with into the 'to' field. Add a message at the top of the email if you want.

Select the image size to large to prevent the message from being too large.

Click the 'send' icon on the top left when you're done.

384

Shared Albums

A shared album creates a shared area where you can share photos with people. You can add photos to the shared album and you can allow others to add photos as well.

Select the photos and videos you want to share. Click the share icon on the top right of the toolbar, then click 'shared albums'.

Click 'new shared album'.

Type a name for the shared album (eg 'promo'), then type the email addresses of the people you want to share the album with. Click 'create'.

Now the people you shared the album with will get an invite in their email.

385

You'll find your shared album under 'shared albums' on the sidebar. You can add photos and videos by dragging the photos to the shared folder on the sidebar.

To edit the sharing options, click the shared folder on the sidebar, then click the 'people' icon on the top right of the toolbar.

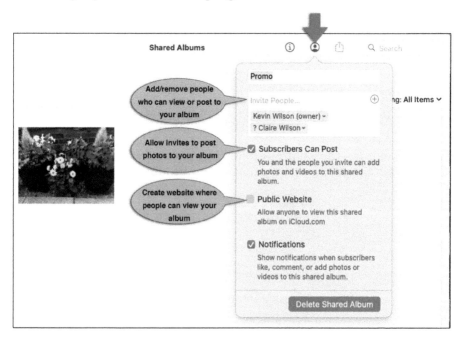

Click 'delete shared album' to delete the album. This only deletes the album not the actual images.

Printing Photos

To print photos, select the photos you want to print.

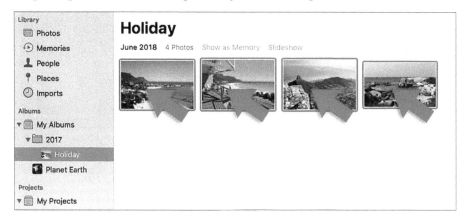

From the 'file' menu, then select 'print'.

From the print preview screen, select your printer on the top right, select paper size (eg A4), then select 'photo on photo paper'.

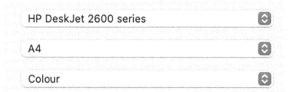

To get 4 photos on a page, select 'custom' from the layout options on the right hand side.

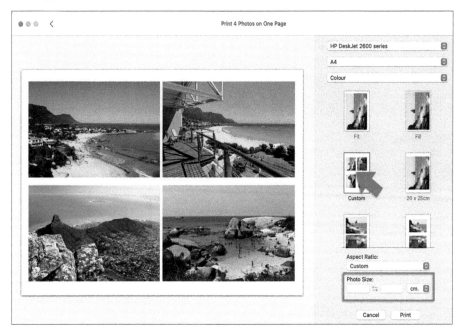

In the 'photo size' section, change the size of the photos to 9cm by 13cm. This will crop and fit four 9x13 photos onto a page.

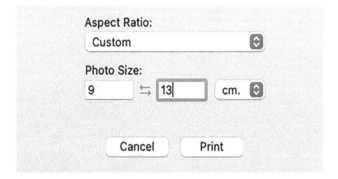

You may need to adjust the sizes slightly to fit your page - adjust until all four photos appear on the page.

Load your printer with some photo paper.

Click 'print' when you're done.

Creating Slideshows

Select the photos you want, hold down the CMD key to select multiple photographs. Right click on the selection.

From the drop down menu select 'slideshow', go down to 'create' and select 'slideshow'.

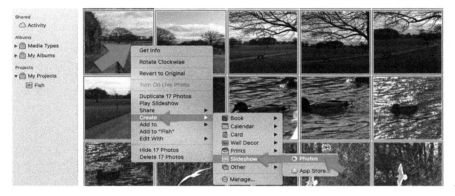

Give your slideshow a name

Double click the title text to edit the title.

Add some effects by clicking on the effects button on the right hand side, circled below far right.

In this example, I am going to apply a nice vintage photo look.

Click the music icon on the right hand side, indicated by the arrow, to add some music. You can add music from photos or you can use music from your music library.

Hit the play button to run your slideshow. Now you won't have to bore your friends and family with your holiday/vacation pictures - you can create a more interesting slideshow.

Printing & Publishing Photos

Using the printing and publishing extensions you can create personalised projects such as photo books, calendars and greeting cards.

Installing the Apps

First you'll need to install the extensions, hover your mouse over 'my projects' on the left hand side of the screen. Select 'books', then click 'app store'.

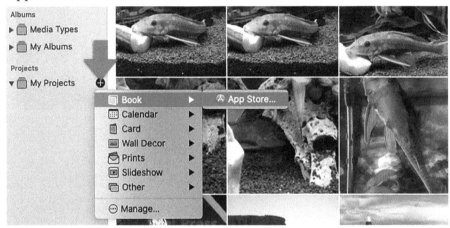

Scroll down the 'print and publish your photos' screen until you see the apps. Install both 'mimeo photos' and 'motif'.

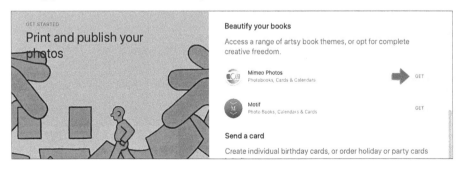

Click 'get' next to the app name. Click the green install button. Scroll down and install 'ifcolor photo products'.

Enter your Apple ID username and password if prompted.

Creating Photobooks

These make nice gifts at weddings, birthdays and special events. Select your photos from the main screen, hold down the command key to select multiple photographs. Right click on the selection, go down to 'create', select 'book' from the slideout, then click 'mimeo photos'.

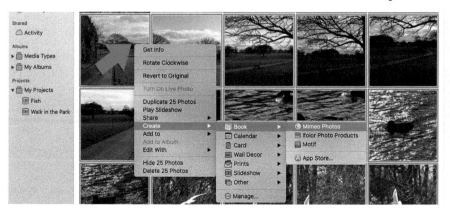

Select a style then click 'create'.

Select 'autofill my photos' on the top right.

Select a theme.

Within the app, you can now start to create your book. You'll notice that the app has automatically added all your photos.

Double click 'add title here' and type in the title of your book.

Use the left and right arrows to move between pages.

Click 'photos' on the top right. From here you can drag and drop photos onto the pages to put them into the correct order.

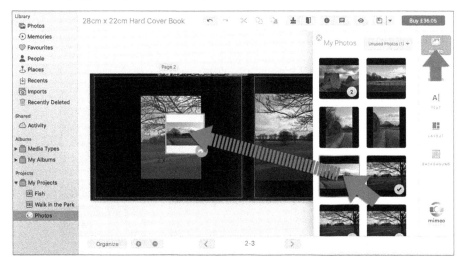

Click the 'right' arrow to browse to the next page.

Chapter 6: Using Multimedia

To change the layout of the page, click the photo on the page where you want to change the layout, then select 'layout' from the right hand side panel.

Click 'page', select your page layout (eg 3 photos on page), then select how you want the photos arranged.

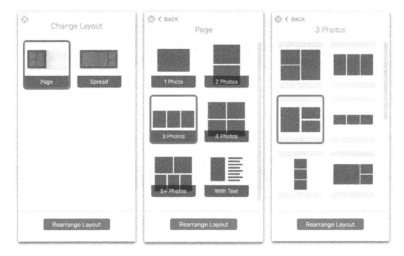

Now, select photos from the panel on the right. Drag and drop the photos you want into the placeholders.

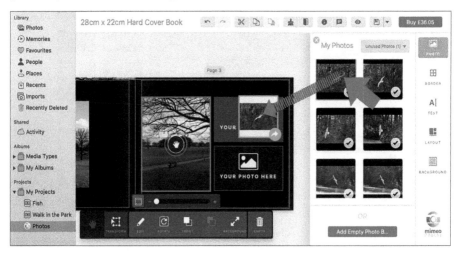

To add a text caption, click the photo, then select 'text' from the panel on the right hand side. Click 'add empty text box'.

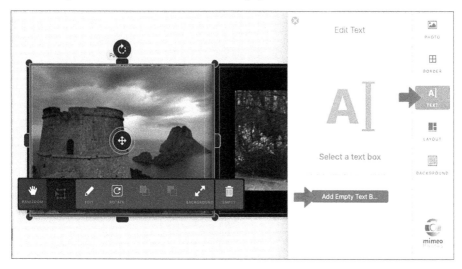

Drag the text box into position using the drag handle.

Change the font, size, color using the 'edit text' panel on the right. Type your text into the textbox.

Click 'buy' on the top right when your book is complete.

Ordering Prints

Select the photographs you want to print, hold down the command key to select multiple photographs. It's best to order at least 10 to make the order worthwhile for the cost of printing and shipping.

Right click on your selection, go down to 'create'. From the slideout select 'prints', then click the 'ifcolor photo products' app.

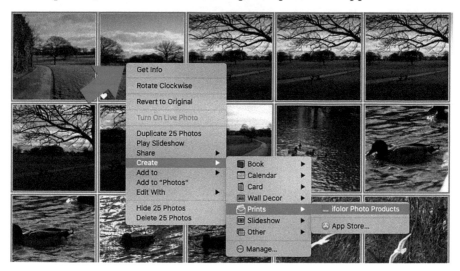

Select your country, click 'next'.

Select 'create'.

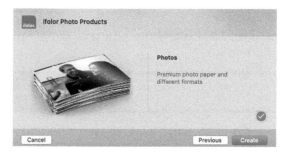

If you want a bigger size, click on a photo, select a size.

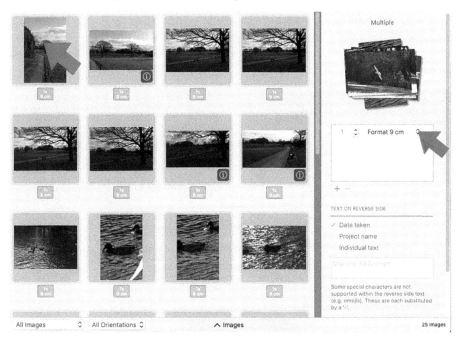

Click the photos you want. Hold down the control key on your keyboard to select multiple photos. To select them all, press the command key on your keyboard, then press 'A'.

Click 'order' on the top right when you're done. Review your order, then click 'order' on the bottom right to confirm.

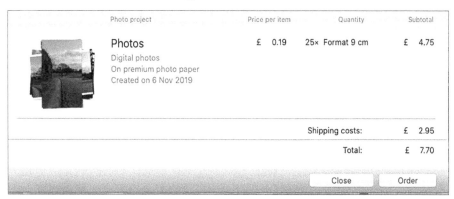

They'll post the prints to your address. You can frame and display them in your home if you wish.

Greeting Cards

You can create personalised greeting cards that are professionally printed. To create a card, select the image you want to use. Right click, select 'create' from the popup menu. Select 'card', then click 'mimeo photos'.

Select the type of card you want, eg 'folded landscape'.

Click 'create'.

Click 'autofill my photos', then select a theme.

Click the 'next' arrow on the bottom to jump to the interior of the card.

Here you can write your message. Double click in the grey placeholders and type your message in the text box.

Click 'buy' on the top right when you're done.

Live Text

Live Text detects text in photographs. It allows you to look up information, or copy handwritten and printed text from a picture to your clipboard. Useful for extracting text, names or places from photos.

Copy Text

You can use Live Text in Image Preview, Quick Look, or the Photos app. Here in the image below, I have a photograph of a sign with some text.

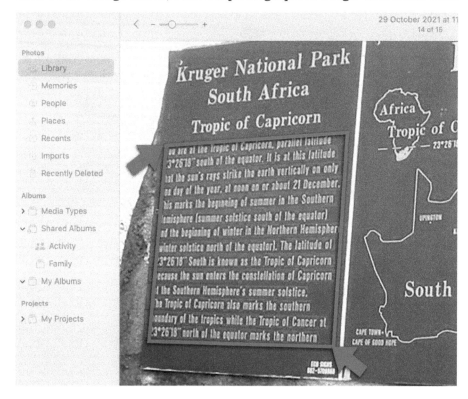

First highlight the text. To do this, click and drag the mouse over the text you want in the photograph.

Press Command C to copy the text to the clipboard.

Press Command V to paste it into another app, such as a note. Depending on the quality of the original photo, the live text feature may not recognise the text at 100% accuracy, so you may see some strange words etc. You can easily edit this.

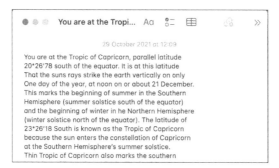

Lookup Text

You can look up words that appear in a photograph. To do this, highlight the text with your mouse, then right click. Select 'lookup' from the popup menu. *Or select 'search with google' if you want to do a google search.*

You'll be able to find articles from the dictionary and the web.

Use the slider at the bottom of the window to select a source.

Visual Lookup

Visual look up identifies popular landmarks, art, plants, flowers, pets and other objects that appear in your photos. You can use visual lookup in the photos app and image preview..

Lookup an Object

First open a photo in the photos app.

If visual lookup has identified an object in the photo, on the top right of the toolbar, you'll see an info icon with a sparkle.

Once you click on this icon, you'll see the Visual Look Up info marker appear on the photograph. Click on this to reveal information.

You can also use this feature in the preview app. You can open the image from finder.

If visual lookup has found some information, you'll see the info icon with a sparkle on the toolbar.

Once you click the info icon you'll see the Visual Look Up info marker appear on the photograph. Click on this to reveal information.

Separate Subject from Background

You can also separate the subject from the background. To do this, open the image in the photos app.

Here in this example, I want to remove the lion from the background. Hold down control, then click on the image. Select 'copy subject' from the popup menu.

Once you've copied the subject, you can paste into any app you like. For example, I'm going to paste the lion into my report document I've opened in Pages. To do this, hold down the control key on your keyboard, then click on the position where you want to paste in the image

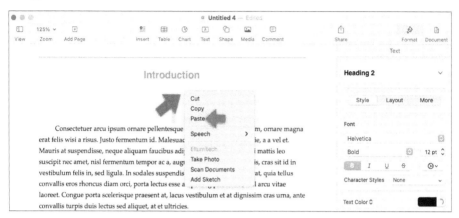

Once you paste in the image, you can move it into position. Notice that only the subject has been copied and not the background from the original photo.

Continuity Camera

To use Continuity Camera, you will need to sign into all your Apple devices with the same Apple ID (eg Mac and iPhone). Also they will need to be connected to the same Wi-Fi network with Bluetooth enabled.

You can use continuity camera to quickly snap a photo with your iPhone or iPad and have it appear instantly on your Mac. This can be useful if you're writing a Pages document and need to insert a quick photo of something. You can also use continuity camera as a scanner, to scan in photos or documents and add hand drawn sketches.

Insert Photo from iPhone/iPad

In this demo, I'm going to insert a photo taken with an iPhone directly into a Pages document.

First open your Pages document. Right click where you want the photo to appear. From the popup menu, select 'take photo'.

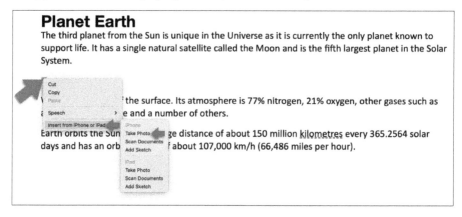

You'll see a place-holder appear asking you to take the photo with your device

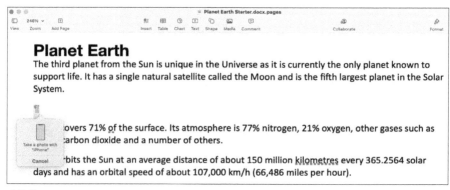

The camera app will open on your iPhone. Line up your shot, then tap the white circle to take the photo.

The photo will appear in the document.

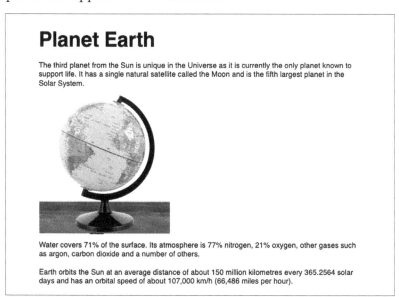

You can also scan documents using this feature, just choose 'scan documents' from the drop down menu instead of 'take photo'.

Add Sketch

For this demo, I'm going to insert a sketch from my iPad into a Pages document. To add a sketch, right click in the document where you want the sketch to appear, go down to 'insert from iphone or ipad', then under iPad click 'add sketch'.

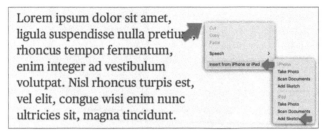

Draw your sketch on your iPad with your pencil or finger.

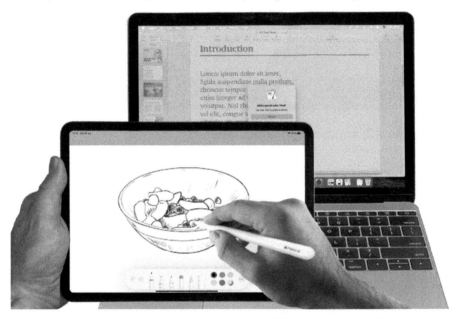

Tap 'done' on the top right of your iPad/iPhone screen. Your sketch will appear in the document on your Mac.

Scan a Document

To scan a document, right click in the desktop, go down to 'import from ipad or iphone', then select 'scan document'.

Use your iPad/iPhone to scan the document. Line the document up in the yellow outline.

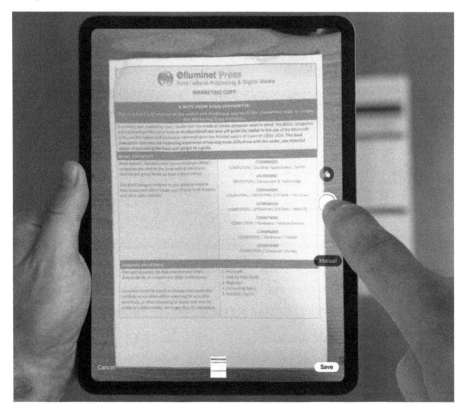

Tap 'keep scan', then scan the next page. When you've scanned all the pages, tap 'save' on the bottom right.

The scanned document will appear as a PDF on your Mac's desktop.

409

iMovie

iMovie is great for editing together your home movies. Perhaps you've just come back from your vacation/holiday, maybe a family member or friend has just got married, or maybe just collecting precious memories of your kids. You will find iMovie on launchpad or in finder.

If it's not installed, go to the app store and download it.

Importing Footage from your Camera

Connect the camera to your Mac with the USB cable. Turn your camera on and set it to 'PC Connect Mode' if required.

Now on your Mac, launch iMovie. Go to the file menu and select 'new movie'. Tap 'import media'.

Select your camera on the top left of the screen under the 'cameras' section. You'll see a thumbnail list of all the clips on your camera.

Select which video clips to import then click 'import selected'. To import all clips click 'import all'.

410

Importing Footage from your iPhone

To import video clips from your iPhone or iPad, you'll need to connect your device to your Mac using the USB cable.

Plug the cable into the bottom of your device, then plug the other end into a spare USB port on your Mac. You'll need to unlock your device with your Touch ID/Face ID, or passcode. When you do, you'll see a 'trust' prompt appear. Tap 'trust' to allow your Mac to access the media on your device.

Now on your Mac, launch iMovie. Go to the file menu and select 'new movie'.

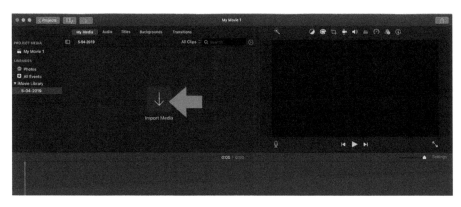

Tap 'import media'.

Select your device on the top left of the screen under the 'cameras' section. In this example, my iPhone is called 'ElluminetPress', so I'd select that one.

Here you can preview any clips and select the ones you want. Click 'import all' to import all your clips to your Mac.

Once imported, you'll see all your clips in the project window.

Now you can start to drag and drop your clips into the timeline at the bottom of the screen to create your movie.

Adding Clips

To begin editing, click and drag a clip from your photo library or imported footage to the time line at the bottom of the screen.

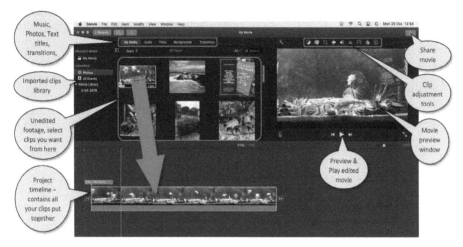

Continue to add the clips you want to appear in your movie. You can also trim or cut out bits of the clips you don't want. For example, I want to add a part of the clip below. If you hover your mouse pointer over the clip, you'll see a yellow box appear with two handles either side - this is your trim box.

Click and drag the handle to mark the part of the clip you want. You'll see a preview of the clip play as you move your mouse - this is so you can see where in the clip you currently are.

Do the same for the end of the clip also.

Click and drag the clip you just trimmed to the time line. The clip will snap into place at the end.

Do the same with any other clips you want to add to your video.

Adding Titles

To add a title, select 'titles' from the icons along the top of the screen.

Click and drag the title you want to the position on the timeline where the title is to appear.

On the preview window on the right hand side, you'll see the title text markers. Type in your titles here.

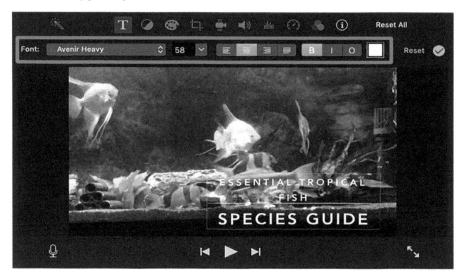

Use the tool controls along the top to change font, size, color, and so on.

Adding Music

To add a title, select 'audio' from the icons along the top of the screen.

From your music library, click and drag the track you want to the position on the timeline where the music is to start.

Transitions

You can also add transition effects between the clips. You can add a crossfade, wipe, or cut, along with various other transitions.

To add a transition, click the 'transition' icon along the top of the screen.

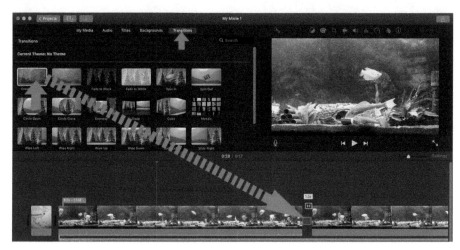

Drag the transition you want to one of the gaps between the clips on your timeline

To change the length of the transition, right click on the transition marker, and select 'precision editor' from the menu.

Now click on the yellow marker and drag it to the right to increase the length of the transition.

Click 'close precision editor', when you're done.

Animations

The only decent animation that is available is the map or globe. This is a nice feature to include in vacation/holiday videos, as you can set the location on the map to indicate where you've travelled to. You can also add backgrounds to titles.

To add an animation, click the 'backgrounds' icon along the top of the screen. Click and drag one of the map/globe animations to the position on the video the animation is to appear.

Double click on the animation in the timeline. You'll see a preview of the animation in the preview screen on the right hand side. Here you can customise it

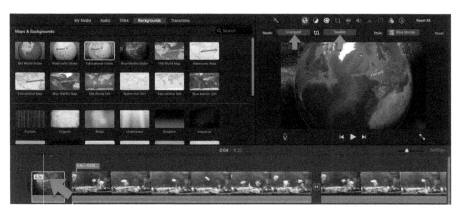

Add your travel destinations in the route options at the top of the preview window.

Now when you play the animation, you'll see a map of your route.

Music App

Apple have split iTunes into three different apps: music app, podcasts app, and TV app. In this section we'll take a look at the Music App.

There are two ways you can buy your music. You can subscribe to Apple Music and stream any track you like from the music library for a monthly subscription fee. Or you can purchase and download the albums or tracks individually from the iTunes Store.

Subscribing to Apple Music

Let's take a look at Apple Music. With Apple Music you need a constant internet connection. At the time of writing, there are three subscription options for Apple Music.

- £4.99 a month gives you full access to the music library and is only available for University/College students.

- £9.99 a month gets you full access to the music library and many radio stations available. This is an individual account and allows only one account access to the iTunes Store.

- £14.99 a month gets you full access to the music library and radio stations and allows up to 6 people to sign in and listen to their music. This is ideal for families.

To sign up, open the Music App. From the list on the sidebar, select 'listen now'.

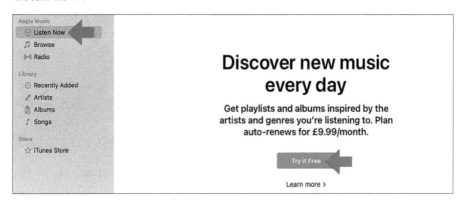

To get started, tap 'try for free', or 'start listening'.

Choose a membership programme, then tap 'start trial', or 'join Apple music'.

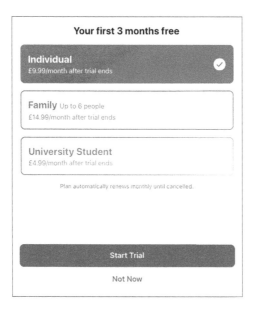

Enter your Apple ID username and password, or confirm with touch ID, if you have this enabled, by placing your finger on the home button.

The Main Screen

You can use the links under the 'Apple music' section of the sidebar.

Here under 'listen now', you'll find curated playlists that have been compiled according to your listening habits. Click on the icons to view albums and tracks. Click 'browse' to browse through all the latest music releases. Click 'radio' to listen to various radio stations

Searching for Music

To search for an artist or band, type the name into the search field on the top left of the screen. Select the closest match from the list of suggestions.

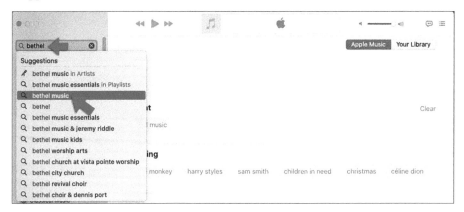

From here you can click on a song to listen to it, click and album to open it.

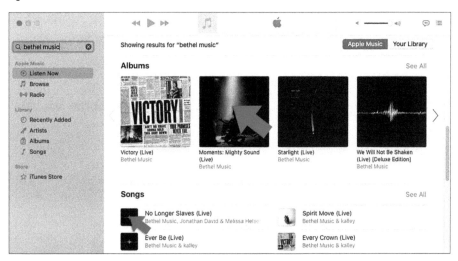

You'll see the track start to play at the top of the screen.

Add to Library

You can start to create a library of your favourite music, so it's easy to find. You can create a list of songs you want to listen to. To do this, tap the + sign next to the song you want to add to your library. If you want to add the whole album tap '+add'.

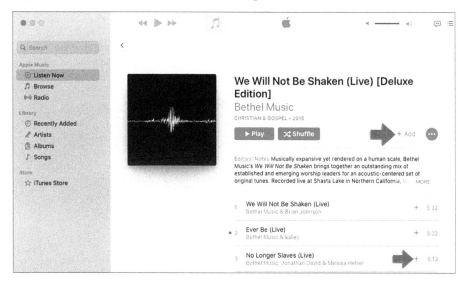

You can access your music library using the links under the 'library' section on the sidebar.

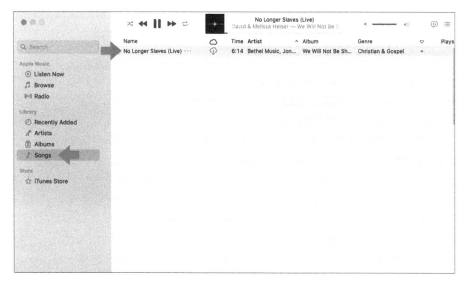

Select 'songs' to view the tracks you've added as a list, click albums to view as an album, click artists to view as artist.

Creating Playlists

You can create playlists to play all your favourite tracks from any album or artist.

To add a track to a playlist, click on the track in the list of songs, then from the popup menu, select 'add to a playlist.

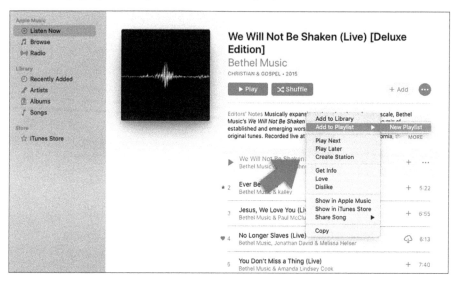

Select the playlist you want to add the track to, if it exists. Or tap 'new playlist' to add the track to a new playlist.

You'll find the playlists under the 'playlist' section on the sidebar. Click the playlist to view the tracks. Click a track to start playing.

Importing CDs

Somewhat outdated technology nowadays, but if you still have audio CDs, you can import them. First you'll need an external CD drive. Plug the drive into a USB port on your Mac and insert a CD.

Open the music app on your Mac, your CD will appear under 'devices' on the left hand panel. Click on the CD to open. Click 'import CD' to begin.

Click 'ok' on the 'import settings' popup.

Adding Tracks to your iPhone, or iPad Manually

Tracks you download from the iTunes Store or stream from Apple Music will automatically synchronise across your devices. If you want to add music you've imported from a CD or other source you can add the tracks to your device. To do this, plug your iPad or iPhone into your Mac using the USB cable.

On your Mac, open finder.

Select your iPad/iPhone from the left hand pane. Click 'trust' if prompted on your Mac and iPad.

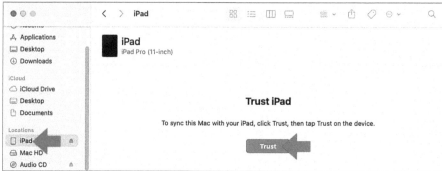

Now, open the music app.

Select the tracks you want, then drag them to your iPad/iPhone under the devices section on the left hand side.

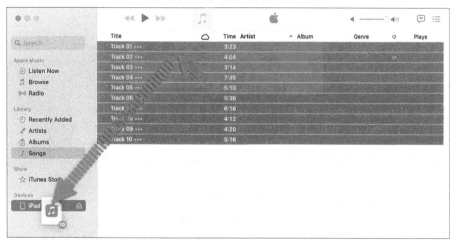

You'll be able to find the tracks on your iPad/iPhone.

Burning CDs

CDs are somewhat outdated technology nowadays however, it is sometimes useful to burn tracks to a CD. Macs no longer include DVD/CD drives, so you'll need an external CD drive.

To do this, first you'll need to create a playlist with all the tracks you want on the CD. When adding music to your playlist, as a guide, keep an eye on the status bar at the bottom middle of the main window, an 80 minute CD will hold 1.2 hours. If you go over this, you'll need more than one CD.

'Use Sound Check' is useful when you have made a compilation of songs from different albums. It makes sure all the songs are at the same volume level, so you don't have to raise or lower the volume too much when you're listening to the CD in the car or on a CD player. Make sure 'Gap Between Songs' is set to none or automatic.

Insert a blank CD-R then click burn.

Podcasts App

A podcast is a series digital audio files and sometimes video files you can listen to. You can listen to all sorts of podcasts. To begin, click the podcasts icon on your dock or on launchpad.

Once the app starts, you can browse through the latest podcasts. Along the left hand side of the screen you'll see a side panel.

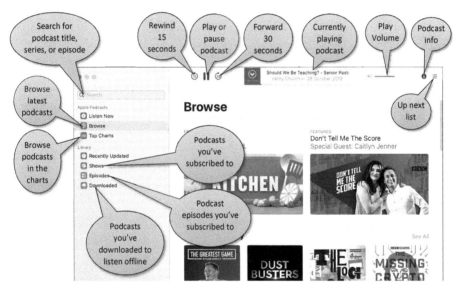

The best way to find your podcasts is to search for them. You can search for artist name, program name, or any area of interest. To search, click the search field on the top of the sidebar panel on the left hand side.

Type the podcast you're looking for in the search field at the top of the screen, the select the podcast you want from the results.

Click 'subscribe' to get updates when new episodes are posted.

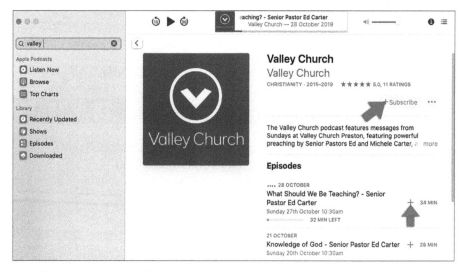

You'll find all your subscribed podcasts in your library or on the 'listen now' tab.

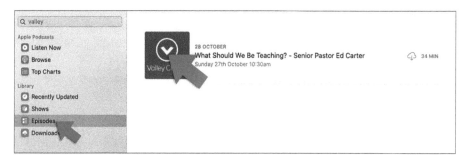

Click 'episodes' on the left hand side. You'll see a list of the episodes you've added. Click the podcast thumbnail to listen.

Hit the cloud icon next to the episode if you want to download the podcast to listen offline.

To delete a podcast, right click on the podcast and select 'remove'.

iTunes Store

If you've subscribed to Apple Music, you won't see the iTunes Store. To access the iTunes Store, open the Music App then click on 'iTunes Store' on the side panel on the left hand side of the screen.

Once the app has loaded you can browse through music, movies and tv shows - tap the category icons across the top of the screen. You can also type what you are looking for in the search field on the top right of the screen.

To search for your favourite tracks, artists and albums, click on the search field on the top left, then select 'iTunes Store' on the top right.

Type your search into the field at the top. Then select the closest match from the suggestions.

Along the top of the search results, you can view by song or album. Scroll up and down the list to see the songs and albums.

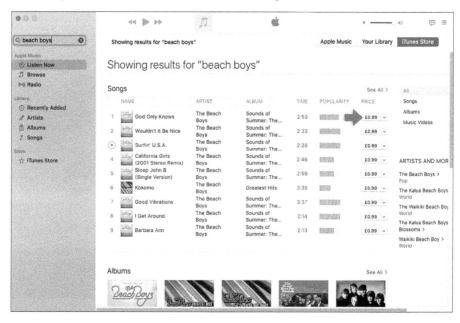

Click on the price tag to download the song. You'll need to enter your Apple ID email address and password to verify and confirm the purchase

Once the songs are downloaded you will find then in your recently added playlist under the 'library' section of the sidebar.

Apple TV App

Gearing up for Apple's new streaming service Apple TV+, the Apple TV App becomes your entertainment hub where you'll find all your purchased or rented films, music, and TV programmes. You'll find the app on your home screen.

Here, you'll be able to subscribe to Apple's streaming service and stream the latest TV Programmes and movies direct to your iPad.

Watch Now

When you first start the app, you'll land on the 'watch now' page.

Along the top of the screen you can select movies, tv shows, kids shows and your library of media you've purchased or rented. In the middle of the screen, you'll be able to scroll through current TV Shows and movie releases. Tap on the thumbnail icons to view details, or tap 'see more' on the top right to see more content.

Chapter 6: Using Multimedia

Searching for Media

To search for a specific movie or tv show, type the name into the search field on the top right.

In the search results, click on the thumbnail cover to view the details.

On the film details screen you'll be able to read details about the film, reviews and ratings. Click 'rent' or 'buy'. Verify your purchase using your Apple ID username and password.

You'll find your downloaded films and TV programmes in the library section of the TV App.

Library

Select 'library' from icons along the top of the screen.

Select 'movies' to see movies you've rented or purchased, similarly select 'tv shows' if you've downloaded a tv show.

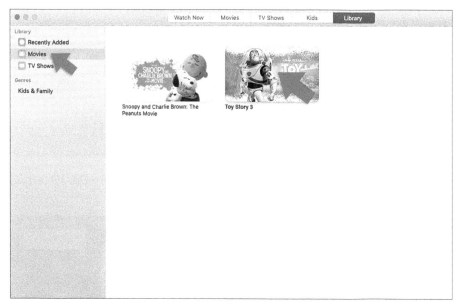

Tap on the movie or tv programme to begin playback.

Apple TV+ Streaming

Apple TV+ is a video streaming service where you can subscribe and watch TV shows and movies.

Select 'watch now' from the icons along the top of the screen

Scroll to the Apple TV channels section and choose Apple TV+.

Select 'try it for free'.

Click 'confirm' on the dialog box, then enter your Apple ID email address and password when prompted.

434

Airplay

Airplay allows wireless streaming of audio and video data to Apple TV, a Mac, or compatible receiver on your TV.

Apple TV

For this to work, both your Mac and Apple TV will need to be on the same WiFi network. This is usually the case in most homes.

To mirror your Mac, click the airplay icon on the bottom left of the play window during playback.

Select the tick box next to your Apple TV. Enter your Apple TV passcode if prompted.

Chapter 6: Using Multimedia

If you don't know the Apple TV passcode, go on your Apple TV, then go to settings > Airplay, select 'Onscreen code'. You can turn off the code or set a new one.

Now you can watch your program on the big screen. Here below I have my Apple TV plugged into a digital projector. The Macbook on the right is streaming a movie to Apple TV.

AirPlay to Mac

This feature turns your Mac into an AirPlay receiver. This means you can stream music and video from an iPhone or iPad to your Mac.

To activate 'AirPlay to Mac', open the system preferences.

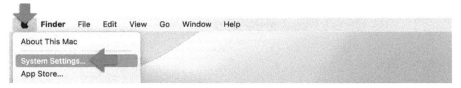

Select 'general' from the list on the left hand side, then click 'airplay & handoff'.

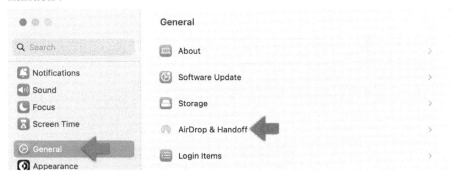

Turn on 'airplay receiver'. Under 'allow airplay for', selecting 'anyone on the same network' will allow anyone connected to the same WiFi network to stream media. Selecting 'everyone' will allow anyone to stream media.

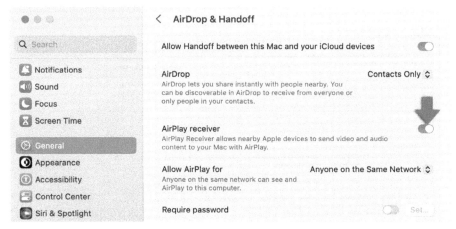

You can also set a password. Turn on 'require password', then enter the password you want to use.

To stream media, on your iPad/iPhone select the music track or video, then tap the 'airplay' icon at the bottom of the screen. Select your Mac.

You'll hear the media play on your Mac.

AirPlay will stream from any iPhone or iPad running iOS / iPadOS 15 or later. This feature works on all Macs released in 2018 or later.

Cancelling Subscriptions

First open the system settings.

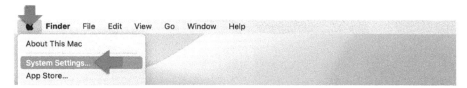

From the settings app, select 'Apple id' on the top left. Select 'media & purchases'.

Next to 'subscriptions' click 'manage'.

Click 'edit' next to the subscription you want to cancel.

Click 'cancel subscription'.

Maintaining your Mac

In this section we'll take a look at some of the security aspects of Macs and how to go about putting it into practice.

In this chapter, we'll take a look at

- Firewalls
- Do Apple Macs get Viruses?
- Downloading MacOS Sonoma
- Installing MacOS Sonoma
- Create a Boot Drive
- Booting from a USB Drive
- Internet Restore
- App Updates
- System Updates
- Mac Storage Management
- Disk Utility
- FileVault
- Encrypt External Drive
- Decrypt External Drive
- Reset SMC
- Reset NVRAM

To help you better understand this section, take a look at the video resources. Open your web browser and navigate to the following site:

elluminetpress.com/mac-sys

Firewalls

A firewall helps prevent unauthorised access to your Mac and works by monitoring incoming and outgoing network traffic according to a set of rules.

A firewall won't protect you against malware and viruses, so adequate anti-virus software is still necessary but it is your first line of defence against a hacker trying to gain access to your computer or some malicious software trying to send data.

Enabling the Firewall

To set up your firewall, open the system settings, then select 'network' from the list on the left.

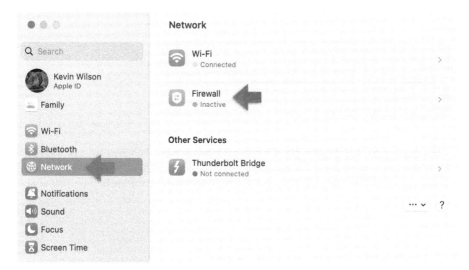

Click the switch to turn on the firewall if it is inactive.

Firewall Settings

To change the firewall settings, allow or block an app, follow the steps in the previous section, then click 'options' on the bottom right.

Here, you can block all incoming connections, allow signed apps to automatically connect, or block an app. Just click in the selection box to the right of the app in the list - set it to allow or block.

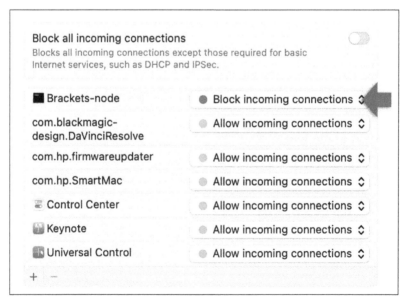

To remove an app from the list, select it, then click the '-' icon on the bottom left. If you want to add an app, click the '+' icon on the bottom left.

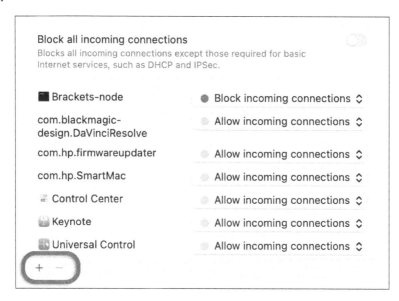

Select the app, then set the selection box next to the app to either block or allow.

Underneath you can automatically allow any built in software such as Mail, FaceTime, Safari, as well as software from trusted suppliers such as Microsoft, Adobe, Apple and Google.

Stealth mode hides your mac and prevents it from responding to probe requests from other machines on the internet.

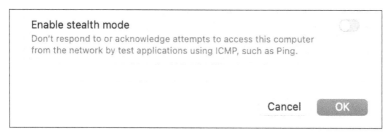

Do Apple Macs get Viruses?

Yes they do! The likelihood of a Mac getting a virus when compared to a Windows user is less, since there are more Windows users than Mac users. Although MacOS is more secure than many versions of Windows, it still has its own security vulnerabilities.

As Macs become more popular, more and more malware is being developed to target MacOS. Even though Macs are more secure, make sure you are protected, as you can still be a victim of trojan horses, phishing, ransomware and other online fraud. So don't fall victim to the 'macs don't get viruses' myth. Hackers and cyber thieves aren't after your computer, they're after your personal information so they can steal your identity, pin numbers and bank or credit card details. They'll try and trick you into handing this information over by pretending to be your bank, the IRS, or someone in authority. This is known as phishing. Learn to protect yourself, don't click on links in emails as these can be spoofed. Go directly to the site using the official URL and sign in.

A free simple anti virus for mac is Avast. There are a lot of different ones out there, but this one is free, small, fast and up to date so is a good place to start. It has a web shield to help protect you when you are browsing the web and warns you about websites that may have been compromised or reported as fake or fraudulent. It also has a email shield that scans incoming emails for worms and other threats.

You can download it here.

www.avast.com/mac

Once on their website, click the 'free download' link.

Go to the downloads folder in your finder and double click on the following file. `avast_security_online.dmg`

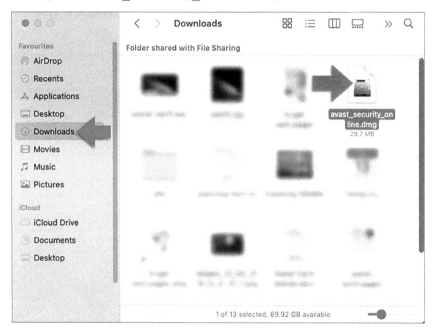

In the finder window that appears, double click on 'avast security' to install.

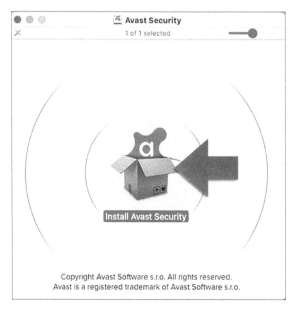

Follow the instructions on screen.

Downloading & Installing Sonoma

You can download MacOS Sonoma free of charge from the App Store and upgrade your Mac automatically.

Go to the App Store and click the download link. If it isn't on the home page you can search for it. Type in 'macOS Sonoma'.

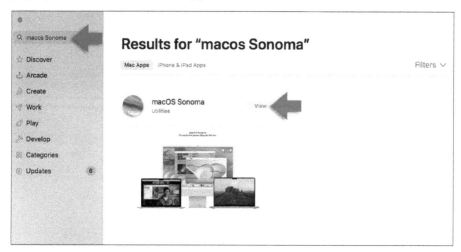

Click on 'view' next to 'macOS Sonoma'. On the details page click 'get' to start downloading Sonoma.

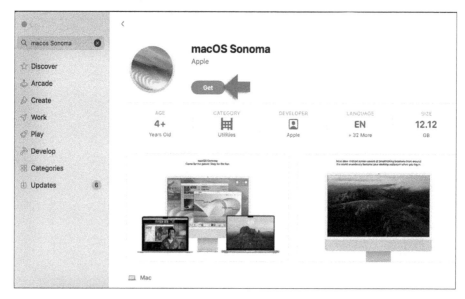

This download will take some time as it is over 10GB.

Once you have downloaded the installer from the app store, you'll see the MacOS installer screen.

If you don't see the installer screen, you will be able to find it in finder/applications. Click finder on the bottom left of your dock, then select 'Applications'.

Double click the installer circled above to start the installer.

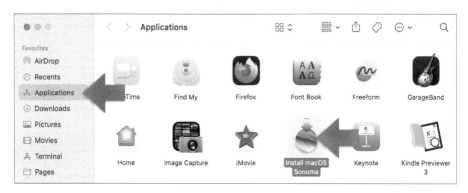

Click 'continue' on the installer screen, follow the on screen instructions to complete the installation.

The installation will take a while. This is automated so you don't need to do anything.

Your mac may reboot a couple of times.

Once MacOS has installed, you'll need to run through the initial setup covered in 'starting your mac for the first time' on page 30.

Create a Boot Drive

Creating a boot drive or recovery drive is always a good idea in case your mac crashes or your hard drive fails.

To begin, plug in a USB flash drive formatted using Mac OS Extended. See page 461 for information on how to format a drive. Here I've used disk utility to format the drive using 'mac os extended'. I've also named it 'Untitled'. Keep note of the name for later.

You'll need a drive that is at least 32GB.

Open the App Store from the dock. Type `macos Sonoma` into the search field on the top left of the screen. Click 'view' next to 'macOS Sonoma'

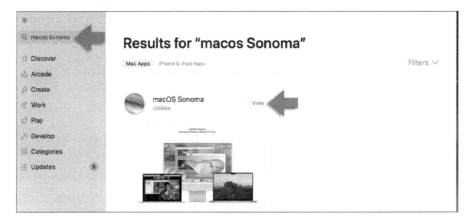

Then click 'get' to download.

If the 'software update' window, click 'download' to begin downloading the macOS installer. This will take some time to download depending on how fast your internet connection is.

Once the installer launches, ignore the install screen. Open launch pad from the dock, then click on 'other'.

Select 'terminal' from the folder.

You'll see a window appear with either a white or black screen where you can type in commands.

```
admin — createinstallme ‹ sudo — 80×24
Last login: Tue Nov  1 09:49:24 on console
admin@Mac ~ %
```

You'll need to be logged into your mac using an account with administrator privileges.

Type the following command in one full line - note that the command is case sensitive. Replace 'Untitled' with the name of your USB drive if you named it something else when formatting. **Note this will erase the entire drive.**

sudo '/Applications/Install macOS Sonoma.app/ Contents/Resources/createinstallmedia' **--volume** '/Volumes/Untitled'

Press enter on your keyboard. Type in your account password - usually the password you use to log into your mac.

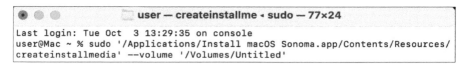

```
●  ●  ●              user — createinstallme ‹ sudo — 77×24

Last login: Tue Oct  3 13:29:35 on console
user@Mac ~ % sudo '/Applications/Install macOS Sonoma.app/Contents/Resources/
createinstallmedia' --volume '/Volumes/Untitled'
```

Press Y, then hit enter on your keyboard to begin.

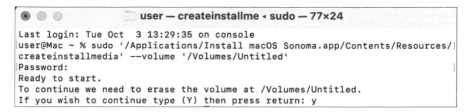

```
●  ●  ●              user — createinstallme ‹ sudo — 77×24

Last login: Tue Oct  3 13:29:35 on console
[user@Mac ~ % sudo '/Applications/Install macOS Sonoma.app/Contents/Resources/]
createinstallmedia' --volume '/Volumes/Untitled'
[Password:                                                                    ]
Ready to start.
To continue we need to erase the volume at /Volumes/Untitled.
If you wish to continue type (Y) then press return: y
```

If prompted, click 'ok' to allow the terminal app access to your removable device.

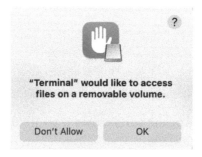

"Terminal" would like to access
files on a removable volume.

Don't Allow   OK

This will take some time to complete.

```
Ready to start.
To continue we need to erase the volume at /Volumes/Untitled.
If you wish to continue type (Y) then press return: y
Erasing disk: 0%... 10%... 20%... 30%... 100%
Making disk bootable...
Copying to disk: 0%... 10%... 20%... 30%... 40%... 50%... 60%... 70%... 80%... 9
0%... 100%
Install media now available at "/Volumes/Install macOS Ventura"
admin@Mac ~ %
```

Booting from a USB Drive

Now, to boot your Mac from the flash drive, insert the drive into a USB port and restart your mac.

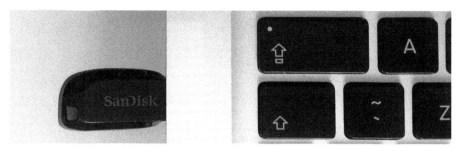

If you're using a new Mac with the **Apple Silicon (M1, M2 etc)**, press and hold the power button until you see the boot menu.

If you're using an **Intel Mac**, when you hear the start up chime, hold down the Alt or Option key on your keyboard.

This will bring up the start up options menu.

Select your USB drive from the start up options.

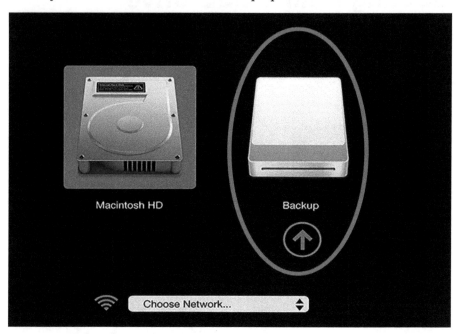

Now you'll need to run through the set up procedure. Hit 'continue', and follow the on screen instructions.

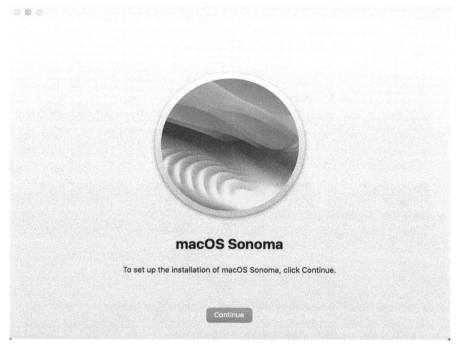

Agree to the terms and conditions. Click 'agree'.

Select the disk you want to install Sonoma onto. This is usually your system disk and is already selected. Click 'install'.

Now, if you have a time machine backup, plug in your external drive, and select 'restore from time machine backup', otherwise click 'install macOS...' to install a brand new system from scratch. Click 'continue'.

If you selected 'restore from time machine backup', select your time machine backup disk from the list, then select the latest backup from the list.

Follow the instructions on the screen to finish installing MacOS Sonoma. Your Mac will restart itself a few times...

You'll need to run through 'starting your mac for the first time' on page 30.

Internet Restore

If you have replaced the hard disk on your Mac, or need to re-install MacOS, you can do this over the internet rather than creating a restore disk.

If you're using a new Mac with the **Apple Silicon (M1, 2 etc)**, press and hold the power button until you see the boot menu. Then select 'options'.

Select your username from the list if prompted.

If you're using an **Intel Mac**, start your machine, then quickly hold down **Command-Option-R** until you see the Spinning World Logo on the screen.

Once started, you'll land on the MacOS Options screen.

From here, you can install MacOS. Select 'reinstall macOS Sonoma'. Follow the instructions on screen. You'll need to run through 'starting your mac for the first time' on page 30.

App Updates

To check if there are any updates for apps you have installed, open the app store and select the 'updates' option from the panel on the left hand side of the screen.

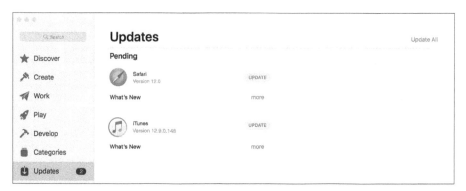

If any updates are available, they will be listed here. To apply all the available updates, click 'update all' on the top right of the screen.

To apply updates to individual apps, click 'update' next to the update in the list.

System Updates

To update Mac OS, open the system settings, select 'general' from the list on the left. Then select 'software update'.

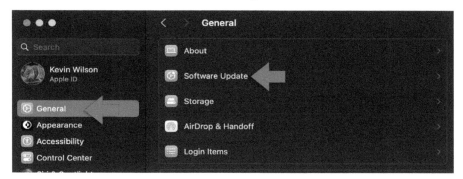

If there are any updates available, they will be listed here. Click 'update now' to apply the updates.

To change update settings, click on the 'i' icon on the top right next to 'automatic updates'.

Enable all the options. Enabling 'check for updates' will automatically check to see if there are new updates.

Similarly 'download new updates when available' will download the updates for you, 'install macOS updates' will automatically install a new update to macOS, 'install application updates from app store' will make sure all your apps are up to date, and 'install security response and system files' will make sure any security issues are fixed.

Mac Storage Management

The Storage Management window shows the current hard drive space and offers recommendations for optimising your storage.

Open the system settings, select 'general' from the list on the left. Click on 'storage'.

Here, you can hover your mouse pointer over each of the colored bars to see how much space it's taking up.

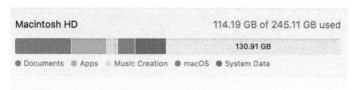

Underneath, you'll see some recommendations.

Store in iCloud moves messages to your iCloud rather than on your Mac. Optimise Storage, automatically remove watched films and TV programmes. When storage space is needed on your Mac, films or TV programmes purchased from the iTunes Store will be removed from your Mac. If you turn on 'empty bin automatically' your Mac will permanently delete files older than 30 days.

Listed underneath, you'll see a list of categories.

Each category contains specific files

- Applications contains all the apps installed on your Mac.
- Documents lists all the documents saved on your Mac.
- iCloud Drive contains all files stored in iCloud Drive.
- iOS files contains iOS backups and firmware.
- TV, Music, Books and Podcasts contains purchases from that specific app, which can be removed from your Mac and downloaded again.
- Mail contains emails and attachments.
- Messages contains content from Messages conversations, including attachments.
- Photos contains all the photos saved in the Photos App.
- Trash contains items you have deleted

To see details of each of these categories, click on the 'i' icon to the right.

Here in the 'large files' tab, you'll see a list of files saved on your mac or sorted by size. You can go through these and delete the ones you don't want. To do this, select the file, click 'delete'.

Under 'downloads' you'll see a list of all the files you've downloaded. In 'unsupported apps', you'll find a list of apps that wont run on your mac.

Disk Utility

You can use the disk utility to partition, format or erase a hard disk. You can also use the disk utility to scan a disk for errors and effect repairs. This utility should be used with caution as misuse can cause data loss.

To start the disk utility, open launch pad and select 'other'.

Click 'disk utility' to start the app.

Lets take a look at the app.

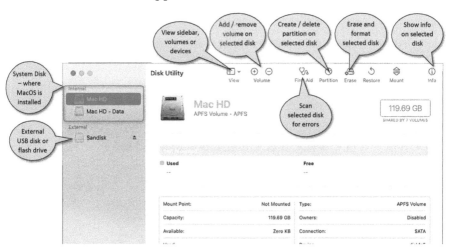

Select a disk from the panel on the left hand side. From here, you can scan your disks for errors using the 'first aid' icon on the toolbar. You can also partition and format new disks as well as external disks and flash drives.

Checking Drives

To check a drive for errors, select the drive from the side panel, then click the 'first aid' icon on the toolbar.

Formatting Drives

If you have a new drive, external drive, or flash drive, you'll need to format it first.

To format a drive, select the drive from the side panel, then click the 'erase' icon on the toolbar.

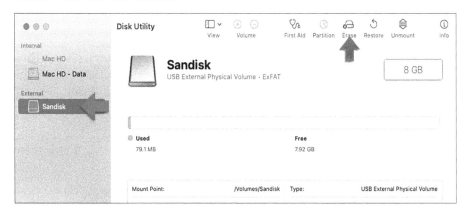

Make sure you select the correct drive as formatting will erase any data on the disk.

Give the drive a meaningful name. Click the drop down menu next to 'format'.

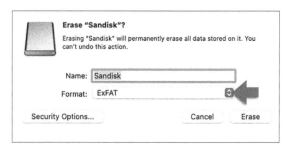

Select a disk format. If you are going to use your drive only on a Mac, choose MacOS Extended (journaled) or APFS. If you are formatting an external drive and intend on using it on different machines such as Windows, Mac, or Linux, use ExFAT.

Click 'security options' on the bottom left.

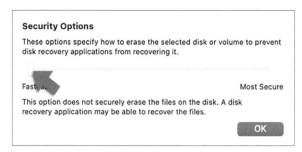

The security options allow you to select how secure the erase operation is. Drag the slider to the right to select the options.

Option 1 does not securely erase the files on the disk. A disk recovery application may be able to recover the files. Useful for every day data.

Option 2 writes a pass of random data, and then a single pass of zeros over the entire disk. It erases the information used to access your files and writes over the data two times. Useful for every day data.

Option 3 writes 2 passes of random data followed by a single pass of known data over the entire disk. It erases the information used to access your files and writes over the data 3 times. Useful if the drive contains sensitive information.

Option 4 erases the information used to access your files and writes over the data 7 times. Useful if the drive contains sensitive information.

Click 'erase' when you're done. The disk utility will format your drive.

Partitioning Drives

A partition is just a fancy word for a storage space on a disk drive. Drive partitioning allows users to divide a physical disk drive into multiple storage spaces.

You can partition a drive using the disk utility. To do this, select the drive you want to partition in the sidebar, then click the partition icon.

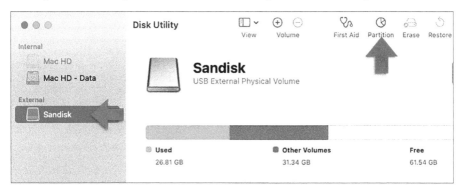

Select 'partition' from the dialog box if prompted.

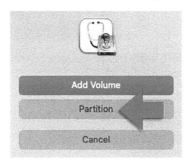

You'll see the current partition information for the drive you selected. .

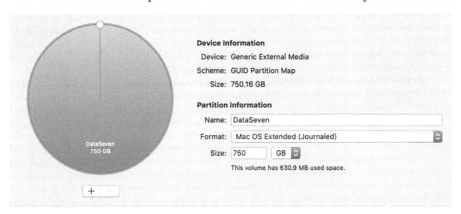

To resize the current partition, hold down the command key on your keyboard, click and drag the resize handle at the top of the pie chart on the left hand side. Note you can't resize FAT or ExFAT formats.

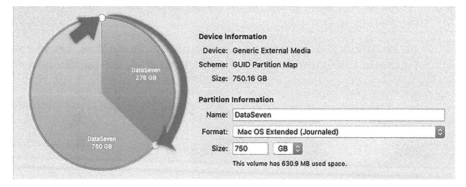

To create a new partition, click the '+' icon on the bottom left.

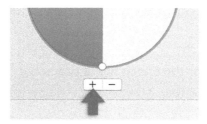

The pie chart on the left will divide into two halves. In the name field on the right enter a name for the partition. Set the disk format (eg MacOS Extended (journaled), APFS or ExFAT).

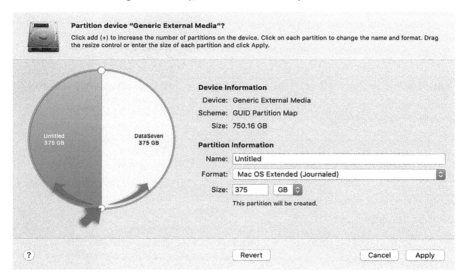

Click 'apply'.

FileVault

FileVault allows you to encrypt the data on your Mac with 256-bit encryption to help prevent unauthorized access to your data. Any subsequent changes to your data will be automatically encrypted. You'll only be able to access the data with your login password or encryption key.

To set up FileVault, open the system settings app, select 'privacy & security' from the list on the left. Scroll down to 'security', then click 'Turn On' next to 'FileVault'.

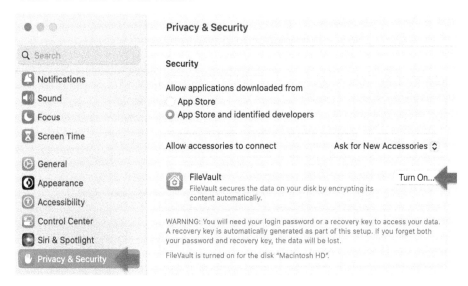

Now select 'allow my iCloud account to unlock my disk', then click 'continue'. This is the safest way. If you lose or forget your password, you can still reset your password and recover your data. If you lose a recovery key your data is lost.

MacOS will begin to encrypt your disk. This can take a while.

Encrypt External Drive

This will work on any external drive formatted using 'APFS' or 'MacOS Extended (journalled)' format with a 'GUID partition map' scheme.

Plug in the drive, open finder, right click on the drive. Select 'encrypt'.

Enter a password for the drive, then click 'encrypt disk'.

Decrypt External Drive

Select the external drive from finder, right-click on the drive, then select 'decrypt'. Enter the password used to encrypt the drive.

Lockdown Mode

Lockdown Mode is designed to protect against the most sophisticated digital threats and cyber attacks. Most people are never be targeted by such attacks, however if you are then this feature will help protect you.

You should keep this feature disabled as enabling it means your Mac won't function as it normally would because certain apps, websites and networking features will be severely limited. Message and Mail attachment types will be blocked and links will be unavailable. Websites load more slowly and wont operate correctly since cookies, scripting and other technologies will be blocked. Also incoming FaceTime calls will be blocked unless you've previously called that person or contact.

Open the settings app, then from the list on the left select 'privacy & security'.

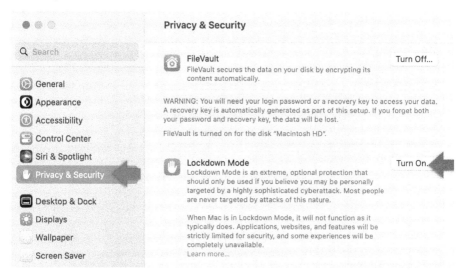

Scroll down to 'lockdown mode', then click 'turn on'. Enter your user password if prompted.

Click 'turn on & restart'.

Allow your mac to restart then sign back in.

When Lockdown Mode is enabled, you'll receive notifications when an app or feature is limited, and a banner in Safari will tell you that Lockdown Mode is turned on.

Mac Password Reset

If you've forgotten your Mac password, you can use your Apple ID reset the login password.

After three failed attempts at signing in, you'll see some options underneath the password box to reset the password with your Apple ID.

Click the arrow next to 'reset and show password reset options'. If you don't know your Apple ID click 'restart and show reset options'.

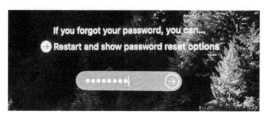

Allow your Mac to restart. Enter your iCloud Apple ID email address and password, then click 'next'.

Follow the instructions to verify your identity and reset your mac login password.

If you have multiple users on your Mac with administrator access, log in with an administrator account, open the settings app, click on 'users & groups'.

Click on the 'i' icon next to the name of the user whose password you want to change. Click the 'reset' button next to 'password'.

Reset SMC

The SMC or System Management Controller, is responsible for controlling the power button, battery, temperature control of internal components, keyboard backlight, video sources, fan speed, and various status indicators.

If your Mac doesn't respond when you press the power button even if it's plugged in, shuts down unexpectedly or is generally running slowly, you can try reset the SMC.

Note there is no system management controller on the Macs with Apple Silicon (M1, M2 etc).

Intel Macbooks (2018+)

For MacBook Pro and MacBook Air models released in 2018 or later with T2 chip

First shut down your Mac.

On your keyboard hold down:

Left Control, Left Option, Right Shift, and the Power Button

Hold these down for 7 seconds.

Release all the keys, then press the power button again to start your Mac as normal.

Older Intel Macbooks

For MacBook Pro models released mid-2009 to 2017 and MacBook Air models released in 2017 or earlier

First shut down your Mac.

On your keyboard hold down:

Left Shift, Left Control, Left Option and the Power Button. Hold these at the same time for 10 seconds.

Release all the keys, then press the power button again to start your Mac as normal.

Intel iMac, Mac Pro and Mac Mini

First shut down your Mac.

Disconnect the power cable.

Press and hold the power button for 5 seconds.

Reattach the power cables and start Mac as usual.

Reset NVRAM

NVRAM or Non-volatile Random Access Memory, is a small memory chip on your Mac that is used to store time zone, sound volume, startup-disk, and other settings.

If you experience issues related to these settings or others, resetting NVRAM might help. For example, if your Mac starts up from a disk drive other than the one selected in Startup Disk preferences, or a question mark icon briefly appears before your Mac starts up, you might need to reset NVRAM.

Note there is no NVRAM controller on the Macs with Apple Silicon (M1, M2 etc).

First, shut down your Mac.

Press the power button to start your Mac, then quickly hold down:

Option, Command, P, and R

Hold these keys for about 20 seconds, during which your Mac might appear to restart. You'll hear two start up chimes.

Release the keys after you hear the second chime or see the Apple logo.

Video Resources

To help you understand the procedures and concepts explored in this book, we have developed some video resources and app demos for you to use, as you work through the book.

As well as the video resources, you'll also find some downloadable files and samples for exercises that appear in the book.

To find the resources, open your web browser and navigate to the following website

`elluminetpress.com/mac-os/`

Do not use a search engine, type the website into the address field at the top of the browser window.

At the beginning of each chapter, you'll find a website that contains the resources for that chapter.

Using the Videos

When you open the link to the video resources, you'll see a thumbnail list at the bottom.

Click on the thumbnail for the particular video you want to watch. Most videos are between 30 and 60 seconds outlining the procedure, others are a bit longer.

You'll also find additional tips and documents in the bonus section. These sections are updated all the time.

As well as some video courses and tutorials for you to try.

MacOS Fundamentals

March 27, 2023

This course is currently running and new lessons will be added each week. If you have a suggestion for a lesson please contact us. Whether you are completely new to Mac...

Files

To save the files into your Mac, right click on the icons above and select 'download linked file as'.

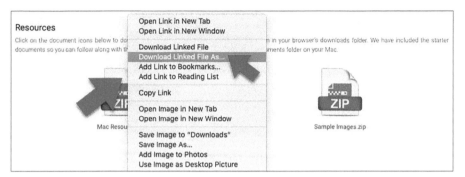

In the dialog box that appears, click the down arrow to show the full dialog box.

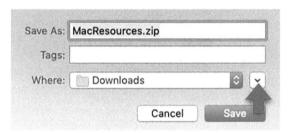

Select the folder you want to save the download into. Use 'pictures'.

Click 'save'.

Once you have downloaded the zip file, open finder and go to your 'pictures' folder. Double click on the zip file to extract all the files.

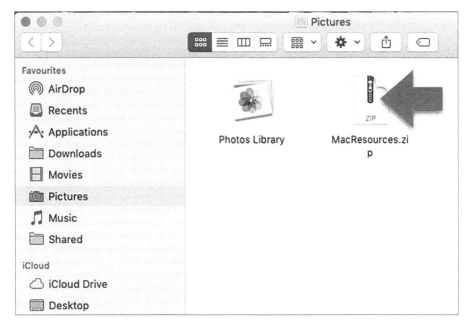

This will create a new folder in your pictures called 'Macs Resources'.

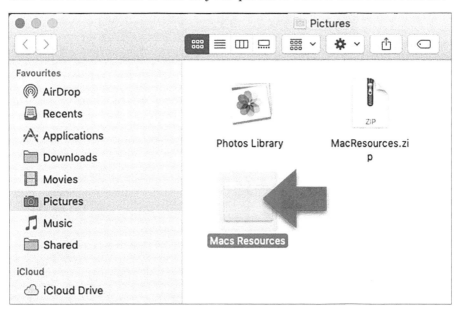

Double click to open this folder. You'll find the images used in the examples in the book.

Scanning the Codes

At the beginning of each chapter, you'll a QR code you can scan with your phone to access additional resources, files and videos.

iPhone

To scan the code with your iPhone/iPad, open the camera app.

Frame the code in the middle of the screen. Tap on the website popup at the top.

Android

To scan the code with your phone or tablet, open the camera app.

Frame the code in the middle of the screen. Tap on the website popup at the top.

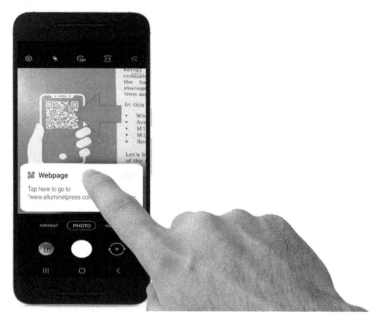

If it doesn't scan, turn on 'Scan QR codes'. To do this, tap the settings icon on the top left. Turn on 'scan QR codes'.

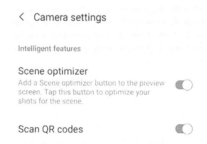

If the setting isn't there, you'll need to download a QR Code scanner. Open the Google Play Store, then search for "QR Code Scanner".

Index

Index

Index

Index

Index

Index

SOMETHING
NOT COVERED?

We want to create the best possible resources to help you learn and get things done, so if we've missed anything out, then please get in touch using the links below and let us know. Thanks.

 office@elluminetpress.com

 elluminetpress.com/feedback